MOY QUI ME VOY

to John Cruickshank

MOY QUI ME VOY

The Writer and the Self
from Montaigne to Leiris

EDITED BY

GEORGE CRAIG AND
MARGARET McGOWAN

CLARENDON PRESS · OXFORD
1989

Oxford University Press, Walton Street, Oxford OX2 6DP

Oxford New York Toronto
Delhi Bombay Calcutta Madras Karachi
Petaling Jaya Singapore Hong Kong Tokyo
Nairobi Dar es Salaam Cape Town
Melbourne Auckland

and associated companies in
Berlin Ibadan

Oxford is a trade mark of Oxford University Press

Published in the United States
by Oxford University Press, New York

British Library Cataloguing in Publication Data

Moy qui me voy: the writer and the self from
Montaigne to Leiris.
1. French Literature. Critical studies
I. Craig, George   II. McGowan, Margaret
840.9
ISBN 0–19–815153–5

Library of Congress Cataloging in Publication Data

Moy qui me voy: the writer and the self from Montaigne to Leiris/
edited by George Craig and Margaret McGowan.
p.cm.
1. French literature—History and criticism. 2. Self in
literature. 3. Autobiography.   I. Craig, George, 1931–
II. McGowan, Margaret M.
PQ145.6.S32M6   1989   840'.9'353—dc19   89–3036
ISBN 0–19–815153–5

Computerset by
Promenade Graphics Ltd.,
Cheltenham

Printed in Great Britain by
Bookcraft (Bath) Ltd.,
Midsomer Norton, Avon

Preface

THE IDEA for this book came from a series of discussions between the editors; starting from very different positions, we had found ourselves sharing a sense that something had gone wrong with the ways in which the notion of self tends to be canvassed in twentieth-century arguments about literature. It is, of course, a notoriously confused and baggy concept; the sort that, every so often, is subjected to more or less ruthless tidyings-up. The result, in our time, has been an increase in clarity, but at the price of a regrettable narrowing. What has happened is a kind of three-way split. Modern literary theorizing, from its earliest stirrings in what the 1930s called the 'New Criticism', has tended increasingly to push the issue aside as part of the unwanted baggage of an earlier, unenlightened era. At the same time, a surge of interest in autobiography has had the effect of linking self with issues of psychology or history. Left in the middle was the worst kind of remainder: the question-begging use of self we find in speculative biography; or in a particular kind of literary history for which the self was not only a transparent and untroubling entity, but a natural term of reference; the kind found in innumerable 'critical editions' such as the *Nine French Poets* of H. E. Berthon.

It may be that the concept is, of its nature, imprecise and shifting; but it would be over-hasty to dismiss it on that account. In the context of writing, in particular, self can have (has had, will go on having) a powerful, even a determining force, as that which every writer has to come to terms with, or fail in his or her enterprise. Indeed, so obtrusive, so immediate a reality is it that it becomes for some writers—one thinks of Montaigne—the heart and matter of their writing. But if there is nothing remote about it, neither is there anything mysterious. The self is, quite simply, that which any writer is brought face to face with when the writing slows down or actually stops; the disconcertingly familiar embodiment of the gap between intention and apparent achievement. Even the humblest of what Roland Barthes called 'écrivants' know this at first hand—when, say, the letter that seemed to be sustained by a tide of excited feeling suddenly and inexplicably grinds to a halt. The relationship between self and letter has, in that moment, been perceived as problematic.

But where, as with established writers, the disturbance is in the very centre of their concern, the activity of writing itself, more is at issue than a mere interruption, or a sudden feeling of inadequacy. No writer can escape awareness of self, since whoever accepts to *be* a writer (to make the move from 'écrivant' to 'écrivain') is accepting a sense of the self as actively and demonstrably engaged in that pursuit. That fact may be viewed very variously (Shelley seeing poets as 'the unacknowledged legislators of the world', Eliot seeing them as caught in a 'mug's game'), but it is seldom troubling. If the self can unexpectedly, unacceptably obtrude as stumbling-block, in spite of the writer's long-sharpened sense of the self's activities, the effect is likely to be both profound and disorientating: a kind of lostness. The apparent course has run into a vast and uncharted sea. Each writer will react in his or her own way: this is not a problem to which there might be a solution. It is an experience.

But if there is no answer, there are approximations, horizons, beams of witness that throw light on the dark water we have ourselves all seen. The writers studied in the present volume are as widely separated in time as in preoccupation, but each in his own way has had to respond at first hand to this urgent, pressing awareness that, somehow, central design had been circumvented, the easy route lost. It is the large version of another, apparently trivial discovery we have all made: that for stretches of time (seconds, certainly; longer intervals, perhaps) we may be unaware that we are writing; unaware that writing is going forward, until suddenly the words become apparent. The design, in other words, has not netted or contained the experience. What is it that is going on?

Montaigne provides an almost obligatory beginning since he raised most of the issues which come into play in any scrutiny of the self and which later writers will take up, issues such as time, memory, complexity, resistance, prejudice and public gaze. He attempted to meet these problems by a process of self-measurement against past experience, whether it was embodied in the writings he admired from the Ancient World or in the experiences he encountered in his own life. Tracing thoughts and pinning down feelings were formidable yet passionate tasks for, as Montaigne discovered, the self resists such analysis and charting, and, he found, can best be revealed by probing backwards, by opposition and by recognition of difference.

Pascal's violent reaction against Montaigne's 'sot projet de se peindre' came from the conviction that not only was such a centring of the self invidious to others, it also led inexorably to those general social ills of pretence and deceit. However, pitiless self-study which sees the 'moi' as 'haïssable' could, Pascal argued paradoxically, open out to include all men (as Montaigne's *Essais* had shown), and thus involve both love of a self ('un moi'), and of a man. In such circumstances, self-love finds its proper place, loses its negative connotations and prepares the way for love of God.

While Pascal's reluctant self-exposure drew its substance from metaphysical preoccupation and from observation of general human traits, Rousseau's self-concern is fed by violent reactions against prevailing social structures and norms. If the self is to be freed from the social constriction which the eighteenth century saw as inevitable and indeed desirable, how can/should it be trained? Interestingly different approaches to this problem are offered by Rousseau and by Adam Smith, who both seek to retain individual happiness as the universal goal. For the equable Scotsman, innate self-interest is counterweighted by sympathy to provide for harmonious social living in which success is guided by propriety, defined and judged by the impartial spectator. Rousseau's voice is quite different; although he too, in *Emile*, starts from self-love and accepts human weakness and pity as the forces which open up the individual to another's emotions, he remained suspicious and fundamentally hostile to society. His judge of behaviour is the individual self and his ultimate aim, the education of the man, not the citizen.

Readers of poetry expect and accept that self-assertion and self-revelation is part of the experience. Yet we are barely prepared for the kind of embarrassment provoked by Hugo's vast literary production which, with its sustained opposition of ferocity and gentleness, challenges assumed norms of poetic utterance. Although the presence of Hugo the poet is disturbingly intrusive, we cannot but be moved by the manner in which the extravagant public voice of the demagogue abruptly softens into the intimate, whispered tones of self-confession. Analysis of several poems from *Les Contemplations* shows how the language of self-regard has changed into the humbler tones of a witness who, none the less, neither loses his identity nor his sense of poetic mission.

While Hugo's presence in his work is evident, it has been argued that Flaubert marks a new departure in writing: that of removing the self from a fiction destined to be impersonal and realistic. The tensions between Flaubert's ideas and his temperament are fully recognized, and a study of the interactions between his letters and *Madame Bovary* (in particular) reveals how Flaubert's taste for the larger than life, his predilection for certain words, and his incurable desire to enter his characters and influence their views and perceptions ensure that in the creating of his novel he has, in fact, been writing himself. The will to disappear from his text was theoretically strong in Flaubert; in Rilke it became a practical necessity. His poems, presented here as a mirror of a 'modern' dilemma, show the shift from expressions of the self's sense of fragility and of feelings of anguish and terror when confronted by a world without transcendence, to a serene and even confident projection of things made. Poems, independent of their author, like the sculpture of Rodin or the paintings of Cézanne, have become objective artefacts; and, released from subjectivity, they carry their own existence and, indeed, their own sense of transcendence. The self has been joyously surrendered, rendered invisible so that that which is made or sung can remain and inspire.

The death of the self is, of course, not a specifically modern notion; it had been anticipated by Ovid. Yet, how marvellously, through a complex play of echo and reciprocity, does Wordsworth give a living presence in *The Prelude* to the Boy that died; while Edgar Allan Poe's exploration of similar themes reinforces feelings of horror at the power of echo, escape from which can only end in death. In Proust, however, echo and time are deliberately blurred to give a reality to the author in his novel which he is denied in the process of creation. At the same time, Proust's novel, while it does indeed end on a note of resolution, a recuperation of unity from multiplicity, is just as much concerned with the mobility and contradictions of possible selves as with the wholeness of one self.

Sartre's vast bulk of writing about the self covers up more than it reveals. He is seen manipulating the image of the self; the motives are diverse and include: self-justification; revenge; countering charges of ugliness; or self-protection—establishing in his sexual relations the dominance of the male self, or securing the tenderness and serenity of a shared intimacy between mother and son.

André Frénaud's exploration is altogether different and (despite the ironies of tone) is more akin to Rilke's findings in its attempt to recover and construct the self in a world without God. The quest is a complex one, and this self-engrossed poet subjects himself to vigilant self-criticism and recognizes the multiple, fragmented and provisional nature of what he finds and, moreover, accepts that other, equally acceptable selves may be created by his reader.

Unease and uncertainty dominate the perspectives on the self offered by Camus in *L'Exil et le royaume* where positive possibilities—environment, communication, journey or location—are disrupted, denied or absent. The traces of selves interacting, of crises overcome, or of expression regained are insufficient to fix the nature of the self which, in each of the six stories, remains resistant to analysis, and problematized.

In the work of Leiris, autobiography is seen anew, presented as immediate experience captured by the fortuitous and discontinuous nature of the writing. The self is created as the words of confession spin, but these are so protean and multitudinous that what began as a kind of therapy turns into an end in itself.

Each of the writers studied here has brought his own resolution to the problem of self, but all share a readiness to follow it through, however demanding it turns out to be. Unfailing commitment, scrupulousness, courage: their marks, but those too of the man to whom this book is dedicated: John Cruickshank.

George Craig
Margaret McGowan

Contents

Montaigne: the Self Discovered—*au rebours*

MARGARET MCGOWAN

C'EST une espineuse entreprinse, et plus qu'il me semble, de suyvre une
alleure si vagabonde que celle de nostre esprit; de penetrer les profondeurs
opaques de ses replis interieurs; de choisir et arrester tant de menus airs de
ses agitations . . . Il n'est description pareille en difficulté à la description
de soy-mesme, ny certes en utilité . . . Je peins principalement mes cogi-
tations, subject informe, qui ne peut tomber en production ouvragère. A
toute peine le puis je coucher en ce corps aërée de la voix . . . Je m'estalle
entier: c'est un SKELETOS où, d'une veüe, les veines, les muscles, les tendons paroissent, chaque piece en son siège . . . Le supreme remede de le
[amour de soi] guarir, c'est faire tout le rebours de ce que ceux icy ordon-
nent, qui, en defendant le parler de soy, defendent par consequent encore
plus de penser à soy. (11. 6, 378–9)[1]

In this celebrated late addition to *De l'Exercitation*, Montaigne
displays in one extended sweep the multiple elements at play in his
exploration, discovery, assessment and depiction of his own self.
The passage opens with the accent firmly placed on the difficulties
associated with the enterprise of self-study; it ends with surging
tones of personal confidence and defiance: the body's structure has
been so revealed as to be accessible at a single glance through a process akin to the operation of X-rays, and the resultant exposure of
the self, Montaigne recognizes (with some glee), runs counter to
established norms and practices. Conscious working against the
grain is much more than simple opposition to prevailing views; for
Montaigne, it involves the discovery of identity, the projection of
the self in flesh and blood, and it draws the reader into the making.
Montaigne's 'ticklish undertaking' immediately grants a presence
to his/our mind ('nostre esprit'), drawing attention to its wandering
gait, stressing the role of both visual penetration—piercing the dark
depths of the mind's inner folds—and aural acuteness—picking up

---

[1] All quotations are taken from the Presses Universitaires edition of the *Essais*,
published in 1965.

and pinning down the tiny sounds of the mind's movements. The whole person is involved in the chase; and, however the means of recording discovery, 'faire tout le rebours' plays a major part in enlightening and persuading.

Despite the confidence expressed in *De l'Exercitation*, Montaigne has not underestimated the difficulties of his task. Although these problems have been examined variously by a range of critics (notably Starobinski),[2] they must be noted here too if we are to assess the nature of the self's resistance to full discovery and appreciate the unusual, oppositional approaches adopted by Montaigne to counter that resistance. If we consider man's condition from a general point of view, Montaigne observes that man is so constituted as to make any analysis of his present state virtually impossible. Fears, regrets and hopes continually occupy his mind, fill it with events from the past and with future anticipations: 'Nous ne sommes jamais chez nous, nous sommes tousjours au delà' (I. 3, 15). The extraordinary distorting power of feelings over judgement, and of the imagination over facts are accepted by Montaigne, who sets his personal analysis against this general shifting backcloth. Yet even within the apparently more limited sphere of self-preoccupation, the problems are numerous.

Initially, they relate to the limitations of man's powers of perception and to the self's lack of control. However keen the eye that pursues manifestations of the self, whether it be a physical gesture—'tout mouvement nous descouvre' (I. 50, 302), or the self's changing posture—'Je me remue et trouble moy-mesme par l'instabilité de mes postures; et qui y regarde primement, ne se trouve guère deux fois en mesme estat' (II. 1, 335), that eye inevitably encounters resistance. In a gait that seems to match the uneven, halting action of his mind,[3] Montaigne's ideas and his judgement are shown in *De l'Institution des Enfans* to hesitate and to stumble before reaching their goal.

---

[2] Jean Starobinski, *Montaigne en mouvement* (Paris, 1982); see also Jules Brody, *Lectures de Montaigne* (Lexington, Ky, 1982), Marcel Gutwirth, *Michel de Montaigne ou le pari de l'exemplarité* (Montreal, 1977), Lawrence D. Kritzman, *Destruction/Découverte* (Lexington, 1980) and André Tournon, *Montaigne. La Glose et l'Essai* (Lyons, 1983).

[3] Described in *De l'Experience* as: 'C'est un mouvement irregulier, perpetuel, sans patron, sans but' (III. 13, 1068), and in *De la Vanité* as: 'La vie est un mouvement materiel et corporel, action imparfaite de sa propre essence, et desreglée; je m'emploie à la servir selon elle' (III. 9, 988).

Mes conceptions et mon jugement ne marche qu'à tastons, chancellant, bronchant et chopant, et quand je suis allé le plus avant que je puis, si ne me suis-je aucunement satisfaict, je voy encore du païs au delà; mais d'une veüe trouble et en nuage, que je ne puis desmesler. (I. 26, 146)

The hesitations are partly attributed to his own incapacity and partly to a more general condition, that is—man's fundamental dissatisfaction with temporary achievement. The point is made again in *De la Vanité* where Montaigne is reflecting on the contribution of Philosophy to our understanding of man: 'l'humaine sagesse n'arriva jamais aux devoirs qu'elle-mesme prescrit et, si elle y estoit arrivée, elle s'en prescriroit d'autres au delà (III. 9, 990).[4]

With regard to the self's lack of control, although Montaigne can detect the changes in the self that each day brings—'A chaque minute il me semble que je m'eschape' (I. 20, 88), as with his will and his utterance, these perceptible changes occur unbidden: 'ma volonté et mon discours se remue tantost d'un air, tantost d'un autre, et y a plusieurs de ces mouvements qui se gouvernent sans moy' (III. 8, 934). In fact, it is man's own make-up—a collection of small, shapeless pieces, each one different and playing an independent role[5]—which incites such change and which allows these pieces to multiply within any given individual. Montaigne's quest is then not a single identity, but the holding in play of the different beings of the self on the move and interacting. His search thus involves the acknowledgement of otherness; 'if circumstances change, if my enterprise changes me, I will be a different I tomorrow', Montaigne declared, in substance, in *De l'Institution des Enfans* (I. 26, 148). When in *De la Vanité* he made the same point, 'Moy à cette heure et moy tantost sommes bien deux' (III. 9, 1964), he illustrated difference by visualizing once again the wayward, drunk and uncontrolled walk of the self; now in old age it has a gait as swaying and as involuntary as the movement of reeds played upon by the breeze: 'C'est un mouvement d'yvroigne titubant, vertigineux, informe, ou des joncs que l'air manie casuelle-

---

[4] For an account of Montaigne's own speculations, see Ian Maclean: 'Le païs du delà: Montaigne and philosophical speculation', in *Montaigne. Essays in Memory of Richard Sayce*, ed. I. D. McFarlane and Ian Maclean (Oxford, 1982), 101–32.
[5] Montaigne's text runs as follows: 'Nous sommes tous de lopins, et d'une contexture si informe et diverse que chaque piece, chaque moment y fait son jeu. Et se trouve autant de différence de nous à nous mesmes que de nous à autruy' (II. 1, 337).

ment selon soy' (ibid.).[6] Increasingly, the stress is placed on captur-
ing the fact of change, of showing variety and difference, of accepting the unfinished, and tolerating even contradictory images of the
self, as Montaigne explains at the beginning of *Du Repentir*:

> C'est un contrerolle de divers et muables accidens et d'imaginations irre-
> soluës et, quand il y eschet, contraires: soit que je sois autre moy-mesme,
> soit que je saisisse les subjects par autres circonstances et considerations.
>
> (III. 2, 805)

Montaigne sees the range and complexity of the difficulties
involved in the search for the self and its presentation as a challenge.
In the *Essais*, the more the self resists discovery, the more importance Montaigne's enterprise acquires in his eyes,[7] and the greater the
chance of achieving some tracings of identity, however modest.

Montaigne's general approach is laid out most obviously in *De la
Diversion* where, bluntly admitting the ease with which his attention wanders, and acknowledging the seductive and dissipating
powers of 'l'imagination', he spells out his own ruses of pursuit:

> Si je ne puis la combatre, je luy eschape, et en la fuyant je fourvoye, je
> ruse: muant de lieu, d'occupation, de compaignie, je me sauve dans la
> presse d'autres amusemens et pensées, où elle perd ma trace et m'esgare.
>
> (III. 4, 836)

Flight, feints, manœuvres, withdrawals and distancing are means
which obscure Montaigne from the forceful glare of the imagination and which free him in turn to gain a clearer view of his object.[8]
In order to see better, Montaigne distances the subject self from the
observing I and studies it as though it were a separate object. He
watches from afar, reminding the reader that he is not so bound up
with self-love or self-preoccupation as to be unable to detach his
gaze, or select and differentiate, and view himself with the same dis-
cretion and indifference as he would a neighbour or a tree:

---

[6] The emphasis on Life as physical manifestation is important here and is stressed
many times in the *Essais*, notably later in this essay (III. 9, 988); cited in note 3
above.

[7] The point is cogently made by Gérard Defaux in 'Rhétorique et représentation
dans les *Essais*: de la peinture de l'autre à la peinture du moi', in *Rhétorique de Montaigne*, ed. Frank Lestringant (Paris, 1985), 21–49.

[8] For consideration of oblique approaches to his subject, see my *Montaigne's
Deceits* (London, 1974); Barbara Bowen, *The Age of Bluff* (Illinois, 1972); and
Richard Barrett, *Dynamics of Detour* (Tübingen, 1987).

Je ne m'ayme pas si indiscretement et ne suis si attaché et meslé à moy que je ne me puisse distinguer et considerer à quartier: comme un voisin, comme un arbre. (III. 8, 942)

This doubling of the self occurs in many places where Montaigne shows us observing himself: 'Je m'ordonne à mon âme ... ' (III. 13, 991); in catching himself and his writing unawares—*se regarder, se taster* and *se controller*;[9] and in seeing himself seeing, in Glauser's fine phrase: 'Il se voit se voyant.'[10]

Montaigne comes closer to enlightenment, however, when instead of splitting the self into subject and object, he introduces and multiplies voices contrary to his own. They may be the real voices of ancient writers: Plato arguing for the separation of body and spirit, for example (1. 14, 58), or Socrates on the ability of man to change inherent vice (II. 11, 429);[11] or, more often (and, in my view, more effective because they are more unusual), voices imagined by Montaigne and set in opposition—*au rebours*—against himself. *De la Vanité* provides numerous examples of this 'opposing voices' approach. Throughout his long discussion on the delights of travel, a barrage of different voices assails him: his wife's complaints, his dependants' fears and his friends' anxieties as well as the voice of Montaigne's own conscience. Opposition does not merely confirm the initial determination, it also exposes complex motives for travel (escape, pleasure and enlightenment, among others); similarly, the counterpoint of argument for and against 'la Vanité' brings a significant shift from general and traditional condemnation to personal appropriation of the theme.[12] Perhaps most startling of all in this essay are the voices that come in at the end, reminding the reader of the Delphic oracle's advice 'Know Thyself'. At first, through the re-pronouncing of this well-known injunction, the voices seem to support Montaigne's views on the value of self-study, of turning in upon oneself, and of resisting the otherwise

[9] On Montaigne's interest in involuntary physical responses, see Carol Clark, 'Talking about souls: Montaigne on human psychology', in *Montaigne. Essays in Memory of Richard Sayce*, op. cit. 57–76.
[10] Alfred Glauser, *Montaigne paradoxal* (Paris, 1972), 49; see also Tournon, op. cit., for the effect of the habit of commenting on Montaigne's writing and thought.
[11] Michel Jeanneret's recent work, *Des mets et des mots* (Paris, 1987) clarifies the complex relationship of writer and source in the *Essais*.
[12] François Rigolot sees this shift as common to all the late *Essais*, 'Les *Incipit* des *Essais*: Structure et Evolution', in *Montaigne et les Essais, 1580–1980*, ed. Pierre Michel (Paris/Geneva, 1983), 247–60.

natural human pressures which disperse and fritter away mental effort. However, with the added words: 'C'est tousjours vanité pour toy, dedans et dehors' (III. 9, 1001), Montaigne's whole enterprise seems thrown back into the melting-pot. But, if we reflect for a moment, we remember that the devastating voice is in fact repeating—more solemnly and more authoritatively, to be sure— that other view of Montaigne which he had argued simultaneously in *De la Vanité*[13] alongside that of the pleasurable benefits of self-study, namely: that all is vanity in the world of man. Contrary voices clarify and do not cancel out.

Like a cubist painter, Montaigne attempts to see and to show his inner self from all sides, and he knows that the picture will be blurred, contradictory and filled with spaces which let the spectator in. The ever-changing nature of the visualizing process is well caught in a passage from *De l'Inconstance de nos actions*: 'Je donne à mon ame tantost un visage, tantost un autre, selon le costé où je la couche. Si je parle diversement de moy, c'est que je me regarde diversement' (II. 1, 335). The diversity which is stressed here, and which must somehow be captured in words, is a force that Montaigne sees everywhere in Nature and in man. It is ever present in the *Essais*, and wherever it occurs, it is presented as the natural source of contradiction, of opposition and of difference, and as a positive source whose many warring features enrich the texture of self-discovery and portrayal. Thus, at the end of Book II, Montaigne argues that others with different views should not be disturbed to find that he advances opposite opinions (here against the value of medicine); on the contrary, since variety is a general fact in Nature, the taking-up of an antithetical stance produces a more accurate (because more complete) reflection of that state. The argument will be pressed again in the opening pages of *De l'Experience*. Here, affirmations about diversity, variety and difference are couched in absolute terms.

– il n'est aucune qualité si universelle en cette image des choses que la diversité et varieté. (III. 13, 1065)

– Nature s'est obligée à ne rien faire autre, qui ne fust dissemblable. (ibid.)

– Jamais deux hommes ne jugerent pareillement de mesme chose, et est

---

[13] For the interweaving of these two and other strands, see my forthcoming article, 'Clusterings: positive and negative values in *De la Vanité*' in *Montaigne Studies: An Interdisciplinary Forum*, I.

impossible de voir deux opinions semblables exactement, non seulement en divers hommes, mais en mesme homme à diverses heures. (III. 13, 1067)

Yet they provide the necessary starting-point for Montaigne's picture of his own individual experience. Recognition of difference clears the way for self-study.

Convinced that the mind is sharpened by opposition—'nostre volonté s'aiguisse aussi par le contraste' (II. 15, 612)—Montaigne often begins his search by a general pronouncement which he immediately contradicts with a phrase such as 'au rebours' (used ninety times in the *Essais*); or 'prenons voye toute contraire à la commune' (I. 20, 86); or again, 'je suis divers à cette façon commune' (III. 8, 935). The conviction is examined at length in *De l'Art de conférer* where Montaigne presents himself as a kind of jouster eagerly advancing for exercise and instruction on his adversary 'qui me contredit, qui m'instruit' (III. 8, 924). Contradiction commands attention, awakens thought, disturbs and then fills the mind. I'm more enlightened, Montaigne adds, 'par contrarié que par exemple, par fuite que par suite'.

Contrary approaches had other virtues too. They served for Montaigne as distinguishing and clarifying modes, separating (for instance) his particular view of retreat from the public arena and from the well-rehearsed debate on the active or contemplative life (I. 39, 237); sharing out responsibility for actions between Fortune and ourselves (I. 50, 303); or discriminating between the harmonious wholeness of the younger Cato's life and the fragmented, piecemeal adjustments of our own (II. 1, 334). They also allowed Montaigne to make plain the greater importance of experience over theory; while philosophers and learned men paint the approach to virtue as an 'image triste, querelleuse, despite, menaceuse, mineuse . . . sur un rocher, à l'écart, emmy des ronces, fantosme à estonner les gens', those who actually possess virtue 'la tiennent, au rebours, logée dans une belle plaine fertile et fleurissante' (I. 26, 161); and while the learned spell out their ideas with precision, and build 'un bastiment solide et entier, dont chaque piece tient son rang et porte sa marque', Montaigne's experience, in contrast, obliges him to write more openly, tentatively—'à tastons', and disjointedly—'par articles decousus' (III. 13, 1076). By measuring his own way against the solid monuments of wisdom, Montaigne has discovered his particular form which can (more faithfully perhaps) reflect the

shifting reality he encounters—'une chose si meslée, si menue et for-
tuite' (ibid.), and which at the same time call into question the completed architectures of the past.

In demonstrating so often the advantages of going against commonly accepted positions, Montaigne is aware of his singularity. 'Je
faicts tout le rebours', he declares with a sense of triumph when elaborating how revealing it is not to accept (as most men do) an argument, however elegant, but to go on challenging and testing its
force; and when describing how he engages in discussion as though
it were a fencing bout. By temperament, Montaigne acknowledged
himself to be combative and to be more impressed by the power of
difference than by the assurances which similarity brings: 'au
rebours du commun, reçoy plus facilement la différence que la res-
semblance en nous' (I. 37, 229).

'Les autres . . . moy, au rebours' is a characteristic structure
within many essays, but never more so than in *De la Praesumption*
where the constant measuring against others brings Montaigne into
the shell of his self:

> Le monde regarde tousjours vis à vis, moy, je replie ma veüe au dedans,
> je la plante, je l'amuse là. Chacun regarde devant soy; je n'ay affaire qu'à
> moy, je me considère sans cesse, je me contrerolle, je me gouste. Les autres
> vont tousjours ailleurs, s'ils y pensent bien; ils vont tousjours avant, *nemo
> in sese tendat descendere*, moy, je me roulle en moy-mesme.
>
> (II. 17, 657–8)

The extent of the development which Montaigne gives to these
successive and sustained contrasts between *autrui/moi* and *dehors/
dedans* is remarkable. It is not just that his eye is keener and more
concentrated, but (unlike others) undistracted from the pull of
outward affairs, Montaigne can indulge not only in the long, considered observation of the self, but make of it a game, bring into
play his judgement and all the relaxed pleasure of rolling over
within himself as if enacting some acrobatic trick. Formally the
essay seeks to justify the amount of self-talk and to ward off anticipated criticisms of the kind which Pascal was to raise,[14] but by the
latter stages of Montaigne's argument (from which the quotation
we are considering was taken), the writing has altogether lost any
defensive tone. Proudly, Montaigne states his discovered difference,

---

[14] In addition to Pascal's remarks in the *Pensées*, there are further condemnations
reported in Antoine Arnauld and Pierre Nicole, *La Logique ou l'Art de penser*, ed.
P. Clair and F. Girbal (Paris, 1965), 267–9.

and like a master of ceremonies, he introduces a supreme performer in the act of self-penetration.

His evident delight in the revealing and recuperative power of adopting an opposite stance Montaigne applies to many spheres; most specifically to his will. In *De Mesnager la volonté*, abandoning the snares of public life—'les hommes se donnent à louage . . . je prens une complexion toute diverse' (III. 10, 1004)—Montaigne seeks to curb the over-enthusiastic appetites of the will. The process began with a comparison: 'pour dresser un bois courbe on le recourbe au rebours' (III. 10, 1006); the act of correcting the bent wood is then transposed direct by Montaigne to his own inner needs: 'où ma volonté se prend avec trop d'appétit: je me panche à l'opposite de son inclination, comme je la voy se plonger et d'enyvrer de son vin' (III. 10, 1014). Although the effect—correction—is the same as in the parallel, the experience is not. Not only is Montaigne performing the adjustment on himself as though that self were distanced from him, he has increased that distance by individualizing the bent will, now transformed into a person drunk with the wine of his enthusiasm.

Notwithstanding the clarifying consequences which Montaigne derives from deliberately pitting his comments against others in the specific contexts of exploring the self, resistances remain. The writing in the *Essais* seems to shift and slide, and examples and anecdotes (which never seem quite to illustrate the point) grow and increase in number, as the diversity which Montaigne sees around him, and in himself, is reflected in multiple observations that intentionally do not add up. However much the reader wants to project an order on to the *Essais*, Montaigne continually thwarts that effort, highlighting the fragmented and incomplete nature of his insights, piling up disparate and contradictory examples, interrupting the flow of thought and alerting us constantly to his wayward style with 'cette farcisseure est un peu hors de mon theme', or 'revenons à nos moutons'. Such interference seems to confirm our bewilderment. But Montaigne will argue that such features, far from dulling our perception, actually enlarge and sharpen the mind. Resistance, obscurity—'mon obscurité', and even muddle—'mon embrouilleure' are put forth by Montaigne as means of enlightenment. In *Des Coustumes anciennes*, he announces:

Je veux icy entasser aucunes façons anciennes que j'ay en memoire, les

unes de mesme les nostres, les autres differentes, afin qu'ayant en l'imagination cette continuelle variation des choses humaines, nous en ayons le jugement plus esclaircy et plus ferme.   (I. 49, 297)

Here he has knowingly drawn together variety teeming in the
mind and a thereby strengthened and improved judgement.[15]

Just as he seeks to rouse his judgement by the challenge of a mass
of material to sift, so Montaigne frequently tries to fire his reader's
attention by presenting himself, his writing and his opinions negatively. He is, he says 'bas, sot, inepte'; his writing he compares to
'excremens'; and the matter of his book is offered as a subject 'si fri-
vole et si vain'. Not so, we want immediately to protest; and, if we
do respond thus, we are confirming the value of Montaigne's use of
arguments 'au rebours'. Contrary or negative approaches not only
enlighten, they involve.

The opening of *Du Repentir* has a familiar disjunctive form: 'Les
autres forment l'homme; je le recite et en represente un particulier
bien mal formé' (III. 2, 804). Initially, it seems that Montaigne is
particularly criticizing his own poor figure in a context where
others can build men solid, handsome and complete. Such a judgement turns out to be misleading, and may even be wrong, as we
note that Montaigne's attention turns suddenly to the theme of 'Le
monde n'est qu'une branloire perenne' (ibid.). In a universe that
shifts without ceasing and in which man's observations are forced
to move perpetually—never secure and never finished—the notion
of the well-formed and coherent whole which educationalists had
argued for seems inappropriate; more natural and fitting is the
unclear, wavering movement of 'un être mal formé' such as Montaigne himself. Thus, by foregrounding his experience of the actual
nature of the world, Montaigne reverses the initial impression
created by the opposition of *forme/mal formé*.

In his analysis of personal motivation, Montaigne customarily
discovers that specific contexts modify judgement and that negative
conditions turn out to have positive qualities. In *De la Vanité*, all
the major themes of the essay—writing, travel, leisure, absence and
vanity itself—are first shown in their darkest colours. Writing is
mere 'vagabondage'; travel is 'tesmoignage d'inquiétude et d'irreso-
lution'; leisure appears as a morally debilitating state: 'je ne cherche

---

[15] This particular conjunction has been well analysed by Kritzman, op. cit., in the
opening section entitled 'Connaissance par entassement'.

qu'à m'anonchalir et avachir' (III. 9, 954); absence implies loss; and vanity which is seen in exactly the same terms as described in Ecclesiastes—that is, as characterizing man's condition—provides the undercurrent of the work; and Montaigne rarely forgets to let us see its flow. Each theme comes alive and is unravelled by association with another,[16] and gradually the negative meanings of the words dissolve. Leisure, for example, becomes a precious condition which provides freedom for thought and protection from the inevitable immoralities necessitated by public office. Similarly, absence/ *voyage*, weighted favourably against presence (which is revealed as physical discomfort and mental apprehension), acquires the entirely pleasurable aspects of possession and 'jouissance'.

By focusing first on negative attributes, and then recovering step by step their opposite positive value, Montaigne persistently (and through the very waywardness of the writing) exposes the force that underlay his interest in all these activities and that animated his own motives—that of pleasure! It looks like an incredible discovery in an essay entitled *De la Vanité*; yet it is clear that Montaigne expects our applause, for it appears that the motives were premeditated and that Montaigne's extraordinary revelation was known by him from the start. At the point in the essay where he sets aside Reason—'cette raison trouble feste'—he has determined a completely contrary approach to received views on Vanity, an approach that, for the sake of pleasure, revels in celebrating vanity and even foolishness: 'Au rebours, je m'emploie à faire valoir la vanité mesme et l'asnerie si elle m'apporte du plaisir' (III. 9, 996). Beside this exhilaration at his ability to manipulate and to create, Montaigne none the less remembers that the pleasure discovered in his own work, the response of a human mind and the creation of his pen are set in a fallen world where all achievement is ultimately vain. While the end of the essay firmly re-established that fact with the voice that reminds Montaigne: 'Il n'en est une seule si vuide et necessiteuse que toy, qui embrasses l'univers: tu es le scrutateur sans connoissance, le magistrat sans jurisdiction et apres tout le badin de la farce' (III. 9, 1001), in spite of that reminder, we cannot forget the delight that Montaigne savoured too.

Long ago. Georges Poulet pointed to the difficulty Montaigne

---

[16] The detailed nature of this interaction is explored in my article, 'Clusterings', art. cit.

often encountered in staying with the present.[17] Despite the robust claims at the beginning of *Du Repentir*: 'Je ne peints pas l'estre. Je peints le passage: non un passage d'aage en autre, ou, comme dict le peuple, de sept ans en sept ans, mais de jour en jour, de minute en minute' (III. 2, 805), Montaigne was the first to recognize the gap that existed between the movement of things and the pace with which the mind could catch them. He also acknowledged another space between reflections already recorded and his present response to them which adds, and inevitably modifies, the original text. Far from hiding such adjustments, he parades the ways his writing comments on itself and shows the process of imitating, digesting and transforming older texts in action.[18] This drawing of attention to the way the text moves and grows suggests not only that Montaigne is aware of the many factors involved in keeping his object of study (the self) in focus, but also might explain why he resorted so often to contrary approaches to his task.

What happens when Montaigne, unaided by the tactics of opposition, presents himself in particular circumstances? In a passage which precedes a little the quotation given at the beginning of this essay, he arrives at the culminating point of his account of his accident, when he had been thrown insensible to the ground after a horse had ridden him down.

> Quant à la façon de ma cheute, on me la cachoit en faveur de celuy qui en avoit esté cause, et m'en forgeoit on d'autres. Mais long temps après, et le lendemain, quand ma memoire vint à s'entr'ouvrir et me representer l'estat où je m'estoy trouvé en l'instant que j'avoy aperçeu ce cheval fondant sur moy (car je l'avoy veu à mes talons et me tins pour mort, mais ce pensement avoit esté si soudain que la peur n'eut pas loisir de s'y engendrer), il me sembla que s'estoit un esclair qui me frapoit l'ame de secousse et que je revenoy de l'autre monde.
> (II. 6, 377)

This is the instant of revelation; Montaigne's memory, acting involuntarily, brings back the whole experience, and the day after the event, recalls the feeling of being dead; but, above all, it conveys the miraculous sense of having come back to life through some divine intervention which Montaigne can only describe in the same

---

[17] Georges Poulet, *Etudes sur le temps humain* (Paris, 1950), 4–5.

[18] On the habit of commenting, see Tournon, op. cit.; Michel Jeanneret, op. cit., *passim*, has most sensitively studied the manner in which Montaigne allows us to see him in the art of transposing another's writing into his own.

way as painters had done—by imagining the divine spirit as a shaft of light entering the brain.

In presenting to us his extraordinary experience—his resurrection—Montaigne has significantly altered the time-scale of his discovery of the real sequence of events. The actual event he describes with the pace and select precision of an expert story-teller; each stage of the subsequent physical traces of the shock and of the mind's recovery is charted with care and in detail; and the unconsciously performed words and gestures are faithfully recorded. All this is done *before* recounting the experience which made his story possible. Thus, in the telling, Montaigne has preserved the real-time succession of events which he has been able to reconstruct through the unbidden activity of memory prompted (as Montaigne admits) by the details elicited later from his servants. By saving the moment of revelation to the end, Montaigne has alerted us fully to the process of recovery and of creation.

Although he attempted to detach himself from the common experience which pulled men ever away from the present: 'le monde regarde tousjours vis à vis, moy je replie ma veüe au dedans' (II. 17, 657), Montaigne did not always dissociate himself from the power of the elsewhere (in time and space)—'Nous pensons tousjours ailleurs' (III. 4, 834); nor did he ignore the consolatory force of distancing his thoughts from present ills: 'Cette opinion et usance commune de regarder ailleurs qu'à nous a bien pourveu à nostre affaire' (III. 9, 1000). The great difference is that Montaigne does not lose himself, as others do, in the process. The past is made to play on his present self's concerns; and distance is brought home to signify.

The matter is best illustrated if we return again to *De la Vanité* where Montaigne collapses into the same flow of writing meditations upon a projected journey to Rome; actual experience of that journey and contact with the imperial city itself; memories of his reading about the lives, writings and thoughts of great Romans of former times; and feelings that endured for his father, his friends and family. The contrary voices that painted the distant, inconvenient and even frightening horizons of the proposed journey, have in the experience of travelling contracted into calm statements about manageable, daily preoccupations, and about unexpected compensations:

– Mon dessein est divisible partout: il n'est pas fondé en grandes esper-

ances; chaque journée en faict le bout. Et le voyage de ma vie se conduict de
mesme.   (III. 9, 978)
   – Absent, je me despouille de tous tels pensemens; et sentirois moins lors
la ruyne d'une tour que je ne faicts present la cheute d'une ardoyse.

                                                                   (III. 9, 954)

By thus conflating space and time perspectives, Montaigne has
produced unanswerable arguments for embarking with equanimity
upon the journey that has just finished. Additionally, he has been
able to represent the enrichments of the self which he has encountered on the way, those benefits which he derived less from actual
meetings of minds than from meditating upon his feelings during a
long absence in which, he concedes, his imagination played a major
role: 'Je sçay que l'amitié a les bras assez longs pour se tenir et se
joindre d'un coin de monde à l'autre . . . la jouissance et la possession appartiennent principalement à l'imagination' (III. 9, 975).
   In *De la Vanité*, it becomes apparent that when Montaigne medi-
tates upon the effects of distance a process of discovery and self-
enlargement is at work similar to that which he experienced when
he was probing the analytical force of difference. His vision of
Rome offers a good example of its intricate nature. In his response
to the imperial city, Montaigne adopts a different stance to the
oppositional and negative ones which we have so far been studying;
his reaction is sympathetic, admiring and many-faceted. It is made
up of reminiscences from books and from walking through the
streets of Rome, and of imaginative reconstructions which are
drawn in the *Essais* to fill the void created around Montaigne by the
unsatisfactory nature of the intellectual companionship provided
by his own contemporaries.
   It is immediately after throwing down the challenge of extolling
vanity, for the sake of his own pleasure—'si elle m'apporte du plaisir'—that Montaigne launches into a deep meditation upon Rome,
as representing the supreme vanity and the symbol of the best that
man can achieve. The ruins of Rome, ambiguous signs of decline
and defeat and of survival and grandeur, rouse Montaigne's rever-
ence and give him consolation and hope for the tottering state of his
native land. They are, however, more than abstract entities, for they
work on his imagination, turning ruined homes and the fragments
of statues from brick and stones into men: 'J'ay veu ailleurs des
maisons ruynées, et des statues, et du ciel et de la terre: ce sont tousjours des hommes' (III. 9, 996). With his own eyes he has wit-

nessed their fallen shape, and with his mind he has conjured up the Roman heroes—dead now, of course: 'Ils sont trespassez', but as much a living presence to him as his father who, although dead and buried himself these eighteen years, none the less continues to be with Montaigne in a real sense.

Ils sont trespassez. Si bien est mon pere, aussi entierement qu'eux, et s'est esloigné de moy et de la vie autant en dix huict ans que ceux-là ont faict en seize cens; duquel pourtant je ne laisse pas d'embrasser et practiquer la memoire, l'amitié et societé, d'une parfaicte union et très-vive. (III. 9, 996)

Montaigne has again collapsed the time-scale; he underlines the closeness of the contact, the friendly fellowship, and the living accord he feels of these figures from the past, figures who provide him not only with substitutes for the present, but with souls with whom he can speak and argue, minds against whose strength he can test his own. The conditions and fortunes of Lucullus, Metullus and Scipio are more familiar to him, for example, than those 'que je n'ay d'aucuns hommes des nostres', in the same way as he had been more thoroughly acquainted (through his reading) with Rome before he knew Paris: 'je sçavois le Capitole et son plant avant que je sceusse le Louvre, et le Tibre avant la Seine' (ibid.).

The strands of association that weave the past into the present so effectively that the inhabitants of the imperial city supplant contemporary Frenchmen are complex, but Montaigne is in no doubt about their reality. He explains the process as a conscious retreat, recognizing himself as useless and inappropriate to his own times: 'Me trouvant inutile à ce siècle, je me rejecte à cet autre' (ibid.). As we follow him in his quest for companionship and consolation, the powerful feelings generated by the search become manifest. Montaigne is bowled over by the past that he touches, to the extent that present affairs seem to belong to the world of imagined things: 'Cette accointance dure encore entre nous; les choses presentes mesmes, nous ne les tenons que par fantasie' (ibid.). Connections with past figures are more real and more substantial than the flimsy shadows of the present. And Montaigne goes further, for he gives an unusually strong characterization of the feelings he has for the Rome he has seen and for the city he imagines; he describes them as *besotted*. When he came to re-read the word 'embabouyné', Montaigne paused to reflect on the strength of the interest and pleasure he derives from Rome:

Est-ce par nature ou par erreur de fantasie que la veüe des places que nous sçavons avoir esté hantées et habitées par personnes desquelles la memoire est en recommandation, nous esmeut aucunement plus qu'ouïr le recit de leurs faicts, ou lire leurs escrits? *Tanta vis admonitionis inest in locis. Et id quidem in hac urbe infinitum: quacunque enim ingredimur in aliquam historiam vestigium ponimus.*[19]   (III. 9, 997)

Here, Montaigne allows us to glimpse how sensitive he was to the Power of Place,[20] to the evocative force of those ancient buildings where his Roman heroes once lived and which have the art of moving more deeply than their deeds themselves or any account of them. Montaigne's words are more touching than the stirring lines of Cicero, for while the Roman philosopher is concerned with treading the streets of History, Montaigne is expressing a personal discovery. It is a discovery that excites him into visualizing the very faces of his Roman friends, their clothes and their gait, and shows himself to himself enjoying their company, his conversation with them, and sharing their meals: 'Il me plaist de considerer leur visage, leur port et leurs vestements ... Je les visse volontiers diviser, promener, et soupper!' (ibid.). No wonder he felt proud to have been granted the citizenship of Rome, 'seule ville commune et universelle ... la plus noble qui fut et qui sera oncques'. The satisfaction is profound, less for the title he gained with such difficulty, much more for the pleasure of a kind of human contact which the civil wars (among other things) had denied him.

Montaigne betrays a certain defiant self-consciousness in revelling so unashamedly in such pleasure: 'Quelqu'un se blasmeroit et se mutineroit en soy-mesme, de se sentir chatouiller d'un si vain plaisir. Nos humeurs ne sont pas trop vains, qui sont plaisantes' (ibid.). However, just as he had discovered pleasure in activities normally associated with negative values, so Montaigne here again re-emphasizes the importance of pleasure, even in the context of that supreme example of vanity—Rome. The putative accuser has little defence against Montaigne's wry humour.

In the opening paragraphs of *Du Repentir*, Montaigne under-

---

[19] Florio gives the translation of Cicero's text as follows: 'So great a power of admonition is in the very place. And that in this City is most infinite, for which way soever we walke, set our foote upon some History.'

[20] For a more detailed discussion of Montaigne's attitude to Rome, the survival of its State, its institutions and its spectacles, see my forthcoming work on the vision of Rome in the French Renaissance.

lined the difference between his own approach towards self-representation and that of other writers. When they expose themselves to the public, they look for some remarkable trait to promote; Montaigne, in contrast, offers a complete view: 'Les autheurs se communiquent au peuple par quelque marque particuliere et estrangere; moy le premier par mon estre universel, comme Michel de Montaigne' (III. 2, 805). The resounding tones of confidence recall the lines from *De l'Exercitation* quoted at the beginning. There is the same insistence on thoroughness and the same sense of the singular nature of what he is doing. Montaigne is here, however, preparing the ground for his unusual views on Repentance, attributing to himself alone the power to see better within himself, to analyse more effectively and to penetrate further:

> Jamais homme ne traicta subject qu'il entendit ne cogneust mieux que je fay celuy que j'ay entrepris, et qu'en celuy-là je suis le plus sçavant homme qui vive; secondement, que jamais aucun ne penetra en sa matière plus avant, ny en esplucha plus particulierement les membres et suites.   (ibid.)

Implicit in these claims are familiar assumptions about his difference. The habit of thinking which runs counter to accepted norms and of writing *au rebours* are both modes of self-discovery and ways of stating uniqueness, and Montaigne explored their dual function again and again; in *Sur quelques vers de Virgile*, for instance, where he refuses to condone false praise of self: 'Ceux qui se mescognoissent, se peuvent paistre de fauces approbations; non pas moy, qui me voy et qui me recherche jusques aux entrailles, qui sçay bien ce qui m'appartient' (III. 5, 847). In addition to the obvious resistance, Montaigne is also establishing here his ability to know and to judge. Elsewhere (in *Du Repentir*, for example), he had expressed similar convictions: 'je n'ay guere de mouvement qui se cache et desrobe à ma raison' (III. 2, 812), promoting that faculty which operated most obviously in the process of re-thinking and of reflexive writing which (b) and (c) additions brought to the *Essais*. Expansion meant continual modification of the original text, changes which could go against first explorations of a topic; in *De l'Art de conférer*, for instance, after re-reading his approbation for the *Annals* of Tacitus, he adds a contrary thought, opening with the words: 'Et me semble le rebours de ce qu'il luy semble à luy' (III. 8, 940).

Such writing which comments upon itself naturally and continuously provides opportunities for enlightenment. Montaigne is aware of making discoveries 'après coup'; 'j'aurai eslancé quelque subtilité en escrivant' (I. 10, 40), he added to *Du Parler prompt ou tardif* in his own hand on the Bordeaux copy of the *Essais*. The unexpected illumination may be unwilled on some occasions, yet the overall impression of Montaigne's writing is of a controlled and supremely conscious mind reacting to words he has already written and to subjects—especially the self—which he has explored.

Writing *au rebours* implies both detachment and a high degree of consciousness; and these qualities—critical distance and conscious application of judgement—are ones to which Montaigne repeatedly makes appeal. At the end of *De l'Art de conférer* where we can actually hear his confidence through the echoing sounds of *Moy/ Roy* (a tone which he immediately modifies and undermines), Montaigne explains how sudden impulses of the mind and unbidden verbal gifts are threaded attentively into the writing:

> Moy qui suis Roy de la matiere que je traicte, et qui n'en dois conte à personne, ne m'en crois pourtant pas du tout: je hasarde souvent des boutades de mon esprit, desquelles je me deffie, et certaines finesses verbales, de quoy je secoue les oreilles; mais je les laisse courir à l'avanture. (III. 8, 943)

The waywardness that he injects into his thinking and the wandering style that matches it are to be commended, for they are the products of a pen that controls wisps of thought that may run counter to the will. In suggesting commendation, Montaigne knows that he is in good company; in *De la Vanité*, referring to Plutarch and to Plato, he writes with undisguised admiration: 'Ils ne creignent point ces muances, et ont une merveilleuse grace à se laisser ainsi rouler au vent, ou à le sembler' (III. 9, 994). The apparent afterthought—'ou à le sembler'—must be given its full weight; the restless surface of thought and writing of these remarkable giants from the past has been achieved through a conscious artistic process which Montaigne admires and emulates. 'Mon stile et mon esprit vont vagabondant de mesme' (III. 9, 994); writing and the self are bound by the same movements and incorporated in the same flow which often runs apart from the common streams—backwards and contrary—and, when it does, it leaves space for observation. It shows Montaigne watching—'moy qui me voy'—distinguishing difference, and overcoming the resistance of self to capture.

2

Pascal et le 'moi haïssable'

JEAN MESNARD

'LE MOI est haïssable' (597–455):[1] s'il est vrai que la meilleure 'manière d'écrire' est celle 'qui se fait le plus citer' (745–18), il est difficile de trouver formule plus réussie dans les *Pensées* de Pascal, puisqu'il en est peu que l'on entende plus souvent répéter. Est-ce à dire que le sens de cette phrase toute simple soit parfaitement limpide? L'idée, en tout cas, est souvent reprise dans les *Pensées*, avec d'innombrables variations. Il faut se placer à plusieurs points de vue pour en saisir tous les aspects.[2]

L'un des commentaires le plus précocement et le plus fréquemment avancés se place sur le terrain de la rhétorique. Il invite à proscrire, dans le discours et dans la conversation, l'usage de la première personne du singulier. Selon le témoignage de Nicole, dans la seconde édition de la *Logique de Port-Royal* (1664), Pascal prétendait 'qu'un honnête homme devait éviter de se nommer, et même de se servir des mots de *je* et de *moi*'.[3] De même, selon un propos recueilli à la fin du XVIIᵉ siècle par Vigneul-Marville, 'M. Pascal disait de ces auteurs qui, parlant de leurs ouvrages, disent: *mon livre, mon commentaire, mon histoire, etc.*, qu'ils sentent leurs bourgeois qui ont pignon sur rue et toujours un *chez moi* à la bouche. Ils feraient mieux, ajoutait cet excellent homme, de dire *notre livre, notre commentaire, notre histoire, etc.*, vu que d'ordi-

---

[1] Nos références aux *Pensées*, inscrites entre parenthèses dans le cours du texte, comportent deux chiffres: le premier renvoie à l'éd. Lafuma, Paris, Ed. du Luxembourg, 1951, 3 vol.; le second à l'éd. Brunschvicg (Paris, 1897).

[2] Sur le sujet on peut consulter Joachim Merlant, 'L'ennemi du *moi*: Pascal', *De Montaigne à Vauvenargues, Essais sur la vie intérieure et la culture du moi*, Paris, 1914, 249–84; Paul Bénichou, *Morales du Grand Siècle* (Paris, 1948), 77–130; A. J. Krailsheimer, *Studies in Self-Interest from Descartes to La Bruyère* (Oxford, 1962), 98–151, principalement pp. 139–151.

[3] *La Logique ou l'Art de penser* (Paris, 1664), 341; éd. Clair et Girbal (d'après la 5e éd.) (Paris, 1965), 267. Voir aussi notre éd. de Pascal, *Œuvres complètes*, t. i (Paris, 1964), 994. Le passage est allégué par Mme Périer dans la seconde version de sa *Vie de Pascal*, ibid. 635.

naire, il y a plus en cela du bien d'autrui que du leur' (1000–43).[4] Le propos dénonce, avec ironie, le manque de discrétion, contraire à l''honnêteté', l'espèce de suffisance bourgeoise que comporte l'emploi du possessif de la première personne. La substitution du pluriel au singulier est l'une des solutions que la politesse traditionnelle à préconisées. Au pronom personnel, la substitution de l'indéfini 'on' fournit un autre moyen de faire preuve de savoir-vivre.

La condamnation ainsi portée atteint évidemment au premier chef l'écrivain qui s'est fait lui-même 'la matière de son livre'.[5] D'un bout à l'autre de ses *Essais*, Montaigne ne cesse de dire 'je'. Pascal tient pour ses deux principaux défauts, dans le domaine de l'expression, 'qu'il faisait trop d'histoires' — il vise par là sa tendance à multiplier les anecdotes — et 'qu'il parlait trop de soi' (649–65), en tenant registre des aspects les plus insignifiants de sa personne. D'où l'exclamation: 'Le sot projet qu'il a de se peindre' (780–62). Dans le passage cité de la *Logique de Port-Royal*, Nicole, interprète de Pascal, dénonce cette référence constante à soi-même comme 'indigne d'un honnête homme'.[6]

Mais, lorsque Pascal déclare 'le moi est haïssable', son propos dépasse de beaucoup la rhétorique. La condamnation du moi, soit comme sujet, soit comme objet du discours, implique déjà une certaine conception des rapports humains et, au-delà, toute une philosophie. C'est sur le terrain de la philosophie qu'il convient de s'établir pour dégager toute la portée de l'idée.

La philosophie se complètera nécessairement par la théologie, car il y a lieu d'appliquer sur ce point, plus que jamais, la distinction fondamentale chez Pascal entre l'homme sans Dieu et l'homme avec Dieu.

Dans la perspective de l'homme sans Dieu, l'analyse est purement psychologique et rationnelle. Comment alors le moi peut-il être haïssable? Il l'est de deux manières, car il possède deux 'qualités', c'est-à-dire, au sens neutre usuel au XVIIe siècle, deux caractères: 'Il est injuste en ce qu'il se fait centre de tout. Il est incommode aux autres en ce qu'il les veut asservir' (597–455).

C'est d'abord en ce qu'il est 'incommode' que le moi est

---

[4] Voir aussi, dans notre éd. citée, 832.
[5] Montaigne, *Essais*, éd. Villey-Saulnier (Paris, 1965), 3.
[6] 1664, p. 342; 1965, p. 267.

haïssable. En son premier sens, cet adjectif désigne, non une situation de droit, mais une situation de fait. Il s'oppose rigoureusement à 'aimable'. Est aimable ce qui se fait aimer; est haïssable ce qui se fait haïr. C'est le propre du moi que d'exciter l'aversion. Chaque moi tend à s'imposer aux dépens d'autrui et à utiliser les autres à ses propres fins; 'Chaque moi est l'ennemi et voudrait être le tyran de tous les autres' (ibid.). D'où une rivalité universelle, qui fait que 'les hommes se haïssent naturellement l'un l'autre' (210–451). Point n'est besoin que cette haine se manifeste sous des formes brutales et violentes, de celles qui appellent la formule célèbre de Hobbes: 'l'homme est un loup pour l'homme.' Elle existe tout autant lorsqu'elle se réduit à de petites jalousies, lorsqu'elle découle de menus conflits d'intérêts.

Exprimé en termes psychologiques, ce pessimisme n'en est pas moins d'origine théologique. Il repose sur la grande distinction opérée par saint Augustin entre les deux amours qui se partagent le cœur de l'homme: l'amour de soi et l'amour de Dieu. Le péché originel, en détournant l'homme de sa fin véritable qui est Dieu, l'a livré à l'amour de soi, ou amour-propre, principe de tout désordre. C'est parce qu'il s'aime lui-même que le moi tend à opprimer les autres et, par là, s'en fait haïr. L'amour-propre ruine l'harmonie entre les êtres et, en premier lieu, celle qui existerait, hors de l'état de péché, au sein de la communauté humaine. En dépit de son extrême simplicité, ce principe se prête à une multitude d'analyses concrètes, comme le prouve, outre l'œuvre de Pascal, celle de La Rochefoucauld.

On ne peut négliger de mettre aussi en rapport de telles vues avec l'esprit général du temps. La ruine du cosmos harmonieux de la pensée médiévale, et, conjointement, celle d'une société organique et hiérarchisée, le développement de l'individualisme apporté par la Renaissance, le progrès de l'absolutisme, où s'affiche une image exemplaire de la puissance inquiétante du moi, les innombrables conflits intérieurs et extérieurs qui ont marqué les débuts de l'époque moderne, étaient propres à éveiller ce désenchantement, à provoquer ces analyses impitoyables.

On peut encore rattacher ces vues à un effort tout moderne pour entrer dans la 'psychologie des profondeurs'. A l'origine des manifestations de l'amour-propre, Pascal, comme La Rochefoucauld, découvre une sorte d'angoisse fondamentale, résultat de la quête perpétuellement insatisfaite d'un bien perdu ou inaccessible, et qui entraîne naturellement l'agressivité envers autrui.[7] Vis-à-vis des autres, le moi de chacun apparaît comme recouvert de multiples aspérités, de pointes menaçantes, moyen de défense peut-être, mais qui déchaîne une violente répulsion.

Cependant, le moi ainsi conçu occupe une situation limite, celle d'un homme réduit à ses pulsions primitives, à une sorte de volonté de puissance élémentaire. Il appartient à ce que Pascal appelle l'ordre des corps (308–793). Or l'homme est aussi esprit. Doué de raison, il cherche les moyens de surmonter cet état de guerre et d'établir une harmonie par l'élimination des menaces que chaque moi représente pour les autres. C'est ainsi que se constitue la société politique.[8] C'est ainsi que, dans les rapports privés, dont l'étude nous retiendra seule ici, des règles s'instaurent visant à rendre le moi, non plus haïssable, mais aimable. Ce sont les règles de la politesse. Dans le dialogue imaginaire qu'il institue avec son ami le libertin Mitton, champion de l'"honnête homme", Pascal lui fait dire: 'En agissant, comme nous faisons, obligeamment pour tout le monde, on n'a plus sujet de nous haïr' (597–455). L'"honnête homme', c'est-à-dire celui qui plaît, celui qui se fait aimer, semble donc avoir éliminé le moi haïssable.

Prétention qui se heurte aussitôt à une fin de non recevoir: 'Cela est vrai, si on ne haïssait dans le moi que le déplaisir qui nous en revient. Mais si je le hais parce qu'il est injuste qu'il se fasse centre de tout, je le haïrai toujours' (ibid.). Le second caractère du moi, son injustice, survit donc à la suppression de son incommodité. Le moi haïssable est simplement 'couvert', dissimulé. Il n'en demeure pas moins fondamentalement présent.

Pour quelle raison le moi peut-il être ainsi taxé d'injustice? Parce qu' 'il se fait centre de tout', si l'on en juge par la formule la plus explicite de Pascal à cet égard. C'est dire qu'il garde toujours le caractère exclusif, accapareur, qui le rendait incommode. Il ne donne que des apparences, et il entend recevoir des réalités. Apparences que des attitudes extérieures qui n'engagent pas le moi profond, réalité que l'amour des autres attendue en échange. Plaire, se faire aimer, c'est d'ailleurs attirer vers son moi les faveurs d'autrui, sans promesse de réciprocité. Voilà ce que signifie se faire centre de tout.

---

[7] On songe en particulier au célèbre fragment de La Rochefoucauld sur l'amour-propre, *Maximes*, éd. Truchet (Paris, 1967), 133–6.

[8] On peut se reporter sur ce sujet aux fragments 106–403, 118–402, 210–451, 211–453.

Les règles de la politesse ne font que masquer l'égoïsme. Elles font imiter un ordre idéal où l'amour serait parfaitement désintéressé et réciproque; elles font découvrir en l'homme une aspiration à cet ordre, signe de grandeur; mais elles ne le procurent pas. Pour y parvenir, il faudrait que le moi ne fût pas seulement 'couvert', mais 'ôté' (ibid.).

Il y a plus. Ce moi qui cherche à se faire aimer est-il vraiment aimable? Tout au contraire, et c'est par là qu'il est foncièrement injuste. Non seulement il se fait haïr mais il mérite d'être haï: le droit s'ajoute au fait. Deux séries de raisons sont employées à le montrer, les unes d'ordre moral, les autres d'ordre ontologique.

Le célèbre fragment sur l'amour-propre (978–100) est tout entier consacré à dénoncer, en termes de morale, l'injustice du moi. 'Il veut être l'objet de l'amour et de l'estime des hommes, et il voit que ses défauts ne méritent que leur aversion et leur mépris.' Objectivement, le moi est haïssable, à cause de ses 'imperfections' et de ses 'vices'. Il est juste que les autres 'nous connaissent pour ce que nous sommes, et qu'ils nous méprisent si nous sommes méprisables'. Mais, comme notre cœur est dénué 'd'équité et de justice', 'nous aimons qu'ils se trompent à notre avantage . . . nous voulons être estimés d'eux autres que nous ne sommes en effet.' L'amour que chacun porte à son moi, les défauts qu'il étale pourtant aux yeux des autres, l'effort intéressé de ces derniers pour lui plaire malgré tout en le flattant créent une situation complexe, d'où il s'ensuit que 'la vie humaine n'est qu'une illusion perpétuelle.' Le mensonge premier que constitue le refus du moi de se reconnaître pour ce qu'il est, c'est-à-dire haïssable, est le principe d'un mensonge généralisé dans tous les rapports humains.

Le moi ne mérite pas davantage l'amour si l'on considère son statut ontologique. C'est l'idée que met en valeur un fragment célèbre: 'Il est injuste qu'on s'attache à moi, quoiqu'on le fasse avec plaisir et volontairement. Je tromperais ceux à qui j'en ferais naître le désir, car je ne suis la fin de personne et n'ai de quoi les satisfaire. Ne suis-je pas prêt à mourir? Et ainsi l'objet de leur attachement mourra . . . ' (396–471). Confidence personnelle, évoquant les rapports de Pascal avec les membres de sa famille,[9] mais aussi réflexion générale sur l'injustice du moi. Son caractère passager, mortel, interdit de lui vouer un attachement dont l'objet, en définitive, se

---

[9] Voir la *Vie de Pascal*, dans notre éd. citée, 592–3, 631–3.

dérobe, et que mérite seul un être subsistant, c'est-à-dire Dieu. L'inconsistance fondamentale du moi est encore plus impitoyablement analysée dans un autre fragment:

Qu'est-ce que le moi? . . . Celui qui aime quelqu'un à cause de sa beauté l'aime-t-il? Non, car la petite vérole, qui tuera la beauté sans tuer la personne, fera qu'il ne l'aimera plus. Et si on m'aime pour mon jugement, pour ma mémoire, m'aime-t-on, moi? Non, car je puis perdre ces qualités sans me perdre moi-même. Où est donc ce moi, s'il n'est ni dans le corps ni dans l'âme? Et comment aimer le corps ou l'âme sinon pour ces qualités, qui ne sont point ce qui fait le moi, puisqu'elles sont périssables? . . . On n'aime donc jamais personne, mais seulement des qualités . . .   (688–323).

Ce qui caractérise en fin de compte le moi, c'est donc, au sens étymologique du terme, sa vanité.

Ces analyses permettent de mieux saisir la portée des critiques adressées à Montaigne. Les indications rapides des *Pensées* sont d'ailleurs développées par Nicole dans les pages déjà citées de la *Logique de Port-Royal*.[10] Si l'auteur des *Essais* a mis en œuvre un 'sot projet', c'est qu'il 'a affecté de n'entretenir ses lecteurs que de ses humeurs, de ses inclinations, de ses fantaisies, de ses maladies, de ses vertus et de ses vices', ce qui 'ne naît que d'un défaut de jugement aussi bien que d'un violent amour de soi-même'. Dans la peinture de son moi, Montaigne n'est certes pas 'incommode'. Mais il s'expose au reproche d'"injustice' principalement de deux manières. Il s'applique à rendre aimables même ses défauts, par les couleurs qu'il leur donne et par la sincérité artificieuse avec laquelle il les reconnaît. Il s'attarde sur des aspects insignifiants de sa personnalité, marque de complaisance en soi, expression d'une parfaite vanité. Si, dans sa manière de se peindre, Montaigne fait preuve d'un raffinement exceptionnel, il ne mérite pas une indulgence particulière.

Pourtant, chez Pascal, la critique de Montaigne n'empêche pas l'éloge, un éloge qui peut même sembler parfois contredire la critique. Ainsi lorsque nous lisons: 'Ce n'est pas dans Montaigne, mais dans moi, que je trouve tout ce que j'y vois' (689–64), la dénonciation de la peinture du moi ne fait-elle pas place à une véritable réhabilitation? Que faut-il en penser?

Le principe d'une réponse se déduit de l'identité que Pascal établit entre son moi et celui de Montaigne. Le fragment cité ne fait que

[10] 1664, pp. 342-5; 1965, pp. 267-9.

reprendre, en l'approuvant, la célèbre déclaration des *Essais*: 'Chaque homme porte la forme entière de l'humaine condition.'[11] Voltaire croyait réfuter Pascal lorsqu'il opposait à la condamnation 'Le sot projet qu'il a de se peindre' la réponse: 'Le charmant projet qu'il a eu de se peindre . . . car il peint la nature humaine.'[12] En fait, Pascal admettrait aisément le point de vue de Voltaire, sans renier pour autant le sien. Ce qui peut légitimer la peinture du moi chez Montaigne, c'est qu'elle est une peinture de l'humanité. S'il est répréhensible de se complaire dans son individualité la plus superficielle, il est important de chercher à saisir en soi-même l'universalité de la condition humaine.

D'autres pensées justifient cette interprétation et invitent au même élargissement: 'Quand on voit le style naturel on est tout étonné et ravi, car on s'attendait de voir un auteur et on trouve un homme' (675–29). Un homme, et non un moi: la distinction est capitale. De même: 'Quand un discours naturel peint une passion ou un effet, on trouve dans soi-même la vérité de ce qu'on entend, laquelle on ne savait pas qu'elle y fût, de sorte qu'on est porté à aimer celui qui nous la fait sentir, car il ne nous a point fait montre de son bien mais du nôtre . . . ' (652–14). Le passage du 'haïssable' à l' 'aimable' s'opère par le passage de l'individu à l'homme en tant qu'échantillon de l'humanité.

Aussi bien si l' 'honnête homme' est effectivement celui qui se fait aimer, ce qu'il convient d'aimer en lui n'est pas ce qui est strictement personnel; c'est ce qui reflète l'humanité en général. C'est par l'humanité que les hommes communiquent sans se nuire et sans se haïr. Le véritable 'honnête homme' est l' 'homme universel': 'Il faut qu'on n'en puisse dire, ni il est mathématicien, ni prédicateur, ni éloquent, mais il est honnête homme. Cette qualité universelle me plaît seule . . . ' (647–35). Ou encore: 'Les gens universels ne sont appelés ni poètes, ni géomètres, etc., mais ils sont tout cela et juges de tous ceux-là.' (587–34). Sans doute l'homme universel est-il ainsi opposé au spécialiste; mais la spécialité est une manière de faire valoir un moi différent. La disponibilité à l'autre, la capacité de s'adapter à lui, c'est-à-dire le refus de s'imposer, voilà le caractère véritable de l'honnête homme. Ce qui est aimable en lui est ce que chacun y retrouve de lui-même. En élargissant le moi aux

[11] Ed. cit. 805.
[12] *Lettres philosophiques*, éd. Lanson, 5e éd. (Paris, 1937), 216.

dimensions de l'universel, il est donc possible, sans quitter l'ordre humain, de le faire échapper à la tare qui le rendait 'haïssable'.

D'un point de vue plus directement philosophique, le retour vers soi pour y trouver l'humanité essentielle, offre une signification capitale. Par là se constitue la pensée, qui est d'abord conscience de soi, et qui 'fait la grandeur de l'homme' (759–346). Or, précise Pascal, qui se souvient du *cogito* cartésien, 'l'ordre de la pensée est de commencer par soi . . . '. Mais il ajoute, sans cesser d'être fidèle à Descartes, tout en le dépassant: 'et par son auteur et sa fin' (620–146).

En effet, l'homme qui, par la pensée, prend conscience de son être, découvre d'abord sa misère. C'est d'ailleurs cet acte même qui permet d'affirmer sa grandeur. Ce n'est pas seulement le moi, c'est l'humanité en lui, qui éprouve son imperfection, associée à un désir de perfection, sa précarité, associée à un désir de stabilité. Pour surmonter cette déception essentielle, pour procurer à l'homme une fin qui comble ses désirs, il faut passer de la philosophie à la théologie et, plus précisément, de l'ordre des esprits à l'ordre de la charité.

C'est pourtant d'abord par une argumentation rationnelle que Pascal montre la nécessité d'opérer ce passage. Une réflexion sur l'être lui en fournit le premier moyen:

Je sens que je puis n'avoir point été, car le moi consiste dans ma pensée. Donc moi qui pense n'aurais point été si ma mère eût été tuée avant que j'eusse été animé. Donc je ne suis pas un être nécessaire. Je ne suis pas aussi éternel ni infini. Mais je sais bien qu'il y a dans la nature un être nécessaire, éternel et infini.

$$(135–469)$$

Dans cette perspective, comme dans celle du *cogito* cartésien, le moi s'identifie à l'humanité.

A ce raisonnement s'en ajoute un autre, portant sur les fins auxquelles l'homme aspire, sur ce qu'on appelle souvent aujourd'hui les valeurs. C'est par erreur que l'homme cherche le Souverain Bien dans les créatures — terme qui définit le statut aussi bien de l'humanité en général que de chaque moi en particulier: le 'gouffre infini' de son âme 'ne peut être rempli que par un objet infini et immuable, c'est-à-dire que par Dieu même' (148–425).

La nécessité d'accéder à l'ordre de la charité s'impose dès lors qu'on s'exprime, non plus en termes de connaissance, mais en termes d'amour. Tout ce qui est créé, fini, particulier, ne peut être l'objet que d'un amour de concupiscence, réductible à l'amour de soi. Seul mérite absolument l'amour l'Etre incréé, infini, 'universel', qui est Dieu. Or l'homme est ballotté entre ces deux amours qui l'habitent: 'Le cœur aime l'être universel naturellement et soi-même naturellement, selon qu'il s'y adonne; et il se durcit contre l'un ou l'autre à son choix' (423–277). Mais le seul choix propre à combler l'homme est celui du premier de ces amours, c'est-à-dire de la charité.

La vraie et unique vertu est donc de se haïr, car on est haïssable par sa concupiscence, et de chercher un être véritablement aimable pour l'aimer. Mais comme nous ne pouvons aimer ce qui est hors de nous, il faut aimer un être qui soit en nous et qui ne soit pas nous. Et cela est vrai d'un chacun de tous les hommes. Or il n'y a que l'être universel qui soit tel. Le royaume de Dieu est en nous. Le bien universel est en nous, est nous-même et n'est pas nous.

(564–485)

Quoique d'origine théologique, cette opposition de l'amour de soi et de l'amour de Dieu et la nécessité de faire triompher le second sur le premier, avec, pour corollaire, celle d'une véritable 'haine de soi', apparaît à Pascal si parfaitement conforme à la connaissance que l'homme, par la raison, peut prendre de lui-même, qu'il en fait un critère déterminant pour distinguer vraie et fausse religion. 'La vraie religion doit avoir pour marque d'obliger à aimer son Dieu . . . la nôtre l'a fait. Elle doit encore avoir connu la concupiscence et l'impuissance, la nôtre l'a fait' (214–491). 'Nulle autre religion n'a proposé de se haïr, nulle autre religion ne peut donc plaire à ceux qui se haïssent et qui cherchent un être véritablement aimable' (220–468). Par là même, la religion chrétienne se trouve justifiée: 'Jèsus-Christ n'a fait autre chose qu'apprendre aux hommes qu'ils s'aimaient eux-mêmes . . . qu'il fallait qu'il les délivrât, éclairât, béatifiât et guérît, que cela se ferait en se haïssant soi-même, et en le suivant par la misère et la mort de la croix' (271–545). Jésus-Christ, se substituant au moi comme fin, devient 'l'objet de tout et le centre où tout tend' (448–559). Il est ce Dieu dont le premier caractère est d'être 'universel' (221–774). La conversion, acte d'entrée dans l'ordre de la charité, consiste à se soumettre à la règle: 'Il faut n'aimer que Dieu et ne haïr que soi' (373–476).

Mais parler de haine de soi n'est-il pas excessif et inhumain? Les premiers éditeurs des *Pensées* ont perçu la difficulté et jugé bon de l'écarter par une explication: 'Le terme de *moi* dont l'auteur se sert . . . ne signifie que l'amour-propre. C'est un terme dont il avait

accoutumé de se servir avec quelques-uns de ses amis.'[13] L'explication est double. Elle concerne d'abord l'emploi de *moi* comme sub-
stantif, nouveauté à l'époque de Pascal et qu'il a contribué à faire
passer dans la langue: c'est une manière de parler qui lui était personnelle. Mais le *moi* ainsi désigné est envisagé dans sa propension
à se faire 'centre', à se rendre exclusif, en somme comme sujet de
cette tendance vicieuse qu'est l'amour-propre. Pascal lui-même con-
firme cette interprétation: 'Qui ne hait en soi son amour-propre et
cet instinct qui le porte à se faire Dieu est bien aveuglé' (617–492).
Le moi ne coïncide donc pas avec l'essence de la personne, selon la
conception qui prévaut aujourd'hui. Mais Pascal admettrait aussi
ce dernier sens: pour lui, comme pour tout le christianisme, c'est la
personne individuelle qui est appelée au salut. Ce qu'il faut haïr
dans le moi, c'est donc uniquement ce qui en lui s'érige en absolu et
refuse de se situer dans un ordre. Dès qu'un ordre véritable met
chaque être à sa place, un certain amour de soi devient légitime,
parce que l'individuel se concilie désormais avec l'universel. Pour
faire comprendre cette idée, Pascal développe la grande image d'un
corps plein de membres pensants. 'Pour régler l'amour qu'on se doit
à soi-même, il faut imaginer un corps plein de membres pensants,
car nous sommes membres du tout, et voir comment chaque
membre devrait s'aimer, etc.' (368–474):

Le membre séparé, ne voyant plus le corps auquel il appartient, n'a plus
qu'un être périssant et mourant. Cependant il croit être un tout et, ne se
voyant point de corps dont il dépende, il croit ne dépendre que de soi et
veut se faire centre et corps lui-même. Mais, n'ayant point en soi de principe de vie, il ne fait que s'égarer . . . Quand il vient à se connaître, il est
comme revenu chez soi et ne s'aime plus que pour le corps . . . En aimant le
corps il s'aime soi-même, parce qu'il n'a d'être qu'en lui, par lui et pour lui.

                                                                    (372–483)

L'image se fonde sur la fable antique des membres et de l'estomac,
mais aussi sur la grande idée de saint Paul, celle du Corps mystique,
dont Jésus-Christ est la tête et les chrétiens les membres. 'On s'aime
parce qu'on est membre de Jésus-Christ. On aime Jésus-Christ
parce qu'il est le corps dont on est membre' (ibid.). C'est par référence à Jésus-Christ devenu centre que la communauté des hommes
se constitue authentiquement.

---

[13] *Pensées*, 2e éd. (Paris, 1670), 278 (voir le facsimile publié par G. Couton et
J. Jehasse, Saint-Etienne, 1971, 392).

Les valeurs humaines prennent consistance à partir du moment
où elles sont ordonnées aux valeurs chrétiennes. 'Nul homme n'est
heureux comme un vrai chrétien, ni raisonnable, ni vertueux, ni
aimable' (357–541). Dans l'état de nature, 'les hommes sont contraires à l'honnêteté' (642–448). L'aspiration si essentielle à l' 'honnête homme' à se rendre aimable n'est satisfaite que pour le
chrétien, qui n'a pas seulement 'couvert' son moi, mais l'a 'ôté'
(597–455), en en extirpant l'amour-propre. Par une dialectique
paradoxale, mais tout à fait rigoureuse, le moi cesse d'être haïssable
à partir du moment où il se hait lui-même.

Bien entendu, dans la vie terrestre, la concupiscence ne peut être
totalement éliminée; l'amour de Dieu ne peut se substituer entièrement à l'amour de soi. Il reste toujours à se défier de son moi. Mais
il importe de tendre vers la 'communion des saints' que réalisera
seulement la Cité de Dieu.

Résultat d'une observation sans complaisance des comporte-
ments humains, l'affirmation 'le moi est haïssable' exprime
d'abord pour Pascal une situation de fait. Mais celle-ci n'est pas
irrémédiable. Le désir qu'éprouve le moi de se rendre aimable ne
peut toutefois se réaliser que s'il renonce à se faire 'centre de
tout', s'il accepte de se plier, dans ses rapports avec les autres, à
un principe d'uni-versalité qui le met de plain-pied avec eux. Ce
principe peut être l'humanité, à laquelle tous les hommes partici-
pent au-delà de leurs différences individuelles: ainsi l'envisage,
sous sa forme la plus élevée, l''honnêteté' mondaine. Mais le véritable Bien, celui qui peut être possédé par tous sans que la part de
chacun en soit diminuée, n'est autre que l'Etre universel, c'est-à-
dire Dieu, seul médiateur d'une communication authentique, où
chaque moi, par le refus de s'aimer égoïstement, devient souverai-
nement aimable.

Telle est la démarche rationnelle, du particulier à l'universel, que
Pascal nous invite à accomplir dans sa réflexion sur le 'moi haïssable'. Cet élargissement, si l'on se place sur le terrain religieux,
devient ascension. Le 'moi haïssable', tout occupé à affirmer sa
puissance, se situe dans l'ordre des corps. La raison, faculté maîtresse dans l'ordre des esprits, montre la nécessité d'une référence
universelle pour que le moi puisse devenir aimable. Mais ce qu'elle
entrevoit ne peut devenir réalité que si l'on accède à l'ordre de la
charité, c'est-à-dire par une véritable conversion, où le moi, désormais animé du seul amour qui puisse le combler, celui de Dieu,
trouve, dans l'universalité des êtres, sa juste place.

3

Rousseau, Adam Smith and the Education of the Self

PETER FRANCE

LUI. De l'homme. Tout ce qui vit, sans l'en excepter, cherche son bien-être aux dépens de qui il appartiendra; et je suis sûr que, si je laissais venir le petit sauvage, sans lui parler de rien: il voudrait être richement vêtu, splendidement nourri, chéri des hommes, aimé des femmes, et rassembler sur lui tous les bonheurs de la vie.

MOI. Si le petit sauvage était abandonné à lui-même; qu'il conservât toute son imbécillité et qu'il reunît au peu de raison de l'enfant au berceau, la violence des passions de l'homme de trente ans, il tordrait le cou à son père, et coucherait avec sa mère.

LUI. Cela prouve la nécessité d'une bonne éducation; et qui est-ce qui la conteste! et qu'est-ce qu'une bonne éducation, sinon celle qui conduit à toutes sortes de jouissances, sans péril, et sans inconvénient.

MOI. Peu s'en faut que je ne sois de votre avis; mais gardons-nous de nous expliquer.[1]

This essay will go into the question that 'Moi' avoids; it concerns the taming and training of the 'little savage'. *Le Neveu de Rameau*, which expresses so many of the worries of the *philosophes*, was begun within two or three years of the first publication of two important books in which the problems of socialization bulk large, one Scottish, Adam Smith's *Theory of Moral Sentiments* (1759) and the other French, Rousseau's *Emile* (1762). These very different works come from quite different environments. Smith's belongs to the clubbable male world of the Scottish Enlightenment,[2] the

---

[1] Denis Diderot, *Le Neveu de Rameau*, ed. Jacques and Anne-Marie Chouillet (Paris, 1982), 163.

[2] The present essay is not concerned with influences; however, it is worth noting that while Rousseau must have been quite unaware of Smith when writing *Emile*, Smith by 1759 certainly knew the Genevan's *Discours sur l'inégalité*, which he had analysed for the first *Edinburgh Review* in 1755. By the time he revised *The Theory of Moral Sentiments* for the sixth edition of 1790 he would presumably have read most of Rousseau's major works, including *Emile*.

world of men like David Hume, William Robertson and Hugh Blair, whereas Rousseau's is the work of a solitary prophet in revolt against the salons and academies of civilized Paris. It is interesting nevertheless to set them side by side, as both propose to their educated readers (in many cases the same readers) answers to the problems that tormented Diderot. Their voices and their private impulses are often worlds apart, but we find them pursuing parallel lines of inquiry about the possibilities of harmonious social living and the dangers of conformism.

Let us first stay a little longer with *Le Neveu de Rameau*. Quite apart from its apparent anticipation of Freud, the extract quoted above gives dramatic expression to a problem that concerned many moralists of the time. If earlier periods had seen human beings as 'encadrés dans des solidarités collectives, féodales et communautaires à l'intérieur d'un système qui fonctionne à peu près',[3] the two centuries preceding Diderot's dialogue had seen a growing emphasis on the separateness of the individual. This is evident from various aspects of everyday life (such as house design, physical taboos enforcing privacy, silent reading, autobiographical writing, the taste for solitude, the stress on individual friendship), which have recently been traced in volume iii of the *Histoire de la vie privée*. As for moral thought, Hobbes in particular had proposed a cynical assessment of the human animal's natural selfishness, which could only be restrained by force. His challenge had to be met by all those eighteenth-century thinkers (Diderot among them) who attempted to work out a natural moral system, independent of religious dogmas and sanctions, that could provide a basis for harmonious social existence. If man was naturally a savage, self-seeking beast, how could human beings live successfully together?

The passage in *Le Neveu* is very close to some lines in Diderot's *Encyclopédie* article 'Hobbisme', where we read of Hobbes's 'sublime' definition of the 'méchant' as an 'enfant robuste'. And in the article 'Droit naturel', Diderot attempts rather desperately to deal with the threat of this wild child who announces: 'il faut ou que je sois malheureux ou que je fasse le malheur des autres; et personne ne m'est plus cher que je me le suis à moi-même. Qu'on ne me reproche point cette abominable prédilection; elle n'est pas libre.

---

[3] *Histoire de la vie privée*, 5 vols, ed. P. Ariès and G. Duby; *De la Renaissance aux Lumières*, ed. R. Chartier (Paris, 1986), iii. 7.

C'est la voix de la nature qui ne s'explique jamais plus fortement en moi que quand elle parle en ma faveur.'[4] Nor did the problem go away if a less pessimistic view of human nature was taken than that of Hobbes. If the individual was the source of value, and individual happiness the universal goal, how could the different claims of individuals be reconciled? How was the self to learn to accommodate to other selves? And if socialization was achieved, what were the costs and dangers of the achievement?

Le Neveu gives two radically different answers to these questions. 'Moi' and 'Lui' agree that what is needed is 'une bonne éducation', but this apparent agreement rests on totally opposed views of human nature. Rameau sees humanity in jungle terms; beast preys on beast, and a good education teaches young human beings to hold their own and obtain their pleasures in this savage world. For those who are not powerful (the great majority), this means flattery, hypocrisy, treachery and similar arts. Nor is this easy. Rameau says at times that his so-called vices, so essential for social success, come naturally to him—in which case we should have a Mandevillean harmony in which private vices bring mutual satisfaction. Elsewhere, however, as he speaks of his pathetic 'dignity', it is clear that the human animal has to be broken in to social conformity. This is emblematically represented by the stiff hand of the violinist, which has to be painfully forced into flexibility:

Ces dix doigts, c'étaient autant de bâtons fichés dans un métacarpe de bois; et ces tendons, c'étaient de vieilles cordes à boyau plus sèches, plus roides, plus inflexibles que celles qui ont servi à la roue d'un tourneur. Mais je vous les ai tant tourmentées, tant brisées, tant rompues. Tu ne veux pas aller; et moi, mordieu, je dis que tu iras; et cela sera.   (ed. cit. 87)

The *philosophe*, on the contrary, is not flexible. He claims exemption from the great pantomime of mutual dependency, even if that means becoming a Diogenes. Unlike Rameau, he has made for himself (or so he says) 'une ressource indépendante de la servitude'. But he too has an ideal of sociability. The education he wants for his daughter is moral and public-spirited, and he sets against Rameau's cynicism an optimistic view of humanity, in which sympathy and benevolence are natural. I have no doubt that he speaks for Diderot when he praises the pleasures of virtue, but in the dialogue he is not allowed the last word. At the end, as the two speakers part, we are

⁴ Diderot, *Œuvres politiques*, ed. P. Vernière (Paris 1983), 31.

still left with the question: what is 'une bonne éducation' for the commercial society of Diderot and his contemporaries?

I say 'commercial society' because for certain eighteenth-century writers, notably those of the Scottish Enlightenment, the move from a predominantly agricultural society to one centred on commerce had brought with it particular problems.[5] In fact the notion of commerce was an ambiguous one. As Hirschman has shown, 'le doux commerce' was seen as a factor moderating such powerful and disruptive passions as anger and ambition, thus leading to greater social harmony.[6] At the same time, for less optimistic spectators, such as Adam Ferguson,[7] a commercial society was one in which individuals pursued their own ends, heedless of the social bonds of traditional society. The very word 'commerce' is interestingly multi-faceted, both in English and in French. Its etymological meaning has to do with the exchange of goods, but from the sixteenth century onwards it became increasingly used metaphorically to refer to all types of social relations (including those between the sexes). Bouhours, in his *Remarques nouvelles* of 1676, notes that this figurative social meaning is 'very elegant'. When used in this way, however, it can equally well carry positive or negative connotations. Bossuet, for instance, in his funeral oration for Le Tellier, speaks of his 'doux commerce avec des amis aussi modestes que lui'.[8] La Bruyère, on the other hand, translating Theophrastus, writes that 'la flatterie est un commerce honteux qui n'est utile qu'au flatteur'[9]—and here commerce seems close to its mercantile sense and consequently appears as a shameful business to an aristocratic seventeenth-century audience. The *honnête homme* does not engage in commerce of this kind.

[5] There is a sizeable literature on this subject; see in particular J. G. A. Pocock, *The Machiavellian Moment* (Princeton University Press, 1975). Pocock's insights have been applied to the Scottish Enlightenment by (among many others) N. Phillipson, 'The Scottish Enlightenment', in *The Enlightenment in National Context*, ed. R. Porter and M. Teich (Cambridge University Press, 1981), 19–40, and Donald Winch, *Adam Smith's Politics* (Cambridge University Press, 1978).

[6] See Albert O. Hirschman, *The Passions and the Interests* (Princeton University Press, 1977), in particular pp. 56–63.

[7] Adam Ferguson, *An Essay on the History of Civil Society* (1767), ed. D. Forbes (Edinburgh University Press, 1966). On Ferguson and Rousseau, see my article 'Primitivism and Enlightenment: Rousseau and the Scots', *Yearbook of English Studies* 15 (1985), 64–79.

[8] Bossuet, *Oraisons funèbres*, ed. J. Truchet (Paris, 1961), 319.

[9] La Bruyère, *Les Caractères*, ed. R. Garapon (Paris, 1962), 21.

It is enlightening to see how the word is used in *Le Misanthrope*, which may be seen as setting the terms for the debate on sociability in the following generations. In the first scene, Alceste anticipates La Bruyère's condemnation when he exclaims:

> Non, vous dis-je, on devrait châtier sans pitié
> Ce commerce honteux de semblants d'amitié.
>
> (i. i. 67–8)

This commerce is the negation of authentic human relations. In Act II, it is Célimène who uses the word to refer satirically to the social pretensions of Géralde:

> Dans le brillant commerce il se mêle sans cesse,
> Et ne cite jamais que duc, prince ou princesse.
>
> (ii. v. 597–8)

Again the word carries connotations of falsity. But to my mind the most interesting use of 'commerce' comes in Act V: Alceste declares his 'misanthropic' intention of leaving 'le monde' in these words:

> Trop de perversité règne au siècle où nous sommes,
> Et je veux me tirer du commerce des hommes.
>
> (v. i. 1485–6)

Here the word seems to be used neutrally ('le commerce des hommes' equals 'human society'), yet all that we have seen of Alceste's world leads us to conclude that the whole web of social relations could well be seen as a 'commerce honteux'. Many moralists of the succeeding century would echo Alceste's words.

At the same time, this century saw a notable rise in the esteem accorded to merchants, or at least the esteem of which certain writers thought them worthy. The commercial society was welcomed by most Enlightenment thinkers, for whom there was nothing shameful in the exchange of goods and services. On the contrary, for a Hume or a Diderot, commerce led not only to increased comfort, but to greater peace, security and cooperation between peoples. Adam Smith in particular is often seen as the champion of commerce; his *Wealth of Nations*, first published in 1776, shows how the self-interest of individuals is directed by the Invisible Hand to work for the general good. Thus he writes in chapter 2:

man has almost constant occasion for the help of his brethren, and it is in vain for him to expect it from their benevolence only. He will be more likely to prevail if he can interest their self-love in his favour, and shew them that it is for their own advantage to do for him what he requires of them . . . It is not from the benevolence of the butcher, the brewer, or the baker, that we expect our dinner, but from their regard to their own interest.[10]

For Smith, however, *The Wealth of Nations* was part of a larger theory which sought to give an empirical account of all aspects of social life. His first published work, *The Theory of Moral Sentiments*,[11] is concerned not with the exchange of goods, but with the way we learn to live in society, forming appropriate moral values by which to act and judge the actions of others and ourselves. One naturally asks, therefore, how far his picture of social relations between individuals is based on the human 'propensity to truck, barter and exchange one thing for another' which is the 'principle which gives occasion to the division of labour' and thence to the whole economic system of *The Wealth of Nations*. At first sight the answer is that *The Theory of Moral Sentiments*, with its stress on the importance of sympathy, gives a much less egoistic account of human nature than *The Wealth of Nations*, and this apparent opposition between the two works has become known as the 'Adam Smith problem'. Scholars have by turns dramatized this problem or sought to lay it to rest, and most recently, in an illuminating article,[12] Laurence Dickey has indicated how it may be 'historicized' and more fully understood if we examine how Smith changed his first work for its sixth edition in 1790. I do not want to venture into this argument here, nor to try to situate Smith in relation to a highly complex tradition of moral thought, but simply to ask how in *The Theory of Moral Sentiments* Smith envisaged the mechanisms, problems and dangers of the socialization of the individual in a modern society.

The first thing to remember is that he was lecturing to students, most of them teenagers, at Glasgow University (even if the theories expounded in *The Theory of Moral Sentiments* go back to his days as a lecturer in Edinburgh some ten years earlier). Naturally

---

[10] Adam Smith, *An Inquiry into the Nature and Causes of the Wealth of Nations*, 2 vols, ed. R. H. Campbell and A. S. Skinner (Oxford 1976), 26–7.

[11] *The Theory of Moral Sentiments* (TMS) is cited in the edition of D. D. Raphael and A. L. Macfie (Oxford, 1976).

[12] Laurence Dickey, 'Historicizing the "Adam Smith Problem": Conceptual, Historiographical and Textual Issues', *Journal of Modern History* 58 (1986), 579–609.

therefore, his 'scientific' analysis of moral behaviour is also aimed at instilling proper values and encouraging proper conduct in the future educated classes. All the time he appeals to a consensual 'we'—when he writes for instance: 'We are disgusted with the clamorous grief, which, without any delicacy, calls upon our compassion with sighs and tears and importunate lamentation' (*TMS*, 24), it may be thought that he is proposing as a model to his students the behaviour and attitudes of adult males of a certain rank in a specific society. The 'we' are for the most part the respectable men (rather than women) among whom his listeners will take their place. Nevertheless, the dominant impulse behind Smith's work (like Montesquieu's) is to give an account of how people (even if not all people everywhere) actually behave. As he puts it, 'the present inquiry is not concerning a matter of right, if I may say so, but concerning a matter of fact' (*TMS*, 77). His book belongs to the science of man which was to stand alongside Newton's physical science.

Smith does not seek to deny the importance of self-interest in human action. The butcher engages in trade for his own ends, and we are impelled to act by what the Stoic tradition described as the principle of self-love, which enables every animal 'to preserve not only its own existence, but all the different parts of its nature, in the most perfect state of which they were capable' (*TMS*, 272). In the case of human beings, this self-love has a very extended definition, and Smith is at pains to refute 'licentious systems' which would reduce all our actions to narrowly selfish motives, and thus negate any real distinction between virtue and vice. Such systems are represented by Mandeville, to whom Smith devotes several pages of criticism which are reminiscent of the *philosophe*'s attempt to deal with Rameau's nephew.

The counterweight to egoism is provided by Smith's master principle, sympathy. His book begins with a description of this instinct:

How selfish soever man may be supposed, there are evidently some principles in his nature, which interest him in the fortune of others, and render their happiness necessary to him, though he derives nothing more from it except the pleasure of seeing it. Of this kind is pity or compassion, the emotion with which we feel for the misery of others, when we either see it, or are made to conceive it in a very lively manner. That we often derive sorrow from the sorrow of others, is a matter of fact too obvious to require any instances to prove it; for this sentiment, like all the other original passions of human nature, is by no means confined to the virtuous and human, though they perhaps may feel it with the most exquisite sensibility. The greatest ruffian, the most hardened violator of the laws of society, is not altogether without it. (*TMS*, 9)

(Note from the outset the use of 'we', suggesting a consensus that a Rameau might well deny.) In Smith's account sympathy enables us to 'bring home to ourselves' all the different feelings of our fellow-men—not just their sorrow, but equally their joy or their anger. The operation of sympathy depends crucially on imagination; on the basis of our own experience, we mentally put ourselves in the place of others. Such sympathy brings pleasure, and a pleasure which according to Smith is so spontaneous that it cannot possibly be traced back to 'certain refinements of self-love'. It is felt equally by those who extend sympathy and by those who receive it: 'As the person who is principally interested in any event is pleased with our sympathy, and hurt by the want of it, so we, too, seem to be pleased when we are able to sympathize with him, and to be hurt when we are unable to do so' (*TMS*, 15).

In such relations of sympathy we can find a stimulus to social co-operation which is different from that of 'trucking and bartering'. Smith admits, it is true, that even without such 'generous and disinterested motives', society may still 'subsist among different men, as among different merchants, from a sense of its utility, without any mutual love or affection . . . by a mercenary exchange of good offices according to an agreed valuation' (*TMS*, 86). But this minimal 'commercial' society is not what *The Theory of Moral Sentiments* is seeking to explain and promote; happy social relations depend on mutual 'gratitude . . . friendship and esteem' (*TMS*, 85). One is struck, however, on reading the first book of *The Theory of Moral Sentiments*, by the problems that may beset the operations of sympathy. What is involved, as often as not, is a process of negotiation between individuals. We do not always naturally feel the sympathy that others feel is due to them. Either we fail to imagine their situation, or their feelings seem to us excessive in relation to the reality of the situation:

When the original passions of the person principally concerned are in perfect concord with the sympathetic emotions of the spectator, they necessarily appear to this last just and proper, and suitable to their objects; and, on the contrary, when, upon bringing the case home to himself, he finds that they do not coincide with what he feels, they necessarily appear to him unjust and improper . . .   (*TMS*, 16)

'Proper' and 'propriety' are the terms used to describe a mutually acceptable level of emotion. Successful and harmonious social living depends therefore on learning 'propriety' in the feelings we express and our expression of them—and also, in so far as we are not directly concerned, in our ability to give due sympathy. This may not be an easy education; we learn by hard experience. If sympathy is refused, we suffer, and will try to do better next time. Smith's description of the process is interesting, and in particular his use of musical analogy:

Mankind, though naturally sympathetic, never conceive, for what has befallen another, that degree of passion which naturally animates the person principally concerned . . . The person principally concerned is sensible of this, and at the same time passionately desires a more complete sympathy. He longs for that relief which nothing can afford him but the entire concord of the affections of the spectators with his own. To see the emotions of their hearts, in every respect, beat time to his own, in the violent and disagreeable passions, constitutes his sole consolation. But he can only hope to obtain this by lowering his passion to that pitch, in which the spectators are capable of going along with him. He must flatten, if I may be allowed to say so, the sharpness of its natural tone, in order to reduce it to harmony and concord with the emotions of those who are about him.

(*TMS*, 21)

This is, in Smith's view, a lesson that 'nature' teaches both the sufferer and the spectator. This personified force (or sometimes the 'author of nature') gives human beings the instincts they need to live together, even if they have to work at it.

So far, so good. There may be difficulties in the negotiation of sympathy (and Smith, in his leisurely lecturing style, gives many examples), but for the most part the mechanism works and 'we' learn to anticipate and respond appropriately to the feelings of others—particularly if 'we' belong to the superior class of men who have a natural sensitivity to those feelings. Smith's account is startlingly optimistic in places, and nowhere more so than when he explains how 'we' naturally take pleasure in identifying with the happy state of the rich and powerful:

It is the very state which, in all our waking dreams and idle reveries, we had sketched out to ourselves as the final object of all our desires. We feel, therefore, a peculiar sympathy with the satisfaction of those who are in it.

(*TMS*, 51)

In this fortunate disposition (unclouded by envy) is to be found the natural foundation for the 'distinction of ranks'. With such feelings the Invisible Hand supports the social hierarchy.

Sympathy, as Smith describes it, is mostly concerned with our reaction to the behaviour of others. As for our own actions, he sees the 'consciousness of being beloved' as the 'chief part of human happiness' (*TMS*, 41). We naturally do our best to merit the love—or at least the sympathy—of others, as well as their approval:

Nature, when she formed man for society, endowed him with an original desire to please, and an original aversion to offend his brethren. She taught him to feel pleasure in their favourable, and pain in their unfavourable regard. She rendered their approbation most flattering and most agreeable to him for its own sake; and their disapprobation most mortifying and most offensive.   (*TMS*, 116)[13]

Smith takes great care in his critique of Mandeville to rebut the suggestion that the desire to be loved, admired and approved (which must be the basis of proper social behaviour) is no more than a form of self-love or vanity. One senses, however, in this section, that he is aware that his position is a tricky one. There is, he admits, 'a certain remote affinity' between disinterested love of virtue, love of true glory, and vanity, and this has allowed Mandeville to 'impose upon his readers' (*TMS*, 310). How is one to draw the line?

The problem is like that faced by Alceste or by the *philosophe* of *Le Neveu de Rameau*. Given the desire for approval, is it not likely, in the school of society, that individuals will learn to play parts for applause? Certainly, when Smith describes the training in the 'great school of self-command' (*TMS*, 145) that has to be undergone by those entering society, one can sense an affinity with Rameau disciplining his stubborn fingers. Or consider the picture of the 'upstart', his attempts to ward off feelings of envy:

---

[13] This quotation is from the sixth edition (1790), but it expresses ideas already present in the 1759 edition.

Instead of appearing to be elated with his good fortune, he endeavours, as much as he can, to smother his joy, and keep down the elevation of mind with which his new circumstances naturally inspire him. He affects the same plainness of dress, and the same modesty of behaviour which became him in his former station. He redoubles his attention to his old friends, and endeavours more than ever to be humble, assiduous, and complaisant.

(*TMS*, 41)

Is this virtue? Yes, if he really does suppress his natural feelings, but more probably 'we suspect the sincerity of his humanity, and he grows weary of this constraint'. It is hard to distinguish between acting virtuously and acting the part of virtue. And things are obviously even worse if the approval of the particular spectators who surround the individual is based on values which to the philosopher appear corrupt and unacceptable. It seems that the individual is at the mercy of public opinion.

It is at this point in the argument that Smith has to bring in his famous 'impartial spectator'. Our social and moral training involves seeing ourselves in the mirror of the gaze of others (see *TMS*, 110), but we can (and up to a point we all do) go beyond the actual approval or disapproval of real spectators and create in our minds an impartial spectator, the 'man within' or 'representative of mankind' (*TMS*, 130). This imagined judge, unlike our neighbours, knows the truth about our actions and motives, and provides us with a truly objective standard (still presumably based on the general opinions of mankind). Thus we are rescued from excessive dependence on the unreliable judgements of our fellow-men. Secure in the approval of the impartial spectator (if we have acted well, that is), we can view with equanimity the 'inferior tribunal' of public praise or blame. Those who do not do this are 'slaves of the world' (*TMS*, 131).

It is important to note that the treatment of this theme was greatly expanded and strengthened by Smith in the sixth (1790) edition of *The Theory of Moral Sentiments*. It is in this edition that we find the celebrated, highly symmetrical passage on praiseworthiness:

Man naturally desires, not only to be loved, but to be lovely; or to be that thing which is the natural and proper object of love. He naturally dreads, not only to be hated, but to be hateful; or to be that thing which is the natural and proper object of hatred. He desires, not only praise, but praiseworthiness; or to be that thing which, though it should be praised by nobody, is, however, the natural and proper object of praise. He dreads, not only blame, but blame-worthiness; or to be that thing which, though it should be blamed by nobody, is, however, the natural and proper object of blame. (*TMS*, 114)

It seems in fact as if the confidence that the earlier edition displays in the natural workings of socialization had dwindled in the intervening years. Laurence Dickey has argued persuasively that in the 1780s—after publishing *The Wealth of Nations*—Smith had become alarmed by the awareness that 'for a commercial society to function properly . . . it would have to maintain a high degree of collective vigilance and "propriety" with regard to its morality.'[14] In the same way, we may note that he added to the sixth edition a section tempering his earlier approval of the sympathy we feel for the good fortune of the rich. Where earlier this natural feeling was the basis of a necessary social hierarchy, Smith now shows himself, in the manner of the 'moralists of all ages', far more aware of the corruption it can engender. Again he is confronting the problem that Rameau set before the *philosophe*: 'We frequently see the respectful attentions of the world more strongly directed towards the rich and the great, than towards the wise and the virtuous. We see frequently the vices and follies of the powerful much less despised than the poverty and weakness of the innocent' (*TMS*, 62). Only the voice of the impartial spectator, bringing with it the pleasure of self-approbation or the pangs of conscience, can be called on to counteract this all too natural tendency. And in the last resort, the virtuous but misjudged man may have to seek consolation by appealing to 'a still higher tribunal', that of 'the all-seeing Judge of the world' (*TMS*, 131). Generally speaking, Adam Smith manages to construct his moral system without God, but, like Rousseau, he has to appeal to him where all else fails.

To sum up, we see in Smith, the habitué of the Edinburgh clubs, an apologist of natural sociability. Children are not little savages for him, though they still have to be broken in to society by an education to which nature prompts them. Generally speaking, as he expounds his system to his Glasgow students, Smith can take satisfaction in the way 'we' behave, the assumption being that he is dealing with people like himself, responsible members of a stable

---

[14] Dickey, art. cit. 608.

society. The description of what is shades into a picture of what
should be. Yet there are doubts. Mandeville's egoism lurks in the
background, and by 1790 Smith is sufficiently worried by the
potential dangers of letting natural socialization take its course to
push the balance back in favour of the individual's autonomous
moral judgement.

When one turns from Adam Smith to his older contemporary
Rousseau, one finds all the Scot's worries writ large. Indeed, they
provide the starting-point for Rousseau's exploration. Jean-Jacques
does not write as a member of the social and literary establishment,
nor as a university professor inducting young men into respectable
adult life. If Smith tends towards complacency when he describes
the way things are, Rousseau, the hermit of Montmorency, is a
fierce nay-sayer. In *Emile*, as in the earlier *Discours sur l'inégalité*,
he denounces a corrupt society. But in *Emile* he also tries to set
what might be against what is, imagining a better form of social
relations, and it is here that we find interesting echoes of *The
Theory of Moral Sentiments*. In what follows, I shall confine
myself almost entirely to *Emile*—and shall of course do no more
than pick out a few threads from this fascinating and complex
work.[15]

Rousseau makes his task extraordinarily difficult with his dramatic opening pages on the incompatibility of the individual and
society. In the *Discours sur l'inégalité*, he had flown in the face of
most contemporary opinion by depicting natural man (hypothetically of course) as a non-social animal, whose evil characteristics
are only acquired through coming into society. It is only in society
that the natural *amour de soi* (akin to the Stoics' self-love)[16]
degenerates into *amour-propre*, the desire to be admired and to
dominate, which is central to Rousseau's account of human unhap-
piness. Once human beings have begun to live socially, however,
there is no going back. In *Emile*, indeed, it is suggested that men,
whatever their original dispositions may have been, were destined
by nature to develop as social beings: 'l'homme est sociable par sa
nature, ou du moins fait pour le devenir' (*E*, 600).

The problem at the beginning of the treatise on education is

[15] *Emile (E)* is cited in the Pléiade edition of Rousseau's *Œuvres complètes*, vol.
iv (Paris, 1969). Spelling is unmodernized.
[16] Smith devotes some interesting pages of *The Theory of Moral Sentiments* to
the Stoic conception of self-love ((pp. 272 ff.)

therefore how best to 'dénaturer' the individual so as to ensure his happiness in society. One answer to this is furnished by Plato's *Republic* or by Lycurgus's Sparta: public education in which the individual is entirely subordinated to the welfare of the group, not an autonomous being but a 'partie de l'unité' (*E*, 249). As J. S. Spink explains in the introduction to the Pléiade edition of the Favre manuscript of *Emile*,[17] this was a favourite topic for discussion at the time, and Rousseau himself was much tempted to follow this line.[18] Later in the *Considérations sur le gouvernement de Pologne*, he gave free rein to this inclination. But in *Emile*, arguing that in what the Scots would have called commercial society there is no place for citizens in the Spartan sense of the word, he opts for educating the man,[19] not the citizen. His aim will be to isolate the child from the corrupting influence of society in order to allow him to grow up in accordance with nature (as Rousseau sees it, of course). Protected as far as possible from the fatal development of civilized *amour-propre*, he will develop his natural faculties in much the same way as a savage.

The important point, for our present purposes, is to see what Rousseau is setting his face against. The enemy is what he calls the 'éducation du monde', described in an early draft of Emile as 'la plus mauvaise de toutes' (*E*, 1268). This kind of upbringing leaves people torn between conflicting impulses, natural love of self and the demands of society; the situation is memorably evoked by Rousseau in these words:

Elle [l'education du monde] n'est propre qu'à faire des hommes doubles, paroissant toujours rapporter tout aux autres, et ne rapportant jamais rien qu'à eux seuls ... ... Entraînés par la nature et par les hommes dans des routes contraires, forcés de nous partager entre ces diverses impulsions, nous en suivons une composée qui ne nous mène ni à l'un ni à l'autre but. Ainsi combatus et flotans durant tout le cours de notre vie, nous la terminons sans avoir pu nous accorder avec nous et sans avoir été bons ni pour nous ni pour les autres. (*E*, 250–1)

---

[17] The Favre manuscript is a first draft of *Emile*; it is reproduced in vol. iv of the Pléiade *Œuvres complètes*. See Spink's introduction, xlii-lvii.

[18] See P. Jimack, *La Genèse et la rédaction de l'Emile*, Studies on Voltaire and the Eighteenth Century 13 (Geneva, 1960), 118.

[19] The first four books of *Emile* are concerned essentially with the education of the male. I have no space here to go into the vexed and fascinating question of his ideas on women and women's education.

No doubt Rousseau is thinking of his own life here; the *Confessions* provide ample illustration of his discontents. When he writes of the 'éducation du monde', however, there is some ambiguity. The Favre manuscript seems to suggest that any society will produce these bad effects[20] but 'le monde' can also be taken in a more limited sense to refer to the polite world in which Alceste had come to grief. It is certain that in *Emile* the fiercest attacks are directed at sophisticated urban society and its education. Paris, the world of Rameau's nephew, is characterized by vanity, flattery and blatant self-seeking disguised behind a hypocritical mask of sociable virtue. Peasant life, by contrast, often provides positive models.

Rousseau's readership, of course, belonged very much to this world he denounced; they and their children had to live their lives there. Inevitably therefore, a work on education directed at them could not confine itself to the 'éducation de la nature'. And immediately after the black-and-white opposition between nature and 'le monde' comes the announcement that Rousseau will try to surmount the terrible split:

que deviendra pour les autres un homme uniquement elevé pour lui? Si peut-être le double objet qu'on se propose pouvoit se réunir en un seul, en ôtant les contradictions de l'homme on ôteroit un grand obstacle à son bonheur   (*E*, 251)

If Emile's early education is that of a savage, the world he has to live in is not that of savage man. As Rousseau writes towards the end of Book III, 'Emile n'est pas un sauvage à releguer dans les déserts, c'est un sauvage fait pour habiter les villes. Il faut qu'il sache y trouver son nécessaire, tirer parti de leurs habitans, et vivre, sinon comme eux, du moins avec eux' (*E*, 483–4). The commitment to community living is hardly very strong here, but Book IV tries to make of Emile more than a foreigner living as best he can in the world of men.

Of course, the first three books do not confine the boy to absolute solitude. For one thing, he is shadowed everywhere by his tutor. But Rousseau's point is that everything must be done to delay the development of social feelings. The child is not yet ready for them and could only acquire them in an inauthentic and corrupt form (saying 'thank you' when no gratitude is felt). Above all, *amour-propre* is

---

[20] For a discussion of this question see Jimack, op. cit. 94–125, in particular pp. 104–5.

to be kept dormant as much as possible (though there are moments, such as the cake-race, where this seems to be forgotten). The child, like natural man, is to act purely out of *amour de soi*, the desire for his own well-being. In his first relations with other people, therefore, there is no question of sympathy as Adam Smith had described it. Every child has a mother of course, and mother-child relations were not a matter Rousseau could take lightly. However, he was concerned above all to delay the education of the feelings. Paradoxically, therefore, although this section contains the celebrated plea for breast-feeding, he deliberately minimizes the role of the mother,[21] so as to bring Emile to the age of puberty as close as possible to the model of solitary natural man that had been worked out in the *Discours sur l'inégalité*.

As for the tutor, he does not figure in the first three books as a fellow-human being with whom the child learns to sympathize. He is seen rather as part of the order of things, from which the child learns by experience in the school of hard knocks. The same is true of the episode with Robert the gardener in Book III, which is meant to teach Emile elementary notions of justice. The boy is not expected to sympathize with Robert (any more than Robert is to sympathize with him) when they destroy one another's crops. Emile's reactions are founded on self-interest; he learns that if you damage someone else's property, you are likely to suffer from the consequences. Before he reaches Book IV and the education of the feelings, he lives in a world where self-love rules and where human relations, such as they are, are governed by the principle of exchange.[22] It is, in fact, a kind of commercial society based on the interests of separate individuals.

In Book III, Emile is specifically introduced to economics, the division of labour and the mutual dependence of all members of a society:

Ainsi se forment peu-à-peu dans l'esprit d'un enfant les idées des relations sociales, même avant qu'il puisse être réellement membre actif de la société.

[21] See the remarks in Book I: 'Emile est orphelin. Il n'importe qu'il ait son père et sa mére. Chargé de leurs devoirs, je succéde à tous leurs droits' (*E*, 267). It is interesting to note that in the Favre manuscript Rousseau had written: 'celui qui ne sait pas être fils et frère ne saura jamais être homme car les liens de l'humanité ne peuvent commencer que par ceux du sang' (*E*, 67), but omitted these words in the definitive version.

[22] Rousseau is not entirely consistent in this matter; in Book II, for instance, he says of Emile's requests for help: 'Il sait que ce qu'il demande est une grace, il sait aussi que l'humanité porte à en accorder' (*E*, 422).

Emile voit que, pour avoir des instrumens à son usage, il lui en faut encore à l'usage des autres, par lesquels il puisse obtenir en échange les choses qui lui sont nécessaires et qui sont en leur pouvoir. (*E*, 467)

As in *The Wealth of Nations*, there is no question of benevolence here. Emile is learning about the 'minimal' just society which Adam Smith envisaged in Book II of *The Theory of Moral Sentiments*.[23] But, like Smith, Rousseau is not content with this 'cold' society. He wants to bring back Robinson Crusoe from his island, to teach his 'savage' real fellow-feeling with others. Only God is happy in solitude, he writes in Book IV of *Emile*, and we are not like God. Human weakness forces us into one another's society, and from this is born the greatest happiness of which we are capable:

Ainsi de nôtre infirmité même naît nôtre frêle bonheur. Un être vraiment heureux est un être solitaire; Dieu seul joüit d'un bonheur absolu; mais qui de nous en a l'idée? Si quelque être imparfait pouvoit se suffire à lui-même, de quoi joüiroit-il selon nous? Il seroit seul, il seroit misérable. Je ne conçois pas que celui qui n'a besoin de rien puisse aimer quelque chose: je ne conçois pas que celui qui n'aime rien puisse être heureux. (*E*, 503)

The problem is to open up the self-sufficient child of nature to this happiness.

Book IV of *Emile* is all about the possibilities and difficulties of connecting the individual to his fellow human beings by the right links of affection and sympathy. Socialization is founded on the vision of nature first expounded in the *Discours sur l'inégalité*, where our basic love of self is accompanied by the capacity for pity, defined as the unwillingness to see others suffer. As in *The Theory of Moral Sentiments*, the force that is needed to realize this potential for fellow-feeling is imagination, a faculty that has been kept stifled in the first three books (sparing Emile the precocious dreams and agonies of his creator). In nature, we are not very aware of the sufferings of others; we have to learn, as Smith would say, to 'bring them home to ourselves'—or rather to get outside ourselves:

En effet, comment nous laissons-nous émouvoir à la pitié, si ce n'est en nous transportant hors de nous et nous identifiant avec l'animal souffrant? en quittant pour ainsi dire nôtre être pour prendre le sien? Nous ne souffrons qu'autant que nous jugeons qu'il souffre; ce n'est pas dans nous, c'est dans lui que nous souffrons. Ainsi nul ne devient sensible que quand son imagination s'anime et commence à le transporter hors de lui. (*E*, 505)

[23] See above, p. 37.

Given that the whole point of Emile's education has been that he should live 'within himself', this is a drastic reversal. The two attitudes are compatible, however. In discussing how the boy is led to perform acts of beneficence, Rousseau insists that this is simply extending self-love to others:

tous ces moyens par lesquels je jette ainsi mon élève hors de lui-même ont cependant toujours un raport direct à lui, puisque non seulement il en resulte une joüissance intérieure, mais qu'en le rendant bienfaisant au profit des autres, je travaille à sa propre instruction.   (*E*, 548)

Except in a Spartan-type public education, the interest of the individual is what matters most.

Sympathy, for Adam Smith, was the capacity to share imaginatively in the emotions of others, pleasant feelings as well as unpleasant ones. It is noticeable that Rousseau puts the accent on the latter. He speaks less of sympathy than of pity, 'la pitié, prémier sentiment rélatif qui touche le cœur humain selon l'ordre de la nature' (*E*, 505). Unlike Smith, perhaps more realistically, he believes that 'l'aspect d'un homme heureux inspire aux autres moins d'amour que d'envie' (presumably this refers to men in the social state), whereas 'nos miséres communes nous unissent par affection' (*E*, 503). The education of sympathy in Rousseau has less to do with learning a standard of propriety such as we saw in *The Theory of Moral Sentiments* than with opening the young man's eyes to the reality of other people's emotions—this being done through experience of the world, but equally through history and other reading.

This is not really a difficult task according to Rousseau. He does not start, like Smith, with an inbuilt ability to sympathize with others, but shows it growing out of the sexual development of the young man:

Sitôt que l'homme a besoin d'une compagne, il n'est plus un être isolé; son cœur n'est plus seul. Toutes ses rélations avec son espéce, toutes les affections de son ame naissent avec celle-là. Sa prémiére passion fait bientôt fermenter les autres.   (*E*, 493)

Moreover, sympathy is an agreeable feeling, bringing immediate rewards to the self, who enjoys simultaneously feeling pity for others and being exempt from their sufferings; the sympathizer 'se sent dans cet état de force qui nous étend au-delà de nous, et nous fait porter ailleurs l'activité superflue à notre bien-être' (*E*, 514). In this way pity leads to active charity. Note how Emile is cast in the role of the giver rather than the receiver of pity. The socialization that Rousseau proposes is concerned not so much with learning how to fit in with other people (who would thereby assume the dominant role) as with feeling and acting generously towards them (and here the self retains something of its independence). In a similar fashion, at the end of Book V, we shall see that Emile's spontaneous reaction to his study of modern society is to withdraw from public life as far as he can. He has to be exhorted by the tutor to allow himself to be called to public service if need be—the implication being that society will be happy enough to allow the man of virtue to go off like Alceste into his desert. Not of course that this means a retreat to solitude; in retirement too Emile will have to live with others (family, friends, neighbours) and exercise the social virtues.

Rousseau's stress is on beneficence, then, but what of the other side of the coin, the desire to be loved (which was so important to him)?[24] Even if it is more important to be 'aimant' than to be 'aimable', the two are virtually inseparable: 'Quand on aime, on veut être aimé; Emile aime les hommes, il veut donc leur plaire. A plus forte raison, il veut plaire aux femmes'. (*E, 668*). As the old notions of chivalry suggest, this is potentially a spur to virtues of all kinds, but equally it leaves the door open to the very type of undesirable social relations ('l'éducation du monde') which it had been Rousseau's aim to avoid in the first place. At the beginning of Book IV, there is a powerful section (which one imagines to be largely based on personal experience) on the dangers of the desire for the love and admiration of others:

Pour être aimé, il faut se rendre aimable; pour être préféré, il faut se rendre plus aimable qu'un autre, plus aimable que tout autre, au moins aux yeux de l'objet aimé. De là les prémiers regards sur ses semblables; de là les prémiéres comparaisons avec eux; de là l'émulation, les rivalités, la jalousie. Un cœur plein d'un sentiment qui déborde aime à s'épancher; du besoin d'une maîtresse nait bientot celui d'un ami: celui qui sent combien il est doux d'être aimé voudroit l'être de tout le monde, et tous ne sauroient vouloir de préférence, qu'il n'y ait beaucoup de mécontens. Avec l'amour et l'amitié naissent les dissentions, l'inimitié, la haine. Du sein de tant de

---

[24] The *Confessions* bear eloquent witness to Jean-Jacques's need for affection; in the pages devoted to his early childhood he writes: 'Etre aimé de tout ce qui m'approchoit étoit le plus vif de mes desirs' (Pléiade, i. 14).

passions diverses je vois l'opinion s'élever un trône inébranlable, et les stu-
pides mortels asservis à son empire ne fonder leur propre existence que sur
les jugemens d'autrui.   (*E*, 494)

Here the horrors of a society based on *amour-propre* spring from
the apparently natural desire to be loved. Rousseau's lessons in the
first three books were designed to forestall this enslavement to the
judgements of others, and the same will be true of Book IV. In
much the same way as Adam Smith, he sets the desire to be worthy
of praise, admiration or love against the desire actually to be
praised, admired or loved. So we read, for instance:

Il ne se dira pas précisément: je me réjoüis parce qu'on m'approuve, mais:
je me réjoüis parce qu'on approuve ce que j'ai fait de bien; je me réjoüis de
ce que les gens qui m'honorent se font honneur; tant qu'ils jugeront aussi
sainement il sera beau d'obtenir leur estime.   (*E*, 671)

Emile has chosen for himself a group of judges who share his own
values; they replace here the imagined 'impartial spectator' of *The
Theory of Moral Sentiments*. In the end, for Rousseau, the true
source of values is in the self: 'Toute la moralité de nos actions est
dans le jugement que nous en portons nous-mêmes' (*E*, 595). And
where does this judgement come from? If it is not the internaliza-
tion of the opinions of others (as appears to be the case with the
impartial spectator), then it must come from 'nature' or the 'author
of nature'. The rules of moral conduct are to be found 'au fond de
mon cœur écrites par la nature en caractéres inéfaçables' (*E*, 594).
Conscience, based on natural feeling rather than on reasoning, is
our individual bulwark against the pressures of a society to whose
false values we should otherwise fall victim. It is conscience, the
consciousness of doing well, that gives us the surest reward for
social virtue. And as in *The Theory of Moral Sentiments*, God is
invoked in the last resort; the rewards of the afterlife are the final
consolation of the innocent in a wicked world.

While Adam Smith and Rousseau seem to start from radically
different positions—for the former sociability is a given, for the
latter it is a human construct, even if on a natural foundation—they
both seek to ground social living on sympathy as well as self-love
and they both run up against the dangers of allowing social conformity ('le règne de l'opinion') to overrule moral autonomy. In
Smith this is clearer in the sixth edition of *The Theory of Moral
Sentiments*; in Rousseau it is a constant and far more insistent

worry. Indeed it may be asked how far he could believe in his 'sauvage fait pour vivre dans les villes'. Certainly *Emile* (not to speak of its tragic sequel, *Emile et Sophie, ou les Solitaires*) paints the way of the world in a much more pessimistic light than Smith. Is it worth the self's while to make the effort needed to live with others? Yes, if one can choose one's company—such is the import of *La Nouvelle Héloïse*. For Rousseau, the life of the social affections seems to be the true life. Book IV of *Emile* is devoted to the 'premier âge où l'homme commence véritablement à vivre', and it is obvious from many of Rousseau's other writings how much he valued the 'commerce' of self and others, *provided it could be achieved on the right terms*. If not, the self was lost. And even in the best of cases, there is an ambiguity in the terms he uses to describe the bonds of sociability. One has only to look at the metaphors of captivity that recur when he writes of the socialization of the young Emile through affection: 'Ses premieres affections sont les rênes avec lesquelles vous dirigez tous ses mouvemens; il étoit libre, et je le vois asservi' (*E*, 520). These are the chains of affection perhaps, but how can one help hearing an echo of 'l'homme est né libre, et partout il est dans les fers'? Whatever Rousseau may write of the advantages of the civil state, one hears again and again in his works what sounds like the stifled protest of the *petit sauvage* against any kind of social education.

If Rousseau's voice is so different from Smith's, this is of course partly due to their very different personal circumstances. Rousseau is the anguished solitary, an exile from his native city, ill at ease in the polite society of France, wanting to be accepted and loved, yet clinging to his individuality. For him, as he tells his story in the *Confessions*, relations with women are both vital and terribly difficult. Smith left no equivalent of the *Confessions*. From what is known, he seems altogether a more equable character, at home in his largely male society of clubs and universities. Unlike *Emile*, *The Theory of Moral Sentiments* has little to say about relations between the sexes.

We should, however, also see in these two works responses characteristic of two different cultural situations. Perhaps one could see in Smith the 'organic intellectual' in his society. In his lecturing and writing, he was contributing to the creation of a new polite culture in the rapidly modernizing commercial society of Scotland. While seeing and foreseeing many of the obstacles this society could present to individual happiness and individual virtue, he was willing to accept it, and his *Theory of Moral Sentiments* offered it an appropriate secular morality in which the self-love that is the motor of commercial society is happily tempered by the great principle of sympathy. *Emile*, on the other hand, is part of a reasoned revolt against a well-established polite world, which to an outsider appeared oppressive and false, casting a veil of insincere sociability over the workings of vanity and self-interest. In a treatise on education meant primarily for French readers rather than for citizens of a virtuous republic, Rousseau could not simply turn his back on this society. The sociability he offers is meant to suggest the possibility of living in this society without being submerged by it. Rousseau keeps his distance from 'le monde'; in the end his education points to the private world of individuals who will be far more divorced than Smith's young men from the commerce of social life.

4

Victor Hugo: the Triumph of Self?

GEORGE CRAIG

IT IS hardly a matter for surprise that the English have not, on the whole, taken to Victor Hugo. Seldom can there have been a poet, a writer of any kind, so apparently sure of having, and deserving, an audience. No trace of irony colours his way of indicating the year of his own birth: 'Ce siècle avait deux ans, Rome remplaçait Sparte.'[1] Then there is the question of volume, where that connotes both the amount and the degree of loudness of the work produced. The plays and their glosses (the 'Préface de *Cromwell*' runs to forty-five pages), the immense novels (*Les Misérables* is close on half as long as *A la recherche du temps perdu*), above all the poetry (editors were still bringing out poems in 1942, nearly sixty years after his death): has anyone, even Balzac, written more? Who else could have moved without discernible strain from the ostentatious pianissimo of:

> Ma fille! va prier. — Vois, la nuit est venue.
> Une planète d'or là-bas berce la nue;
> La brume des coteaux fait trembler le contour;
> A peine un char lointain glisse dans l'ombre . . . Ecoute!
> Tout rentre et se repose; et l'arbre de la route
> Secoue au vent du soir la poussière du jour!
>
> (i. 791)

to the fortissimo haranguing we find in lines such as: 'Bombance! Allez! c'est bien! vivez! faites ripaille!' (ii. 79) or: 'Eunuques, tourmenteurs, crétins, soyez maudits!' (ii. 509)? The likeliest response to all this is, surely, embarrassment; the English, after all, tend to claim as a characteristic of their aesthetic preference a fastidious distaste for the noisy, the showy, the excessive. But where, as here, these come accompanied by what looks like *naïveté*, no great sever-

---

[1] Hugo, Victor, *Œuvres poétiques*, 3 vols (Pléiade, Paris, 1964–74), i. 717. All subsequent quotations from Hugo are taken from this edition.

ity is called for. After all, granted even that Hugo may not always write like that, could any *œuvre* survive such coarseness of judgement? And then again, the French themselves, from Boileau to Valéry, have tended to take a far more severe view than the English of the gross or unbridled. How is it that Hugo has not come to have the status of a McGonagall?

Perhaps that formulation is extreme enough to force a pause. There is, or ought to be, something a little disquieting about the ease with which, on the basis of the argument from embarrassment, a hugely influential writer (and those influenced include Baudelaire and Flaubert) could become a sort of verbal clown. Before turning to specifically literary issues, we might usefully take a closer look at embarrassment itself.

The most vivid, least forgettable experiences of embarrassment come on the whole in adolescence, and take more or less the same form: a sudden and overwhelming glimpse of the self's inadequacy before others, triggering a similarly overwhelming wish to disappear, or to undo the present moment. The distress is virtually always about standing out in some way: being isolated, by physical feature, dress, by some act or the lack of something, from the protection of the now infinitely desirable majority. We will all have our own recollections and stories of this, but I suspect that they have one thing in common: they are tinged with the certainty that we had been hard done by; that we had been exposed to the experience by the unthinking, or even perhaps the conscious cruelty of someone else. That certainty, by dividing the residual rancour, softens its edge (it will be, for most of us, the stuff of anecdote, not of trauma). But it has another, deeper-running effect: that of masking from us the less innocent side of our experience. For, as well as the remembered outrage to our dignity, pride, etc., there will have been a wounding of our narcissism. Just for an instant, there will have been the fear that our secret self might disintegrate; the treasured, unadmitted self that is infinitely beautiful, infinitely potent. It is also because the experience did not correspond to the needs of that fantasy-self that it hurt so much; and that we have to tell the anecdote in the way we do. What follows, for many, is a determination never, so far as it is in their power, to allow such an experience, or anything like it, to arise again. The awkward part is the 'anything like it'. Who knows what forms of behaviour might result in a comparable revealing? For above all one must not be revealed; not least because there is also a secret and perverse longing to be revealed, to stand out, and that wish must be frustrated. But it soon becomes clear that there are two areas in particular where the risk is high: feelings or convictions; and self-presentation. The lengths to which we have been prepared to go in order to forestall danger can be seen when we remember that although eminent Victorians such as the great Arnold of Rugby, Matthew's father, thought nothing of weeping in public, by the time Thomas Hughes wrote *Tom Brown's Schooldays* such behaviour had become unthinkable, in his hero Arnold or in any other self-respecting male.[2]

If we link these elements in our culture to what I called earlier 'fastidious distaste for the excessive', it should be apparent that such an attitude may have to do, not only with aesthetic judgement, but with fear or distrust of feeling. But that is just what we would have to overcome if we were even to begin to see what kind of poet Victor Hugo is. Of course it will no more be the case that displays of feeling in poetry are *a priori* good than that they are *a priori* bad. In that connection, we might usefully consider the view of a French writer who disapproved of Hugo: Paul Claudel. Here is a representative passage:

Les 'Mages' dont il fait défiler devant nous la lugubre procession, pareille à celle des grands hommes que nous admirons aujourd'hui sur nos voies publiques, alternant avec les kiosques à journaux et les vespasiennes ... ne paraissent pas dans le fond l'avoir beaucoup plus excité qu'ils ne nous amusent ... Au contraire, quel intérêt cordial ... quelle attention passionnée pour les monstres, pour tous les criminels, pour tous les bourreaux de l'humanité.[3]

It is clear that it is not the scale of Hugo's conceptions nor his preoccupation with the extreme that troubles Claudel; it is the nature of his choices. Indeed there is a sense in which Claudel loathes Hugo, and, for English readers ill at ease with Hugo, that loathing is instructive, since it presents Hugo in the worst possible light. Hugo, for the Catholic and conservative Claudel, embodies the direst features of France in the nineteenth century: 'la France laïque et républicaine'. Driven by the memory of countless lines like: 'O drapeau de Wagram! ô pays de Voltaire!' (ii. 121) or: 'Le Progrès,

---

[2] On this see David Newsome, *Godliness and Good Learning* (London, 1961), *passim.*

[3] Paul Claudel, *Réflexions sur la poésie* (Paris, 1963), 49–50.

calme et fort et toujours innocent' (ii. 125), we find Claudel writing: 'peut-être qu'une grande partie du succès de l'œuvre victorienne vient de ce qu'elle pourvoyait tant bien que mal aux besoins idolâtriques d'une multitude d'obscurcis.'[4] But hear him most of all when he comes to the core of his feelings:

> Mais on dirait que Victor Hugo ne peut s'arracher à sa bataille contre les fantômes. Je ne parle pas dans un esprit de dénigrement et de moquerie. Personne ne peut contester la sincérité du grand poète et qu'il fut vraiment et réellement un voyant, à la manière de l'Anglais Blake. Non pas un voyant des choses de Dieu, il n'a pas vu Dieu, mais personne n'a tiré tant de choses de cette ombre que fait l'absence de Dieu.'[5]

The breathtaking confidence of that dismissal ('il n'a pas vu Dieu') cannot be separated from the admiration. One notes too that the reference to Hugo's sincerity—in an English writer, almost invariably a coded piece of condescension—is wholly straightforward. The terms of comparison have changed. On this reading, Hugo is a very long way from being like some more resourceful McGonagall. The implication indeed is that he is closer to being a modern version of the Virgil presented in Dante's *Inferno*:[6] a supreme poet, lacking only the true faith. How are we to get a bearing on a writer like this?

The key element is Hugo's voice. We need to be clear what it is like, and why it is as it is. What is in the way of that, I have been trying to suggest, is a largely unspoken, but none the less powerful conviction that there is a norm for poetic utterance; and a sense that, whatever the norm is, Hugo goes well beyond it. We might note too that this kind of restriction affects not only the expression of personal feeling. At least since Johnson there has been a tendency to raise eyebrows at the expression of patriotic fervour.

In order to hear Hugo, in fact, we have to do something to which most readers are profoundly resistant: accept, or at least recognize the possibility of, a different norm. The first constituent of that is the poet's status. When Baudelaire writes: 'Le Poëte est semblable au prince des nuées';[7] we don't believe him for a moment. The image cannot hide the sentiment that drives it: the defensive 'You

---

[4] Ibid. 51.
[5] Ibid. 50.
[6] Dante Alighieri, *La Divina Commedia*, 3 vols (London, 1964), i. 6.
[7] Charles Baudelaire, *Œuvres complètes* (Paris, 1963), 10.

none of you understand me.' Consider on the other hand these lines by Hugo from a poem on Shakespeare (entitled simply 'Le Poëte'):

> Sinistre, ayant aux mains des lambeaux d'âme humaine,
> De la chair d'Othello, des restes de Macbeth,
> Dans son œuvre, du drame effrayant alphabet,
> Il se repose; ainsi le noir lion des jongles
> S'endort dans l'antre immense avec du sang aux ongles.
>
> (ii. 612–13)

Even apart from the striking *rapprochement* that can be made between the final image and the celebrated pronouncement of Stephen Daedalus on the artist's vocation,[8] these words are remarkable, not least in their emphasis. They are the last five lines of a poem marked throughout by a rare veneration, where Hugo can say:

> Dans ce génie étrange où l'on perd son chemin
> Comme dans une mer notre esprit parfois sombre.
>
> (ii. 612)

But what way is this of celebrating a creativity presented as unique? It will be easier to answer that if we set beside these lines part of another, ostensibly very different poem about poets and poetry. A benign, and familiar, tone seems to be set from the start when he speaks of:

> . . . le poëte, épris d'ombre et d'azur,
> Esprit doux et splendide, au rayonnement pur.
>
> (ii. 532)

But for all the abundance of words like 'rêver', 'calme', 'caresse', the poem ends with:

> Il faut que, par instants, on frissonne, et qu'on voie
> Tout à coup, sombre, grave et terrible au passant,
> Un vers fauve sortir de l'ombre en rugissant!
> Il faut que le poëte, aux semences fécondes,
> Soit comme ces forêts vertes, fraîches, profondes,
> Pleines de chants, amour du vent et du rayon,
> Charmantes, où soudain l'on rencontre un lion.
>
> (ii. 532–3)

---

[8] 'The artist, like the God of creation, remains within or beyond or above his handiwork, invisible, refined out of existence, indifferent, paring his fingernails.' In James Joyce, *A Portrait of the Artist as a Young Man* (London, 1956), 219.

It is not just that the lion has reappeared, nor that we are looking at
a preferred image or even a stylistic tic. Hugo's is a poetry of
mutually sustaining opposites, and one of the central oppositions is
that between ferocity and gentleness; not as attitudes or metaphors
but as fundamental constituents of the poet, who, for Hugo, must
be able to *be* these things. There is indeed something strange, even
terrifying about the Shakespeare of Hugo's poem, but these are
features, not of the man, but of the poet; that is, the man who, *as
poet*, dared to venture, further, wider, deeper than any other. The
poet's mission is to see all, then to say all; to penetrate and appre-
hend the brute matter of the world (whether planet or people), then
give it form by uttering it. God sees all; but God does not write
poetry. Small wonder that Shakespeare, who, supremely, does write
poetry, should be such an awesome figure. Even the form of his
fearfulness—the universal predator—is telling. Do we not talk of the
closest kind of attention as 'getting to the heart of things'? Hugo
knows that that cannot always be achieved with the detachment of
the cardiologist or the unworldliness of the mystic. There will be 'vers
fauves' because humans are 'fauves' too; and there is the question of
the poet's desire. For although we may, indeed must, distinguish
between person and poet, more is at issue than our critical categor-
ies. We must look again at the question of the poet's role or
mission. In Hugo's conception it is founded on a kind of primary
awareness that faces two ways: towards the core and cause of
things, of people; and towards the perceptually immediate. In the
service of the first, as the Shakespeare example suggests, the poet
must be able to look into the abyss, to show himself capable of
engaging, open-eyed, with the darkest horrors. It is from this form
of awareness that the 'vers fauves' spring. But he must be able too
to see and say the profoundly harmonious, the intuitions of immi-
nent and immanent glory. Something of what that brings we can
perhaps see in these lines from 'Mugitusque Boum':

> 'Faites tressaillir l'air, le flot, l'aile, la bouche,
> O palpitations du grand amour farouche!
> Qu'on sente le baiser de l'être illimité!
> Et paix, vertu, bonheur, espérance, bonté,
> O fruits divins, tombez des branches éternelles!'

> Ainsi vous parliez, voix, grandes voix solennelles;
> Et Virgile écoutait comme j'écoute, et l'eau
> Voyait passer le cygne auguste, et le bouleau

> Le vent, et le rocher l'écume, et le ciel sombre
> L'homme ... O nature! abîme! immensité de l'ombre!
>
> (ii. 702)

The other direction of attention produces a comparable range of mood and colour. Here what is at issue is the detail (sound, texture, tone) of the physical or human environment. Hugo's love of the natural world is such that there are examples beyond counting of its grimness and grandeur. But we should not think of Hugo as bound or bounded by landscape or seascape. What draws his attention is, quite simply, where he happens to find himself, whether in fact or in imagination, as in these lines from 'Dans un vieux château':

> Ayons une alcôve à trumeaux,
> Ayons un lit à bergerade;
> Hier et demain sont jumeaux,
> Jadis est notre camarade.

—lines which lead forward to the invitation to weave into 'our' fantasies 'Tous ces frais Cupidons cachés/Dans les jupons de nos grand'mères' (iii. 239). And alongside that we might set these rather different reflections:

> Carnage, tas de morts, deuil, horreur, trahison,
> Tumulte infâme autour du sinistre horizon;
> Et le penseur, devant ces attentats sans nombre,
> Est pris d'on ne sait quel éblouissement sombre.

Here the reality he sees is that of France and its army brought low by the ineptitude of Napoleon III: 'Cette ombre de césar et cette ombre d'armée' (iii. 304). The poet, then, is required by the very fact of accepting that extraordinary role to act as a form of free-floating awareness: to be capable of attuning the vigilant self to any feature, grim or gay, general or particular of the knowable world—and not to drop that gaze before signs of a possible beyond. Such a creature is, by definition, extra-ordinary.

Now we can look again at the question of Hugo's voice. It will not, it cannot be an ordinary voice, for its task is to utter the world in a range or words—sounds, shapes, images, patterns—that is at least equal to the range of all those who hear and read them. The exclamations (can anyone ever have used more?) are not, as the incautious sometimes assume, indications of sloppiness or vapidity like the multiple underlinings we find in chatty Victorian letter-writers. Rather they are the transposed form of what actors know as projecting the voice—a technique which ensures that all sounds, the whispered as well as the shouted, will be heard with equal ease. In speaking of the role of the poet we are not merely borrowing an image. Just as the actor is, within the time of his acting, doing that and not another thing (so that there would be no point, for instance, in reproaching him for not getting on with his memoirs, or failing to take a decision about his future), the poet in the exercise of his role is a separate being. The various names Hugo gives him— 'le poëte', of course, but also 'le rêveur', 'le songeur', and 'le penseur'—are not self-flattering or self-advertising badges; they are the names of parts he must play.

Hugo's conception of the poet's role, then, is formidable indeed, and that fact may serve to explain at least one of the odder features of his poetry: its unfailingly surprising yet pervasive mixture of the intimate and the distant. The poet, he will continually remind us, is not as other men. But in spite of, or perhaps indeed because of the sacrificial, almost ascetic implications of the role (the poet, like some prophet, bound to wander through the world, issuing his pronouncements to the people), Hugo the man is not annulled. The analogy with the actor is not perfect. Both actors and poets can become conscious of their own performing, and that consciousness can encourage what amounts to self-display: the decision to indulge preferred aspects of the performance rather than focus on what is being performed. But actors, when they do that, come up against directors, who make very plain whether that is acceptable or not, and who have to be listened to. Poets do not. There are, of course, the critics; but when did Romantic poets ever listen to critics? Hugo, for his part, tends to lump them together with pedants, banishing both in phrases like 'l'essaim des pédagogues tristes' (ii. 499). The sweep and drive of his work seem to command assent, but if at the same time they forbid any other kind of response, Hugo is, in a different sense now, on his own. And it is a dangerous sense. I have laid great stress on the scale of the poet's mission, the weight of the responsibility that falls on him. But these are not simply things that Hugo talks or thinks about, observing their overwhelmingness from below. They are things that he readily, eagerly, irresistibly *takes on*. For this is the great difference from the actor: Hugo has not only to enact the impossibly difficult; he has to create it. But in order that he might do so, overcoming any momentary hesitations or backslidings, Hugo had to see himself as capable of rising to, and staying at, this dizzying height. Nor was this self-valuation to be restricted to mere potential. As the work pours from him in an unstoppable tide, he is faced with the incontrovertible fact that he is indeed 'the poet', in the full and awful sense that he has striven to give those words. We must, of course, remind ourselves that the judgement itself is not made by himself alone. It is abundantly, and crucially, confirmed by younger contemporaries; by, for example, Baudelaire, who will say of him, in the course of a notably encomiastic piece: 'L'excessif, l'immense, sont le domaine naturel de Victor Hugo; il s'y meut comme dans son atmosphère natale. Le génie qu'il a de tout temps déployé dans la peinture de *toute la monstruosité* qui enveloppe l'homme est vraiment prodigieux.'[9] Perhaps more remarkably, given the revolutionary—and by extension iconoclastic—nature of his poetic undertaking, we find Mallarmé (who actually refers to him as 'le géant') writing: 'Comme il était le vers personnellement, il confisqua chez qui pense, discourt ou narre, presque le droit à s'énoncer.'[10] Both literally and figuratively, however, Hugo got there first; and, if judgements such as those of Baudelaire and Mallarmé can be described as generous, we need another word to describe Hugo's estimation of himself.

And so, paradoxically, a wedge is driven between the great, self-abnegating mission and the man who is able and willing to take it on. Through the gap thus opened up we are made to glimpse the signs of a less innocent and less creative self-regard. It is something we see sometimes in *Les Châtiments*, in those moments when it seems as if there are only two identifiable figures in the whole of France: Napoleon III and Victor Hugo. One small instance might be:

> Ecoute, je te dois, Sire, un remercîment.
> Sans toi je n'aurais pas fait ce livre inclément;
> Sans toi je n'aurais pas écrit cette œuvre juste;
> Sans toi je n'aurais pas montré la haine auguste
> Que le méchant inspire au vers mystérieux.
>
> (ii. 371)

But there are more troubling examples too, such as:

> J'avais le front brûlant; je sortis par la ville.
> Tout m'y parut plein d'ombre et de guerre civile,

---

[9] Baudelaire, op. cit. 709.
[10] Stéphane Mallarmé, *Œuvres complètes* (Paris, 1965), 360–1.

... L'air, la plaine,
Les fleurs, tout m'irritait; je frémissais devant
Ce monde où je sentais ce scélérat vivant.
Sans pouvoir m'apaiser je fis plus d'une lieue.
Le soir triste monta sous la coupole bleue;
Linceul frissonnant, l'ombre autour de moi s'accrut;
Tout à coup la nuit vint, et la lune apparut
Sanglante, et dans les cieux, de deuil enveloppée,
Je regardai rouler cette tête coupée.

(ii. 192)

This, like some demented diary-entry, seems a very long way from
the visionary splendour and bitterness we find in, say,'L'Expiation'.
But it is not only in the overheated context of national destiny that
we find Hugo indulging this more self-congratulatory tendency. Let
someone (and it is by no means sure that there actually was a
someone at the bottom of this example) offer a derogatory public
word about Hugo's work and we are caught up in the whirling
invective of 'Réponse à un acte d'accusation'. First, and with a
laboured irony, the charges, whatever they are—Hugo does not
specify—are accepted in lines like 'Vous me criez: Racca; moi, je
vous dis: Merci!'[11] or 'J'en conviens, oui, je suis cet abominable
homme.' But then he gets into his stride:

Et, quoique, en vérité, je pense avoir commis
D'autres crimes encor que vous avez omis,
Avoir un peu touché les questions obscures,
Avoir sondé les maux, avoir cherché les cures,
De la vieille ânerie insulté les vieux bâts,
Secoué le passé du haut jusques en bas,
Et saccagé le fond tout autant que la forme,
Je me borne à ceci: je suis ce monstre énorme,
Je suis le démagogue horrible et débordé,
Et le dévastateur du vieil ABCD;
Causons.

Quand je sortis du collège, du thème,
Des vers latins, farouche, espèce d'enfant blême
Et grave, au front penchant, aux membres appauvris ...

(ii. 495)

<hr>

[11] Matt. 5: 22: 'Whosoever is angry with his brother without a cause shall be in
danger of the judgement: and whosoever shall say to his brother, Raca, shall be in
danger of the council: but whosoever shall say, Thou fool, shall be in danger of hell
fire.'

Only one of the great nineteenth-century actor-managers would have been able to do justice to that 'Causons' and then move, unabashed, to the sort of retrospect that immediately follows. That in turn leads to the recital of his deeds (in a poem of not much more than two hundred lines there are over forty instances of the construction of which the basic form is 'j'ai fait' or 'je fis') in overcoming a literary orthodoxy that had held sway since Malherbe (present by association in another bold line: 'Alors, brigand, je vins; je m'écriai: Pourquoi'), and culminates in the lines:

> J'ai dit aux mots: Soyez république! soyez
> La fourmilière immense, et travaillez! croyez,
> Aimez, vivez! — J'ai mis tout en branle, et, morose,
> J'ai jeté le vers noble aux chiens noirs de la prose.
>
> (ii. 499)

And then, as if in a blush at the enormity of what he has claimed by way of achievement, he writes: 'Et, ce que je faisais, d'autres l'ont fait aussi' (ibid.); though who these others are remains as unclear as the identity of his accuser. Now this is, all the same, Victor Hugo, and not a fool, for all his acceptance of 'Racca'. The poem has enormous verve; is indeed, at moments, disarmingly funny—and it has to be said that the moments overlap occasionally with some of the more extravagant claims ('Et j'ai, sur Dangeau mort, égorgé Richelet'). But extravagant is what the claims are, and they suggest, not aesthetic outrage, but wounded pride. And there is the wonder: why does a poet of such indisputable power need to make fatuous boasts? How can he let by, unrevised, such cheap stuff? (What is that 'morose' doing, apart from helping out with the rhyme?)

Let us come back here to the desire of the poet. By explicitly maintaining the highest possible conception of the poet's role, Hugo has implicitly laid down formidable conditions of acceptability for that role. One side of that is untroubling: since the poet is the divine bow that brings out the music of God's spheres, he is hierarchically subordinate and responsible to God; he is a servant. The other side is different: his mission puts him apart from other humans, answerable *only* to God; he is a master. But we are not simply left to observe a contradiction. When Hugo attributes this mastership to Shakespeare, he does so without reservation, and indeed, as we have seen, with awe. But his doing so does not engage Shakespeare in a moral dilemma; not because Shakespeare is dead, but because Shakespeare is not the attributor, does not have to bear (that is, know) the burden of mastership. The strange, savage, multiple being is not something given or known; it is Hugo's vision. How idiosyncratic a vision it is we can see by comparing it with that of another writer, no less admiring, no less concerned with Shakespeare's protean diversity: the brief parable by Borges called 'Everything and Nothing', in which we read:

History adds that before or after dying he found himself in the presence of God and told Him: 'I who have been so many men in vain want to be one and myself.' The voice of the Lord answered from a whirlwind: 'Neither am I anyone; I have dreamt the world as you have dreamt your work, my Shakespeare, and among the forms in my dream are you, who like myself are many and no one.'[12]

When, however, Hugo grants himself the status of poet, he goes on necessarily to confer mastership. And that is a rather different matter, whether or not he 'deserves' such a rating. It is hard not to be reminded of the act of someone about whom Hugo thought all his life long: the first Napoleon and his placing of the Imperial crown on his own head. If you have given yourself the highest reward, if you have set aside the limits on narcissistic demand (you are next to God), what is your desire? There is only one desire: to be God.

Once you know that that is your desire, you will of course do everything to conceal or play down the fact; you will shower the world with kindnesses and services, and refrain from crushing it with your strength; be, indeed a paragon of gentleness ('je ne fais plus même envoler une mouche'—ii. 531). But, little by little, you will get used to the fact. And then the guard drops for a moment, and the desire shows. Hugo, I am suggesting, split into two in just such a way: being the poet, doing the countless things that only that particular poet could do or have done; and knowing that he was The Poet, with all the implications of near-omnipotence that that brought. And that was to put under enormous pressure the word 'je'. Some sense of how long a road it was that Mallarmé knew he had to go down can be guessed from setting what he strove for—'la disparition élocutoire du poëte'[13]—against the immense 'présence élocutoire' of Victor Hugo—what Mallarmé called 'l'ancien souffle

---

[12] In Jorge-Luis Borges, *Labyrinths* (trans. James Irby, London, 1970), 284–5.
[13] Mallarmé, op. cit. 366.

lyrique'.[14] But the contrast is not absolute. It is not possible to guess what would have become of Hugo if events had not taken the course they did; if, that is, the near-omnipotence had not, like Adam's, been abruptly and irreversibly withdrawn. His reaction to the sudden death of his daughter Léopoldine was not only the grief and pain that all bereaved parents know. The loss brought also the greatest blow that could have fallen on him as poet: he could no longer be the poet, for he could no longer write. It is no matter how long or how short a time that paralysis lasted; it is enough that Hugo had to live this unimaginable fact: he was unable to write. Nor was that to be the end of his suffering, for when he could once again feel the words start to come, they had to compete with the bereaved's feelings that spinning words was trivial, frivolous, traitorously disloyal to the wordless one.

Hugo did indeed come back to writing, and to writing in abundance. And he did not become a creature without pride: there will be instances in plenty of the old arrogance. What disappears is the underlying temptation of being God. It remained to find a way of recreating a poet: of reconstituting a 'je' that could catch up the many energies and preoccupations of the self—and still respect its scale. In a sense, the easier part was the political involvement, for at least it was clear who were the villains, who the heroes; and there were always those great abstractions like Progress and Enlightenment to serve. But what could guide the process of reconstruction in the other areas of experience? The commonest, but not, I think, the most helpful answer has been 'religion'. Rather than follow the twists of that thread, we might instead look at something of what happens to 'je'.[15]

If, as I have suggested, the crucial question is whether he can

---

[14] Ibid.

[15] It is true that there are in his work references beyond counting to beliefs, believers, and the object or objects of these (whole sections of the poetry have titles like 'Dieu' and 'La Fin de Satan'). But it would be hard indeed to say whether 'religion' had any stable sense for Hugo. Even catch-all labels like 'pantheism' merely beg the question. Claudel, with his convert's purism, says dismissively: 'La Religion sans religion de Victor Hugo, c'est quelque chose comme le vin sans alcool, le café sans caféine et le topinambour qui est le parent pauvre de la pomme de terre' (op. cit. 49). And then there is the whole cloudy question of Hugo's involvement with spiritualism. The truth of the matter is surely ... that the truth is inaccessible. The attempt to pursue it seems to me to rest on the confusion of two wishes: to identify what it was 'out there' that Hugo saw, or believed in, or both; and to account for (chart, situate, explain) his believing and seeing.

return to the full exercise of his powers without falling again into the fantasy of omnipotence, it is also the case, as even a glance at the poems of *Les Contemplations* will show, that the old Adam has not simply disappeared. What matters is not the presence or absence of the language of self-regard, but the nature of the enterprise, the verbal whole of which it is a part. What matters is tone. Let us look now at how that operates in two very different poems. The first is:

> Elle était déchaussée, elle était décoiffée,
> Assise, les pieds nus, parmi les joncs penchants;
> Moi qui passait par là, je crus voir une fée,
> Et je lui dis: Veux-tu t'en venir dans les champs?
>
> Elle me regarda de ce regard suprême
> Qui reste à la beauté quand nous en triomphons,
> Et je lui dis: Veux-tu, c'est le mois où l'on aime,
> Veux-tu nous en aller sous les arbres profonds?
>
> Elle essuya ses pieds à l'herbe de la rive;
> Elle me regarda pour la seconde fois,
> Et la belle folâtre alors devint pensive.
> Oh! comme les oiseaux chantaient au fond des bois!
>
> Comme l'eau caressait doucement le rivage!
> Je vis venir à moi, dans les grands roseaux verts,
> La belle fille heureuse, effarée et sauvage,
> Ses cheveux dans ses yeux et riant au travers.

The first two lines have a double charge: one part derived from the 'close-up', which ensures that the eye will see only the chosen image; and the other from the male sexual code, which sees to it that the participle-adjectives (from 'déchaussée' to 'penchants') work cumulatively, to suggest both abandon and gentleness. This association is apparently neutralized in the third line, where the 'I' is given only minimal presence (the surpriser), and invokes the traditionally non-sexual ('une fée'). But it is appearance only; this pivotal line deserves a closer look. The suggested sequence—happening on; tiptoeing by; comparing innocently—neither corresponds to the charge of the first two lines nor prepares us for the fourth. In fact, this third line is far closer than that to the first two; and indeed, as we shall see, to the fourth. Precisely what is at issue is the boundary sexual/non-sexual. If lines one and two play with this by running together neutral and erotic, the third line extends and protracts the play. The essential is for us to think how this third line might be *spoken*. Its possible 'meanings' include not only the literal ('this and this only is exactly what I did and thought'), but a range of others that runs from the self-exculpatory ('It was like this: . . . ') to the boastful ('Listen to this: . . . '). For our chosen way of speaking the line will imply that we are already clear how the next line is to be understood. Hugo, in short, has brought us into the delicate area of decision: on whether this is an ideal or idyllic encounter, or simply an idealized conquest. And he has done so for a reason: this is retrospect; Hugo himself is aware that the episode can be read in more than one way, and that at least one of the ways is not, ultimately, flattering.

Then again, there is more than one tradition of presenting beautiful fairy-creatures (we need only think of Keats's 'Belle Dame Sans Merci'). Much will turn on the further presentation of this one. It is in fact fascinatingly intricate. The weight of 'suprême', following the insistence on gaze, works against any straightforward conquest-meaning for 'nous . . . triomphons'. But it also raises again, in more pressing ways, the issue of how to speak the questions that 'je' asks: as timid venturings, hesitant guesses at what is suitable? as well-calculated promptings by an experienced performer? Hugo's 'answer' is to return the focus to the 'fée': we must look at her even as she looks at the poet-venturer. And the result is, again, the suspense of delay: the slowing and repeating that, excitingly, connote the imminence of decision. And in case that pressure, or the associations of 'folâtre', might seem to make the matter too easy, there is the 'pensive', increasing the force of her gazing, and, of course, bringing back in the question of her power. Is she the maid surprised, who might or might not yield to a man? or the fairy who might or might not choose to consort with a human? Anticipating the romantic cinema by nearly a hundred years, Hugo directs attention, in the pause, at the way in which the scene presses to a 'yes'. And then the resolution. The venturing 'je', still, passive, is granted his wish by the free (she is 'heureuse') choice of his 'fée', who is now not just an 'elle' but a 'belle fille'. To head off any suspicion of unchastity there is the 'effarée et sauvage'; and we are through to the final close-up.

I have looked only at issues of charge and emphasis in this little poem in order to come through to the linked questions of 'je' and tone. Many of the early poems in *Les Contemplations* present memories of childhood and young manhood, but this is the first in which sexuality appears as anything other than that which the remembered 'je' did not understand or failed to come to terms with (see for example 'Vieille chanson du jeune temps'—ii. 520–1—or 'La coccinelle'—ii. 515–16). In terms of the elaboration of a 'je', that matters. This move into the world of adult sexuality, like the one it describes, faces Hugo, if perhaps for the only time, with the realization that he has to find a way of representing his own active sexuality. Memory will have brought the anecdote up as story, adventure, idyll even. But composition requires him to give some view or hint of what the speaking subject is like: eager lad? acquisitive male? lucky man? callous exploiter? The continued representations of the 'fée' are the mirror in which this view is worked out (so that in the end, for example, the subject becomes innocent through the gift of the other). But this, like the suggestion that power lies exclusively with the 'fée', suggests that reflection has not yet reached a point where contradictory aspects of the self can be held together.

The other poem comes from the later stages of the collection, but, rather than focus on the obvious centrality (to his work and to my argument) of, say, 'Ce que dit la bouche d'ombre', I have chosen instead what is virtually the last of the poems to have as context a recognizable and ordinary experience: 'Pasteurs et troupeaux'; too long, unfortunately, to quote in full. Here our pursuit of the evolving 'je' is lined up with the declared direction of movement of the 'je' itself:

> Le vallon où je vais tous les jours est charmant,
> Serein, abandonné, seul sous le firmament,
> Plein de ronces en fleurs; c'est un sourire triste.
> Il vous fait oublier que quelque chose existe,
> Et, sans le bruit des champs remplis de travailleurs,
> On ne saurait plus là si quelqu'un vit ailleurs.
> Là, l'ombre fait l'amour; l'idylle naturelle
> Rit . . .
>
> (ii. 707–8)

Almost any commentary on Hugo could take off from this poem, so many are the features of his writing that we find in it: the seeker of solitude, the 'idylle naturelle', the scenic detail, the progression from indulgence to seriousness, and so on. Some of these can only be touched on in this discussion. The chosen valley is, it is soon clear, not just 'charmant'-pretty, but 'charmant' in an older sense made more accessible by the end-placing: having the force of a spell. For if the 'triste' leaves room still for grimmer awareness or memories, the next line begins to work the magic, which even the sounds of the farm-labourers cannot dissipate. Attention is drawn closer and closer in because here are, and are only, beauty and innocence. No accident either that it is a valley: the way in which hollows can screen out sounds from outside is the perceptible form of another beneficent isolation—the cocooned warmth and safety of pulling the bedclothes over one's head. This, in short, is a retreat; and whatever is in it is good. It is even possible, the rhetoric runs, to lift the attention away from immediate detail to reflect on pattern and proportion, and even to play:

> Une petite mare est là, ridant sa face,
> Prenant des airs de flot pour la fourmi qui passe,
> Ironie étalée au milieu du gazon.

But such play lets in the things of the mind (here, the observed 'ironie'); and, as so often in Hugo, the tree of knowledge has bitter fruits. The magic valley can no longer keep us from, or from us, the 'océan grondant à l'horizon'; and with that reminder the poem moves into its second phase, and 'je' moves to the encounter with the human.

Indeed it is here that 'je' reappears in the literal sense, after the excursus into the valley:

> J'y rencontre parfois sur la roche hideuse
> Un doux être; quinze ans, yeux bleus, gardeuse
> De chèvres, habitant, au fond d'un ravin noir,
> Un vieux chaume croulant qui s'étoile le soir;
> Ses sœurs sont au logis et filent leur quenouille;
> Elle essuie aux roseaux ses pieds que l'étang mouille;

and, almost at once (the warning note sounded in 'roche hideuse'), shifts attention over to the girl with her goats. The sudden meeting, the charm of the girl, the bare feet among the reeds echo oddly the surface detail of 'Elle était déchaussée . . . ', but we are in a different world now. There is still the girl's innocence—' . . . quand, sombre esprit, /J'apparais, le pauvre ange a peur et me sourit'; but the 'sombre esprit' knows now that that is what he is for others: a speaking subject, not a spoken hero (or villain) in some shared adventure. More is at issue here than a growth in seriousness, or simply a growing older. The same knowledge that brings him up out of the valley (the knowledge that that valley, for all its offer of pre-lapsarian bliss, is something he must leave behind on his way to something else) takes him on beyond the little goatherd: not just the child she is, but the woman she will be. The perfect, pivotal moment when the self is poised between the remembered—by regression to childhood or invention of the consoling—the immediate present and the time that lies ahead: this moment is caught in the lines that follow:

> Et moi, je la salue, elle étant l'innocence.
> Ses agneaux, dans le pré plein de fleurs qui l'encense,
> Bondissent, et chacun, au soleil s'empourprant,
> Laisse aux buissons, à qui la bise le reprend,
> Un peu de sa toison, comme un flocon d'écume.

Hugo is on the edge of his own great discovery: almost all the elements are present now. It is the next line which perhaps best explains why this, the penultimate section of *Les Contemplations*, is entitled 'En Marche':

> Je passe, enfant, troupeau, s'effacent dans la brume;

Hugo's movement onwards will mean leaving them and their like behind, but not losing them; they disappear from the poet's view, but not from the poem. He knows now that he cannot be God, but also that he cannot retreat to the time before that discovery. He must go on, with all the remnants of the past clinging to him, as for a while the goats' hairs cling to the bushes, until he finds a place or a position where past, present and future converge. That place is figured in the final lines of the poem, where, with the voice of the little goatherd still in his ears, he looks out to where:

> Le pâtre promontoire au chapeau de nuées,
> S'accoude et rêve au bruit de tous les infinis,
> Et, dans l'ascension des nuages bénis,
> Regarde se lever la lune triomphale,
> Pendant que l'ombre tremble, et que l'âpre rafale
> Disperse à tous les vents avec son souffle amer
> La laine des moutons sinistres de la mer.

The 'pâtre promontoire' is one of Hugo's most powerful metaphors; not only because of its intrinsic charge, but on account of the new accent it brings. The characteristic images in which Hugo casts his most deeply felt perceptions of the world form two main networks: those, like 'gouffre' or 'abîme', that carry the dread or the splendour of the limitlessly deep; and those which—the range is wider here—evoke the grandeur or remoteness of the highest things ('Dieu' and 'ciel', of course, but also 'sommet', 'hauteurs' and more). But this image is, of its nature, *intermediate*. The 'je' of the poem must indeed make his way up out of the valley to this higher ground; but only to find himself between sea and sky, sea and pasture or culture. Here at last is an image adequate to the full scope of Hugo's visionary power, yet not depending on any confusion of God and man, God and poet. To stand between the great extra-human forces and the loved world, actual and remembered; to protect as far as he may, to intercede for, to speak for the rest: that will be the mission. But it is something that Hugo can achieve, not by suppressing or denying his own humanity, but by accepting it, with its strengths and its weaknesses, its conquests and its collapses. Whatever backslidings there may be, Hugo, then, has had his founding vision. In the genuineness of this seeing beyond the self he has indeed achieved, against both the temptation of omnipotence and the reality of loss and defeat, the triumph of self.

5

Self-Effacement and Self-Expression in Flaubert

BRIAN NICHOLAS

'L'ARTISTE doit s'arranger de façon à faire croire à la postérité qu'il n'a pas vécu,' Flaubert writes to Louise Colet early in 1852.[1] If by nothing else this aspiration to anonymity was to be thwarted by his massive correspondence, the richness and fascination of which ensured its preservation and eventual publication; though his existence had already been detected by the authorities who prosecuted *Madame Bovary* and who had no doubts about the identity and character of its author.

The range and tone of the correspondence defy summary. Particularly during the years of the composition of *Madame Bovary*, it is a source-book for those formulations of the doctrine of impersonality which have been quoted ever since criticism of Flaubert began: the notion of 'le beau' as being independent of subject-matter; the ideal of 'un livre sur rien', sustained only by style, which is 'à lui tout seul une manière absolue de voir les choses' (ii. 31); the author present in his work only 'comme Dieu dans la création, invisible et tout-puissant' (ii. 691); and so on.

We also have a day-by-day account of the miseries to which this belief in the indifferent subject-matter condemned him: the problems of finding a style which could treat the everyday without either inflating it lyrically or presenting a raw triviality unshaped by art. The complaints are endless: 'Les phrases les plus simples me torturent . . .' (ii. 93); 'franchement *Bovary* m'ennuie . . .' (ii. 104); 'j'en suis physiquement malade' (ii. 134); 'je passe des journées à changer des répétitions de mots, à éviter des assonances' (ii. 311); 'les fétidités bourgeoises où je patauge' (ii. 360).

But the letters themselves, while referring to the 'affres' of writing, show none of this constipated agony. Fluency, spontaneity and explosiveness are their constant characteristics. The bourgeoisie

---

[1] Flaubert, *Correspondance*, 2 vols (Pléiade, Paris, 1973, 1980), ii.62. Subsequent page-references in the text are to this edition.

and the political and social scene are the object of splendid tirades. Love, women, life itself are treated with an unsparing, generalizing scepticism. Yet while the general is bleakly viewed, there is immense enthusiasm and generosity for the particular. His attempts to define his love for Louise, that 'attache supérieure' (ii. 206), do not shrink from phrases which put Emma's effusions in the shade. After a day's struggle with the words he sits down to a line-by-line commentary on Louise's verses. The mocking observer of the bourgeois family is, as a correspondent, an affectionate and dutiful son, brother, nephew and uncle. The letters abound in nicknames, schoolboy jokes, private allusions, merry obscenities, pastiches of sixteenth-century French (ii. 215); and everywhere there is a zest for the grotesque and the extravagant, and an ability to find it and render it in everyday life. *Enorme* (which he likes to spell *hénaurme*) is one of Flaubert's favourite epithets. It is the large, too, that he loves in literature. Homer, Rabelais, Cervantes and above all Shakespeare ('le grand William') provide the authentic *ébahissements* (ii. 192), and, in his own time, Hugo ('le Crocodile') and Balzac: 'Quel homme eût été Balzac, s'il eût su écrire! Mais il ne lui a manqué que cela. Un artiste, après tout, n'aurait pas tant fait, n'aurait pas eu cette ampleur' (ii. 209). Beside these giants the 'bonshommes du siècle de Louis XIV' were not 'des hommes d'énorme génie'; Molière in the end is something of a conformist, 'il est toujours pour les majorités, tandis que le grand William n'est pour personne' (ii. 175).

These preferences put Flaubert's own literary enterprise in an interesting light. If he exalts form it is in large part because he cannot emulate the 'souffle' of an Hugo and of the truly great who 'écrivent souvent fort mal. — Et tant mieux pour eux'. 'Mais nous, les petits, nous ne valons que par l'exécution achevée' (ii. 164). We are 'des nains'; 'comme on se sent petit, mon Dieu! comme on se sent petit' (ii. 179). 'Tout ce qu'il y a de beau a été dit et bien dit,' he writes (i. 433), echoing La Bruyère. The ideal is impossible, 'il faut être correct comme Boileau et échevelé comme Shakespeare' (ii. 511).

But the reservations, and the modesty, are all the same limited. The formal perfections of the seventeenth century can move Flaubert to enthusiasm: 'Mais quelle conscience! . . . Quel travail! Quelles ratures! . . . Comme ils savaient le latin! Comme ils lisaient lentement!' (ii. 292). Only Flaubert could make crossings-out matter for an exclamatory eulogy. And he is happy to take his place in the second rank, and to be remembered for his own *ratures*, 'parce qu'il me semble en ma conscience que j'accomplis mon devoir, que j'obéis à une fatalité supérieure, que je fais le Bien, que je suis dans le Juste' (ii. 77). 'Fatalité', a word which on the lips of Rodolphe and Charles will have heavy ironic resonance, seems here to be used with complete seriousness.

It would be odd if these hectic and often contradictory passions and aspirations, both in life and literature, did not surface in Flaubert's work. In recent years, however, there has been a trend in criticism[2] to play down the possibility of traditional and subjective elements, to see Flaubert as making a sharp break with the past, and inaugurating the superior concerns of 'modernism'. In place of the chatty, knowing novels of Stendhal and Balzac, which aim to explain to the reader a complex but ultimately intelligible world, Flaubert is seen to be—with greater or lesser conscious awareness—questioning the conventions of the novel, rejecting the traditional claim to—and demand for—'meaning', casting doubt on the referential adequacy of language, intent on producing a 'text' of no recognizable provenance; in short becoming something of a 'nouveau romancier' before his time. In one way Flaubert invited this fate, with his talk of 'un roman sur rien'; in another he would hardly have welcomed it. Writing is not there for its own sake, he says in other moods: 'il faut que cela batte, que cela palpite, que cela émeuve' (ii. 557). Wit and cleverness (that characteristic of the 'experimental' novelist) are antipathetic to him (ii. 385). Though he persistently advocates the neutral style it is almost always with a note of apology: 'Nul lyrisme, pas de réflexions, personnalité de l'auteur absente. Ce sera triste à lire.' But in fact Flaubert—in *Madame Bovary*, at least—is never 'triste à lire'. As cheerfulness did with Dr Johnson's aspiring philosopher, so with Flaubert, in spite of the austerity implicit in his expressed ideals, readability keeps breaking in.

'Et la lourde machine se mit en route.' With this sentence Flaubert opens the celebrated description of Léon's and Emma's cab-ride

---

[2] See especially Jonathan Culler, *Flaubert: the Uses of Uncertainty* (London, 1974). For Leo Bersani, *Balzac to Beckett* (New York, 1970), 144, 'what Flaubert's novels are most interestingly about' is 'the arbitrary, insignificant, inexpressive nature of language'.

('ma baisade', as he likes to call it in the letters). Two or more years earlier he had used the same rather odd phrase metaphorically: first to describe the novel, 'quelle lourde machine à construire qu'un livre' (ii. 156), then to characterize himself, 'et puis je suis une si lourde machine à remuer' (ii. 246). One should not, perhaps, get too excited by these minor pleasures of recognition, and there may be no profound significance in this particular recurrence. Nevertheless it exemplifies a striking feature of Flaubert's writing—the constant interaction between his epistolary style, which runs easily, and happily, to metaphor, and the laboriously hammered-out words of the novels.

The passage is stylistically interesting in other ways. Flaubert was something of a connoisseur of horse-drawn transport, an interest reinforced, no doubt, by his impatience with the new breed of railway bores (ii. 560). We remember Charles's *boc* which, when refurbished, 'ressembla presque à un tilbury'; and the vehicles which brought the guests to Charles's and Emma's wedding, and the crowd back from the races in *L'Education sentimentale* are lovingly detailed (in the former case Flaubert's exuberance leads him to provide far more than would have been needed to convey forty-three people). So, if Flaubert says that a certain sort of cab, in his own Rouen, is a 'lourde machine', he is almost certain to be right. Yet once the machine gets under way, the impression we have is of great speed, as the coachman presses his horses and wonders what this 'fureur de la locomotion' on his clients' part can mean. It appears that the number of sightings made of the cab is in excess of what the stated time would have allowed.[3] Flaubert is lured by his taste for the epic, the larger than life, and by that love-hate of Rouen, so frequently attested in the letters (e.g. ii.574–5), which makes the naming of familiar places an incantatory pleasure.

This love of enumeration is perhaps due to the influence of Rabelais. But, whatever the source, we have in the passage a heightened sense of life to which the spectators themselves contribute: 'Et sur le port, au milieu des camions et des bourriques, et dans les rues, au coin des bornes, les bourgeois ouvraient de grands yeux ébahis devant cette chose si extraordinaire en province, une voiture à stores tendus . . . '. 'Ebahi', 'ébahissement' are favourite words of

---

[3] See Léon Bopp, *Commentaire sur Madame Bovary* (Neuchâtel and Paris, 1951), 384.

Flaubert's, used to characterize the effects both of great literature and great love (ii. 292); whether the citizens of Rouen would have experienced such wonderment is less certain. We notice also the (far from impersonal) formula, 'cette chose si extraordinaire en province' – reminiscent of Balzac's appeals to the reader and his knowing distinctions between what goes on in Paris and elsewhere. The scene has engaged critics in other ways (Sartre has a trenchant criticism of its 'dehumanizing' quality).[4] What I want to emphasize here is its stylistic vigour. In defiance of realism or aesthetic principle the 'lourdes machines'—cab, novel, author—occasionally take wing. The vigour, however, is considerably less than that of the private Flaubert, and a letter to Louise Colet reminds us of the way in which he had to tame the zestful forms of expression which came naturally to him. Rouen is indeed only a pale reflection of Paris:

As-tu réfléchi quelquefois à toute l'importance qu'a le Vi dans l'existence parisienne? Quel commerce de billets, de rendez-vous, de fiacres stationnant au coin des rues, stores baissés. Le Phallus est la pierre d'aimant qui dirige toutes ces navigations.   (ii. 471)

The cab scene occurs late in the novel. But had not a similar vigour of style sustained us earlier, had the novel been 'si triste à lire', we might not have read on so far.[5] In fact that vigour sets in with the opening of the novel. And the opening reminds us of the way in which critical concerns can obscure, or at least diminish the enjoyment of, what is going on in the text. A novel launched in the name of impersonality, but which begins with the pronoun *nous*, offers succulent material for the critic who wants to cast *Madame Bovary* as an anti-novel; and a few pages later the narrator remarks that 'il serait maintenant impossible à aucun de nous de se rien rappeler de lui [Charles].' Remembering the unmemorable over five hundred pages—what could be a more overt subversion of the Balzac novel, in which the apparently banal is raised by the author's interpretation to the status of the tragic?

There are other ways of looking at the opening. The *nous* might be seen as a rather mischievous *ave atque vale*; poised for an exercise in self-effacement, Flaubert slips himself into the narrative, as some painters smuggle a self-portrait into a crowd-scene. Whatever

---

[4] *L'Idiot de la famille*, ii (Paris, 1971), 1275–85.
[5] *Madame Bovary*, it may be worth remembering, was first published in instalments.

the motivation for this fictional strategy, we should not lose sight of the most important thing, the sense of lived experience. The vivid detail of the throwing of the caps into the corner, and of the conventions governing that throwing, perhaps deserves some of the attention that has been given to that overworked critical object, Charles's own cap: the *nous* adds to the sense of immediacy.

The scene can be linked, if only in a general way, with Flaubert's memories of his own youth. His school and student days remained with him vividly throughout his life; and the intense friendships which compensated for servitude and boredom find their fictional echo in the saga of Frédéric and Deslauriers who, at the end of *L'Education sentimentale*, though their paths had diverged and though their characters had never really been compatible, are 'réconciliés encore une fois par la fatalité [again, surely, unironical] de leur nature qui les faisait toujours se rejoindre et s'aimer'; and who spend an evening joyfully recalling episodes of their youth and the idiosyncrasies of their mentors. The turbulent behaviour of the class on Charles's arrival, and the master's desperate recourse to a *pensum* ('cinq cents vers à toute la classe'), in fact echo an episode in Flaubert's own schooldays: a letter to the *proviseur* of the Collège de Rouen (i. 56–7), passionately argued but carefully respectful, signed by him and others, complains about a *pensum* ('mille vers' this time) administered, equally desperately, to the whole class; and about the arbitrary and selective measures which followed their refusal to submit to the punishment. The *proviseur* reappears some fifteen years later in a letter to Louis Bouilhet, when Flaubert discovers that he has become a near neighbour:

Ah! sacré nom d'un nom! J'oubliais. Devine qui est l'homme qui habite à Dieppedalle? Cherche dans tes souvenirs une des plus grotesques balles que tu aies connues et des plus splendides.
                              Dainez!
Qui, il est là, *retiré*, le pauvre vieux … Enorme! Juge de ma joie … Quelle visite nous lui ferions si tu venais! — Et quel petit verre, ou plutôt quel cidre doux! … car je suis sûr qu'il brasse lui-même, *pour s'occuper*.
                                                                    (ii. 603)

The memories must be strong to provoke such verve; and it is good to know (ii. 1296) that Flaubert acknowledged Dainez' indirect contribution to the novel by sending him a complimentary copy.

Another sprightly passage in this dense opening chapter is the description of Charles's pre-school days:

Il suivait les laboureurs, et chassait, à coups de mottes de terre, les corbeaux qui s'envolaient. Il mangeait des mûres le long des fossés, gardait les dindons avec une gaule, fanait à la moisson, courait dans les bois, jouait à la marelle sous le porche de l'eglise, les jours de pluie, et, aux grandes fêtes, suppliait le bedeau de lui laisser sonner les cloches, pour se pendre de tout son corps à la grande corde et se sentir emporter par elle dans sa volée.

$(576)^6$

One would hardly recognize here the plodding *collégien* or the somnolent husband; though a last moment of aberrancy, and even of Emma-like yearning ('Qu'il devait faire bon là-bas! . . . Et il ouvrait les narines pour aspirer les bonnes odeurs de la campagne . . .') and sensuality (he puts his hand on the door-knob of the domino-hall 'avec une joie presque sensuelle') returns during his days as a medical student and leads to his examination failure.

The coherence or otherwise of Charles's character (relegated, for the greater part of the novel to the level of a simple *repoussoir* for Emma's feelings, then at the end given almost tragic status) poses, like the opening *nous*, interesting critical problems.[7] But the pre-college characterization seems to me to be able to be considered on its own, as an early example of that love of enumeration, often implying a certain epic enlargement, of which examples recur in the novel. The wedding-feast and the cab-ride have already been mentioned; one could add the rehearsal of Charles's surgical predecessors ('Ni Ambroise Paré . . . ni Dupuytren . . . ni Gensoul . . . ') as he poises his *ténotome* over Hippolyte. More clearly than in the cab scene the influence of Rabelais seems to be present in the listing of Charles's youthful pastimes. And if there is a pull away from fictional purposefulness here, this may be the explanation. The enumeration faintly echoes the account of Gargantua's *vagabondage* (*Gargantua*, ch. xi) before he too, though less repressively, was brought into line. In the same way the description, a page or two earlier, of Bovary *père*'s improvidence ('il montait ses chevaux au lieu de les envoyer au labour, buvait son cidre en bouteilles au lieu de le vendre en barriques, mangeait les plus belles volailles de sa cour et graissait ses souliers de chasse avec le lard de ses cochons') recalls Panurge who 'despendit en mille petitz bancquets et festins joyeux . . . abastant boys, bruslant les grosses souches pour la vente

---

[6] Page-references for *Madame Bovary* are to *Œuvres complètes*, i (Paris, 1964).
[7] See Graham Falconer, 'Flaubert, assassin de Charles' in *Langages de Flaubert* (Paris, 1976), 115–36.

des cendres, prenent argent davance, achaptant cher, vendent à bon marché, et mangeant son bled en herbe' (*Tiers Livre*, ch. ii). The whole of this opening has extraordinary verve—Flaubert is not yet facing the major problems of presentation which will assail him later. Homais and Bournisien are yet to come; and Homais's suspicions of clerical conspiracy are playfully prefigured in the description of Charles's mother's machinations for securing the widow Dubuc, with its delightfully intrusive 'même'—'elle déjoua même les intrigues d'un charcutier qui était soutenu par les prêtres.'

These quietly relished formulations do not disappear as the novel goes on, and Flaubert continues, occasionally, to take time off from the 'affres du style' and allow himself a transparently mischievous intervention; as when he makes Charles write to Rodolphe, once Emma's *amazone* has been purchased, 'que sa femme était à sa disposition et qu'ils comptaient sur sa complaisance'. But, however much this mode pleases Flaubert, and us, it has to give way to the rendering of Flaubert's permanent convictions—'l'éternelle monotonie de la passion', 'l'éternelle misère de tout'. The richness and comedy of life is clouded for Flaubert by a sense of its pitifulness and poverty—and *pauvre* is probably the most frequently recurring adjective in his letters: 'Ma pauvre Louise', 'ma pauvre mère', 'pauvre vieux bougre' (Bouilhet), 'mon pauvre Narcisse' (his servant). Moving to the hypothetical, he evokes the condescension of those who will note 'la calvitie de ce pauvre Flaubert' (ii. 121) and the reactions of the 'pauvres âmes obscures' (ii. 147), who, he hopes, will be solaced by his work. Sometimes *pauvre* refers to a particular predicament, often one for which Flaubert feels the need to apologize (especially towards Louise). Sometimes, too, it is used in the pejorative sense of impoverished: 'Quelle pauvre création . . . que Figaro à côté de Sancho' (ii. 417). Places, too, qualify for the epithet: 'on l'a bien changé, notre pauvre Trouville' (ii. 73). Tone and context differ, but the vast accumulation of examples (even allowing for the possibility of a stylistic tic) seems to point to an embracing meaning on Flaubert's part: *pauvre* characterizes the human condition, becomes a sort of honorific epithet for all those who are doomed to partake in it.

When we turn to the novels, and in particular to *Madame Bovary*, we find an equally high incidence of *pauvre*, and here not naturally occasioned by the vocatives of correspondence. Almost every character is paired with every other in according or receiving the epithet (and occasionally it is self-bestowed—'nous autres, pauvres femmes'). For his mother Charles is her 'pauvre enfant', Charles pities the sacked Nastasie, 'il l'aimait un peu, cette pauvre fille'; Bournisien evokes 'ces pauvres mères'; Félicité weeps over 'ma pauvre maîtresse'; Léon bids farewell to Berthe with 'Adieu, pauvre enfant'; while Charles wonders how 'ce pauvre Léon' will fare in Paris. Later Emma herself effuses over her daughter— 'Comme je t'aime, ma pauvre enfant'—and imagines (though she never in fact makes it) the confession she will offer Charles—'C' est moi qui t'ai ruiné, pauvre homme.' Larivière puts an end to Charles's hopes for Emma's survival with 'Allons, mon pauvre garçon . . . il n'y a plus rien à faire.' There arc also pejorative and malicious uses of the word: for Emma, before her final despair, Charles is 'un pauvre homme, de toutes les façons'; while Lheureux callously refers to him, in relation to Emma's 'petit vol', as 'ce pauvre cher homme'. For Homais, the mayor, 'ce pauvre Tuvache', is completely lacking in 'ce qui s'appelle le génie des arts'; and Emma hypocritically refers to the abandonment of her 'pauvre piano' as she engineers a pretext for the weekly trips to Rouen.

These are only a few examples. What do we make of them? Obviously they are not, usually, straight authorial intervention, since most of them occur either in direct speech or in *style indirect libre*. Flaubert lends his characters his own favoured word, but commonly calls in question their right to use it. In the majority of cases, *pauvre* does not indicate depth of feeling or disinterested sympathy, but rather points back to the speaker's or thinker's own deficiencies: Emma is aware that she neglects her daughter; Charles's fears for Léon are grounded in his own timidity (and in fact Léon proves well able to look after himself). But the matter is not quite so simple. There is sometimes a doubt as to whether the *pauvre* is in the *style indirect* or not—there is the possibility that Flaubert endorses the character's feeling or, indeed, projects on to him his own valuations; as when, in relation to Charles's self-deception about his visits to Les Bertaux, the explanation is offered that 'parmi les pauvres occupations de sa vie' they made 'une exception charmante'. Flaubert can be almost as malicious as Lheureux, as when he makes Charles say in his letter of congratulation to Léon on his marriage 'comme ma pauvre femme aurait été heureuse'. And straight authorial uses of the word can have an element of condescension as well as of sympathy. When Bournisien persuades

Hippolyte that a few prayers could do no harm, 'le pauvre diable promit'. Charles's worries over his wife's health are aggravated by the fact that 'le pauvre garçon avait, par là-dessus, des inquiétudes d'argent.' Justin, 'le pauvre enfant', looks on in astonishment as Emma unfurls her hair in front of him for the first time. But, all irony and self-protection finally put aside, Flaubert tells us that, as she died, Emma 'n'entendait plus que l'intermittente lamentation de ce pauvre cœur'; and that 'ses pauvres mains se traînaient sur les draps, avec ce geste hideux et doux des agonisants qui semblent vouloir déjà se recouvrir du suaire.' And the 'pauvre garçon' at last comes of age: 'il souffrait, le pauvre homme, à la voir [Berthe] si mal vêtue.'

Flaubert repossesses here the word which he had distributed, with varying intent, among his characters, and which he had used ambivalently himself. But the cumulative, and unobtrusive, effect of all these uses perhaps transcends the individual ironies and open-nesses, and supports Flaubert's claim that 'si la *Bovary* vaut quel-que chose, ce livre ne manquera pas de cœur' (ii. 84). At least we are nearer to the 'Alas, poor Yorick' of 'le grand William' than to Mr Woodhouse's 'poor Miss Taylor' in *Emma*.

There is no danger of Flaubert's complicity with his characters becoming sentimental. The possibility of his going in that direction remains, all the same, credible. 'Ce qu'il y a de fort dans *Manon Lescaut*, c'est le souffle *sentimental*, quoiqu'ils [les deux héros] soient des fripons' (ii. 432). And, after *pauvre*, the most frequent adjective in the letters is probably *bon*—itself often linked with *pauvre* ('ma pauvre bonne mère'). Flaubert's acerbity goes with a large generosity towards some of the living—Maxime du Camp is 'une bonne, belle et grande nature' (i. 388)—and of the dead—'ce bon Racine! Honnête poète' (ii. 382). Flaubert's nature and verbal habits lead him to bring these simple, evaluative epithets into his novels; but in *Madame Bovary* there are no obvious contenders (though 'le bonhomme' Rouault comes very close) for the unironic qualification of *bon*. Irony, on the whole, prevails. Emma's use of *bon* points back, more clearly than in the case of *pauvre*, to the inadequacies of the speaker: 'il est si bon', she says of Charles, as she tries to resist Léon. 'Tu es bon . . . ' she tells Rodolphe; and, as she is dying, she repeats the same words to her husband, 'tu es bon, toi.' Nor is she the only one who reaches for this simplest and least discriminating of words. When Homais, to ease his embarrassment after Emma's death, waters the geraniums: 'Ah, merci, dit Charles, vous êtes bon.'

The only unequivocal, authorial uses of *bon* are about places rather than people. The hotel in which Charles and Emma stay when they go to the opera is 'une de ces auberges comme il y en a dans tous les faubourgs de province — bons vieux gîtes . . . continuellement pleins de monde, de vacarme et de mangeaille'; while the other hotel room, which becomes almost a home for Emma and Léon, is 'cette bonne chambre pleine de gaieté, malgré sa splendeur un peu fanée'—a memory, perhaps, of the hotel at Mantes (ii. 102) where Flaubert and Louise sometimes met. Nevertheless we should not go to the extreme of seeing irony everywhere: one of the features of Flaubert's pessimism which makes it acceptable is the sense that, while he relishes examples of *la bêtise*, he is also constantly on the look-out for *le bon*. He simply finds himself defeated by the evidence. Nevertheless he discharges some of his (perhaps condescending) good will on minor characters like Bournisien, a 'brave homme' in the text and 'très brave homme, excellent même' in the correspondence (ii. 304); and on 'cette excellente Mme Homais', 'la meilleure épouse de Normandie'. Boring though she is and, like the more significant 'lourdes machines', 'si lente à se mouvoir', he can afford, and seems glad to take, a genial approach, as he might in life, to someone who threatens neither him nor the central concerns of his art. In contrast, the unremittingly hostile treatment of Binet, who plies his lathe 'avec la jalousie d'un artiste et l'égoïsme d'un bourgeois', is perhaps dictated by Flaubert's lurking fear—and need to defend himself against it—that his own way of life is not all that different.

Trickier to interpret is the reference to 'ce bon Homais', whom Emma meets 'presque avec joie' as she returns from Rouen after her vain attempt to incite Léon to crime so that she can pay her debts. The style is not clearly indirect or ironical; and perhaps Flaubert, for the moment, is willing to ally himself—and us—with Homais, whose domestic order contrasts so strongly with the emotional and financial squalor of Emma's present life. That possibility is reinforced by the lines that follow, in which Homais is shown, uncharacteristically, as the solicitous husband: he is bringing his wife some of her favourite pastries, 'six *cheminots* . . . ces petits pains lourds en forme de turban' which she 'croquait héroïquement malgré sa détestable dentition'. We come close, here, to two realities of

Flaubert's life. A letter to Bouilhet (ii. 575) announces his nostalgic determination to get these Rouen specialities into the novel; and he too had bad teeth, not very numerous, and blackened by the mercury treatment for syphilis (ii. 562). Here he transfers his own, frequently admitted, physical deterioration ('mes pauvres cheveux tombent comme des convictions politiques'—ii. 80), rather ungallantly, to his fictional creation; the strength of his feeling about it, and the relief at its artistic sublimation, may account for the presence of the startling alliteration, which would normally have been the occasion for an immediate *rature*. This animated little passage, with its fanciful evocation of the 'robustes Normands' who at the time of the crusades ate these same *cheminots* as if they were the heads of Saracens, provided, no doubt, a welcome interlude for Flaubert as he girded himself for his denouement. And 'ce bon Homais' is perhaps the beneficiary of this momentary waywardness.

On the whole Flaubert deals with his predilection for *pauvre* and *bon* easily and indeed creatively. His vituperative tendency poses a more serious problem, to which he constantly returns in the letters: how to ensure that his exasperation with the subject-matter does not disrupt the—ideally—impassive surface of his prose, in which he hopes that, if anything personal appears, it will be at most 'une rage sereine' (ii. 226). The letters show an almost comic contradiction between the claim not to judge and the surrender to intemperate condemnation. 'Que je sois pendu si je porte jamais un jugement sur qui que ce soit!' is his reaction to a mildly dogmatic assertion by his brother (ii. 585). But the explosive disclaimer is itself a form of judgement. 'Quel imbécile, quelle brute!' is his loyal response to a harmless editor's rejection of Louise's work (ii. 244). He will find it difficult to keep these and similar words at bay in the novels.

One solution he attempted was to write pages of abuse of his characters, not intended for inclusion in the text: an *exutoire* within the valued *exutoire* (ii. 341) of fictional writing itself. Another was to get the words into the text, but to off-load the responsibility for the value-judgements on to the characters, and often, as with *pauvre*, to call in question their right to make them. Emma feels herself surrounded by 'd'imbéciles petits bourgeois'; Binet for her is 'cet imbécile à carnassière' (because he has witnessed her clandestine trip to Rodolphe's home); the cathedral verger is an 'imbécile' for the impatient Léon, as is Justin for Homais. As well as satire of Homais's pomposity there seems to be a degree of vicarious pleasure in the scene (rather self-indulgently extended by Flaubert) of Homais's virtuoso, but hardly realistic diatribe against Justin for breaching the rules of the *capharnaüm*. Flaubert stands in awe, and envy, of his own frenzied creation, and is moved to a comment and a generalizing diagnosis:

Il citait du latin, tant il était exaspéré . . . Il eût cité du chinois et du groënlandais, s'il eût connu ces deux langues; car il se trouvait dans une de ces crises où l'âme entière montre indistinctement ce qu'elle enferme, comme l'océan, qui, dans les tempêtes, s'entr'ouvre depuis le fucus de son rivage jusqu'au sable de ses abîmes.   (658)

But sometimes vicarious pleasure is not enough. Content to delegate the use of *imbécile* to his characters, Flaubert retains authorial monopoly of the word *idiot* (little knowing what would be its future critical fortune!) and brings it out when he can contain himself no longer. Emma's infatuation with Rodolphe is 'une sorte d'attachement idiot'; and Martinon in *L'Education sentimentale* makes a critical decision 'par un de ces entêtements idiots qui sont des actes de génie'.

If Flaubert seems to be aware of the need to be sparing with his adjectives in the well-identified area of stupidity and mediocrity, he is much less inhibited in the use of *brute* and its derivatives. Rodolphe is 'de tempérament brutal', Emma replies to Charles's observations on Berthe's ragged stockings 'avec brutalité', and undresses 'brutalement' in the hotel bedroom with Léon. Homais, intimidated by Bournisien's fierce looks, tempers his attacks on clerical hypocrisy, and replies 'd'un ton moins brutal'. And the guests at La Vaubyessard are characterized by 'cette brutalité particulière que communique la domination de choses à demi faciles'. This unselfconscious use of a powerful word, in differing contexts, suggests a very personal response on Flaubert's part to a certain sort of coarseness or violence which (as the last quotation implies) is the opposite of the artist's attempted mode of detachment and of the domination of what *is* difficult. When 'l'océan s'entr'ouvre' we see worse things than mediocrity and boredom — as Baudelaire puts it, 'une oasis d'horreur dans un désert d'ennui'. In *L'Education sentimentale* Flaubert comes out even more openly with his hatred of both the *profanum vulgus* and its aristocratic enemies, his sympathy for their victims, and his fear of the abyss. A quotation from the Tuileries scene brings together, (fortuitously?) the words and ideas we have mentioned: 'L'égalité se manifestait triomphalement, une égalité de bêtes brutes . . . La raison publique était troublée comme après les grands bouleversements de la nature. Des gens d'esprit en restèrent idiots pour toute leur vie.'

These examples of moral judgement could be multiplied. Flaubert never flinches from the strong word. Like his biographer Sartre (also, ostensibly, an enemy of absolute values) he has a keen sense of the reality and prevalence of *lâcheté* and he attributes this quality explicitly to Léon, Emma, Rodolphe and Frédéric. Similarly with corruption. Rodolphe makes of Emma 'quelque chose de souple et de corrompu', and she passes the infection on. 'Où donc avait-elle appris cette corruption . . . ?' Léon wonders, as he becomes 'sa maîtresse plutôt qu'elle n'était la sienne'; and of Charles's dandyish habits after her death Flaubert comments that 'elle le corrompait au-delà du tombeau.' We may note too that Emma's relationships are roundly referred to as 'l'adultère', a word of rare occurrence in French fiction, considering the number of occasions there are for its use.

There could, of course, be a prudential factor in this moralistic vocabulary, but that seems unlikely. Flaubert indeed almost courts prosecution when, in his celebration of Emma's beauty at the height of her affair with Rodolphe, he, the responsible creator, says that 'on eût dit qu'un artiste habile en corruptions avait disposé sur sa nuque la torsade de ses cheveux.' The free use of these strong words expresses, rather, one aspect of Flaubert's complex attitude to love. And a personal note intrudes in other ways in the text. On the whole he dissociates himself from Rodolphe's cynicism: the latter's 'Quel tas de blagues!', as he sifts through his old love-letters, receives a firmly critical gloss. But Flaubert is no stranger to love's importunities and makes a surprisingly lenient comment, backed up by a worldly generalization, on Rodolphe's refusal of Emma's request for three thousand francs:

Je ne les ai pas, chère Madame. Il ne mentait point. Il les eût eus qu'il les aurait donnés sans doute, bien qu'il soit généralement désagréable de faire de si belles actions: une demande pécuniaire, de toutes les bourrasques qui tombent sur l'amour, étant la plus froide et la plus déracinante. (679)

This may seem a rather distasteful intervention at a dramatic moment. Perhaps Flaubert senses this himself: though he lets the comment stand, he makes immediate amends by lending Emma an eloquent refutation of Rodolphe, more eloquent, surely (see the paragraph beginning '—Mais, lorsqu'on est si pauvre'), than she would have been capable of in her distress, or perhaps at any time. These veerings recur in the text. In a single page Emma's passion is characterized as an 'attachement idiot' and is defended against the scepticism of Rodolphe, who cannot see beyond her clichés or recognize that 'la parole humaine' (as Flaubert knows all too well from his struggles with it) is never equal to the complexity of what we feel and try to express; and that 'la plénitude de l'âme' may translate itself sometimes by 'les métaphores les plus vides'. Elsewhere Flaubert takes a less favourable view of the word in emotional matters, with the rather tired comment: 'D'ailleurs, la parole est un laminoir qui allonge toujours les sentiments.' There are close parallels here with the oscillating reflections on love in the correspondence. Flaubert feels that his relationship with Louise is 'une attache supérieure', but only to the extent that it transcends the normal squalor of heterosexual love. He strongly defends, against her protests, his 'réflexions sur les femmes' (ii. 80). His chief complaint is their 'besoin de poétisation': 'Un homme aimera sa lingère et il saura qu'elle est bête qu'il n'en jouira pas moins. Mais si la femme aime un goujat, c'est un génie inconnu, une âme d'élite' (we are reminded of Emma's compliment to Rodolphe 'tu es intelligent!'). Women have no 'arrière-boutique' of their own, whereas we men, 'dans toutes nos générosités de sentiment', keep for ourselves '*in petto* un petit magot pour notre usage exclusif'. But 'cette infériorité' of women, 'la cause des déceptions dont elles se plaignent', is also 'au point de vue de l'amour en soi une supériorité' (ii. 80). Rodolphe has a spacious *arrière-boutique*—but his exploitation of Emma is scathingly described as 'cette supériorité . . . appartenant à celui qui, dans n'importe quel engagement, se tient en arrière'. These parallels and verbal echoes point to a long and inconclusive meditation on men and women in love (the letter from which all these quotations come was written in 1852). There are strong suggestions, too, of the influence of Montaigne, whom he reads as devotedly as he does Rabelais (would Louise have recognized the allusion in *arrière-boutique*?). The drive towards impersonality is constantly tempered by the lure of discursiveness.

Generalizations, moral reflections and implicit appeals to the reader are, in fact, very common in Flaubert (less so in *Madame*

Bovary than in *L'Education sentimentale*).[8] Jonathan Culler may be right to say[9] that the phrase 'une de ces coiffures' in the description of Charles's cap parodies the Balzac mode of engaging the reader's participation in a tour of an intelligible fictional world. But to base on this example an argument for Flaubert's rejection of the aims and modes of the traditional novel is to ignore a great deal of evidence. He is often talking very clearly in his own voice. Sometimes he seems to want to mitigate the harshness of his own satire, as when, in the inn scene, he follows up the cruelly stylized Léon–Emma exchange with the gentler comment that 'ils entrèrent dans une de ces vagues conversations où le hasard des phrases vous ramène toujours au centre fixe d'une sympathie commune.' But there are also bold moral generalizations, which strike equally at both sexes: Emma feels before Charles 'cette lâche docilité qui est à la fois la rançon et le châtiment de l'adultère'; while Rodolphe avoids Emma after their rupture 'par suite de cette lâcheté naturelle qui caractérise le sexe fort'.[10] Flaubert's generalizations constantly invite us to consider moral issues, to put the particular in a larger context, to reflect on the largeness or smallness of his characters' transactions. Their variety is consonant with his desire to 'faire rêver' and to avoid, and make us avoid, the ultimate *bêtise*—'conclure'.

At the technical level (*ce /cette*) the influence of Balzac is obvious. And one or two parenthetical comments could come straight from that earlier study of *mœurs de province*, *Eugénie Grandet*. When Emma sits at the window Flaubert notes: 'elle s'y mettait souvent: la fenêtre, en province, remplace les théâtres et la promenade.' Here Flaubert is simply relaxing, letting a little air into the dense text. But in other ways he is bolder and more personal, sometimes more devious, than Balzac, whose generalizations usually derive from some sociological or political theory, however bogus. When Flaubert writes of 'cette indéfinissable beauté' which irradiated Emma at the height of her affair with Rodolphe, he can only, since there is no consensus in these matters, be making, under an almost impudent claim to general truth, a highly subjective celebration of his heroine.

---

[8] See Jean Bruneau, 'La Présence de Flaubert dans *L'Education sentimentale*', op. cit. in note 7 above, 33–42.

[9] *Flaubert: The Uses of Uncertainty*, 92–3.

[10] Flaubert and Bouilhet collaborated in a play on male cowardice entitled *Le Sexe faible* (see Bopp, op.cit. 486).

Léon's allowing himself to be detained by Homais is attributed to 'cet inqualifiable sentiment qui nous entraîne aux actions les plus antipathiques'—a passing word of dissent, perhaps, from Homais's belief in science and rationalism as the solution to all our problems.

The modernist criticism seems, by its selectivity, to be in danger of misrepresenting the prevailing modes of Flaubert's text. Culler's analysis of the description of Yonville[11] as almost parodic of earlier procedures, as emanating from no identifiable or imaginable narrator, is persuasive up to a point. On the other hand it could be argued that this set-piece is untypical and not particularly successful Flaubert. Much more typical are the evocative descriptions of Rouen and Paris seen through the characters', but also, very obviously, through Flaubert's own eyes. The description of certain minor figures also shows a brisk, confident, direct attempt to explain them to the reader in political or regional terms. The Marquis d'Andervilliers (the Bovarys' host at La Vaubyessard) 'secrétaire sous la Restauration . . . cherchant à rentrer dans la vie politique, préparait de longue main sa candidature'. Lheureux, 'né Gascon mais devenu Normand . . . doublait sa faconde méridionale de cautèle cauchoise'. And the sense of an attempt to draw the reader in and make him share Flaubert's local knowledge is reinforced by the use of the conversational *or*, a common feature of Balzac's narratives ('Or, les cerisiers poussaient mal à la Vaubyessard', 'Or il y a, de Tostes aux Bertaux, six bonnes lieues de traversée').

In *Madame Bovary*, then, there are few dull moments; and Proust's characterization of the novelty of Flaubert's narrative style (not at all in a hostile tone) as 'ce grand *Trottoir roulant* . . . au défilement continu, monotone, morne, indifférent'[12] seems, again (even allowing for the fact that he is chiefly concerned with *L'Education sentimentale*), to be the product of selective reading. He does, however, make a more interesting point, when he locates for us what *can* be dull and lifeless in Flaubert's writing: metaphor is the hallmark of the great writer, and 'il n'y a peut-être pas dans Flaubert une seule belle métaphore.'[13] Flaubert would have agreed with this assessment of the primacy of analogy in art (ii. 545).

---

[11] Op.cit. 75–8.
[12] 'A propos du "style" de Flaubert', in *Contre Sainte-Beuve, Pastiches et Mélanges, Essais et Articles* (Paris, 1971), 587.
[13] Op.cit. 586.

Metaphor and simile not only come naturally to him, their creation is a physical need. He tells Louise Colet (ii. 351) that he has just completed a 'comparaison soutenue' two pages long, and which will not survive in the text, but 'physiquement parlant, j'avais besoin de me retremper dans de bonnes phrases'. He knows that analogy involves the dangers of inflation, and perhaps has no place in the impersonal, realistic novel. On the other hand he cannot exclude it. The outcome is unhappy, and perhaps throws further light on the tense relationship—seen so far as fairly successfully resolved—between the man and his fictions.

Though metaphors and similes abound extraordinarily in the letters, a large proportion of them are not suitable for inclusion in, or adaptation for, a published work, even if an appropriate context presents itself. Flaubert's metaphorical characterizations of life have a novel harshness which interestingly parallels that of the *Fleurs du Mal*. Baudelaire has his 'vieille orange' and his 'vieux meuble à tiroirs'; for Flaubert 'la vie . . . c'est un potage sur lequel il y a beaucoup de cheveux, et qu'il faut manger pourtant' (ii. 47). But it is in the scatological and the sexual areas that Flaubert's analogical verve is most fertile. *Merde* is probably the most frequently recurrent metaphor in the letters. Though ink, as he puts it is 'mon élément naturel. Beau liquide . . . et dangereux! Comme on s'y noie!' (ii. 395), this is the one in which he is obliged to 'patauger'. The laurels to be gained in Paris, he warns Maxime du Camp (ii. 114), 'sont un peu couverts de merde, convenons-en'; and the ivory tower of the artist is washed by its tides. We need prophylactics in the physical life, but even more, he writes to Louise, in the spiritual:

Ayons toujours à l'intérieur une vaste capote anglaise, afin de ménager la santé de notre âme, parmi les immondices où elle se plonge. — On jouit moins, c'est vrai, et quelquefois la précaution se déchire . . .   (ii. 511)

This exuberant, and neatly post-scripted, image can have no place in the novel. Nor can the exclamatory and grotesque mode which so often (we have already seen Dainez), makes us laugh out loud as we read the letters. Of another former, somewhat apoplectic teacher, whom he has had to dinner, Flaubert writes to Bouilhet:

Quelle grosseur! Quelles sueurs! Quelle rougeur! C'est un hippopotame habillé en bourgeois. Il n'a pas faibli du reste, car il est toujours de l'opposition, *quand même* . . . ennemi des prêtres, et extra-grotesque.   (ii. 585)

Some of the opinions are Homais's, but Homais has not got the physique to provoke the metaphor.

Faced with these exclusions Flaubert has two resources—to try to adapt the more acceptable images produced by his personal experience, or to fabricate purely literary bits of fine writing. Referring to Emma's infatuation with Rodolphe, Flaubert says that 'son âme s'enfonçait en cette ivresse et s'y noyait, ratatinée, comme le duc de Clarence dans son tonneau de malvoisie.' This anecdote clearly appealed to Flaubert and is quoted, quite appropriately, though inaccurately (and again long before its fictional use), in a letter about Musset's drinking: 'Son génie, comme le duc de Glocester [*sic*] s'est noyé dans un tonneau . . . L'alcool ne conserve pas les cerveaux comme il fait pour les foetus' (ii. 119). In relation to Emma the image is absurd; the 'ratatinée', clearly applicable to the foetus, is itself a pickled remnant and sorts oddly with the attribution to Emma of 'plénitude' a few pages later. Similarly in a letter to Louise early in 1852 Flaubert uses a metaphor obviously derived from his recent trip to Egypt:

Sonde-toi bien: y a-t-il un sentiment que tu aies eu qui soit disparu? Non, tout reste, n'est-ce pas? Les momies que l'on a dans le cœur ne tombent jamais en poussière, et, quand on penche la tête par le soupirail, on les voit en bas qui vous regardent avec leurs yeux ouverts, immobiles.   (ii. 32)

In the novel we have:

Quant au souvenir de Rodolphe elle l'avait descendu tout au fond de son cœur; et il restait là, plus solennel et plus immobile qu'une momie de roi dans un souterrain.   (647)

Divorced from the private context the image becomes no more than a bit of fine writing, its pretentiousness emphasized by the spuriously precise 'plus' before the adjectives. When Emma hears Rodolphe's first compliments, 'son orgueil, comme quelqu'un qui se délasse dans une étuve, s'étirait mollement . . . '. This too looks like a memory of Egypt, and specifically of the Cairo bath-houses, where Flaubert had an unusual experience (i. 572-3); but it hardly illuminates Emma's state of mind. When Léon is getting bored by Emma we have an equally weak and indeed puzzling simile: 'et son cœur, comme les gens qui ne peuvent endurer qu'une certaine dose de musique, s'assoupissait d'indifférence au vacarme . . . '. The medical overtones suggest that this may be a distant echo of a passage in the letters where he regrets the nervous condition which made him give up his law studies, and attacks (taking his usual anti-romantic position) the 'faculté de sentir outre mesure' as the enemy of artistic creation. 'Il se trouve des enfants auxquels la musique fait mal . . . Ce ne sont pas là les Mozart de l'avenir . . . Même chose dans l'art. La passion ne fait pas les vers' (ii. 127). The passage is of the highest interest for Flaubert's aesthetics; but the image which seems to be its by-product is ineffective and not fully intelligible.

There are, indeed, some vigorous images in the novels, which capture some of the spontaneity or fancifulness of those in the letters. Léon, back in Rouen from Paris, is confident of seducing 'la femme de ce petit médecin' though he would have trembled before a fine lady:

L'aplomb dépend des milieux où il se pose: on ne parle pas à l'entresol comme au quatrième étage, et la femme riche semble avoir autour d'elle, pour garder sa vertu, tous ses billets de banque, comme une cuirasse dans la doublure se son corset. (652)

And in *L'Education sentimentale*, exasperation with progressives and reactionaries alike issues in an odd but engaging juxtaposition of similes: hackneyed socialist theories though 'neuves comme le jeu d'oie . . . épouvantèrent les bourgeois comme une grêle d'aérolithes'. The homeliest images can equally be effective. The way in which during the street-fighting in Paris ordinary life also continues is typified by the national guard who 'chargeait son arme et tirait, tout en causant avec Frédéric aussi tranquillement, au milieu de l'émeute, qu'un horticulteur dans son jardin'. But too often Flaubert seems to be pursuing a stylistic ideal as awkward for him as it is tiresome for us. Emma's thoughts constantly return to the chemist's house where Léon lodges: 'ses pensées continuellement s'abattaient sur cette maison, comme les pigeons du *Lion d'Or* qui venaient tremper là, dans les gouttières, leurs pattes roses et leurs ailes blanches.' The flat and redundant colour adjectives seem here to be no more than a rather weary way of prolonging the sentence in a dubious aesthetic cause. Whimsical similes can be enjoyed for their own sake, sometimes in defiance of verisimilitude: 'Pauvre petite femme! Ça bâille après l'amour comme une carpe après l'eau sur une table de cuisine.' Though Rodolphe is a sporting man one can hardly believe that this image would have occurred to him. Flaubert's no more than partial success in an area which was for him of the highest artistic importance emphasizes again the tension, often but not always fruitful, between ideals and temperament, writer and man.

I have concentrated on *Madame Bovary*, but other works throw interesting light on Flaubert's procedures. In *L'Education senti-mentale* he seems to be more openly cantankerous about social and political affairs, and his characters' involvement in them: 'Frédéric, homme de toutes les faiblesses, fut gagné par la démence univer-selle.' By contrast, the *Trois Contes* are almost free of authorial intervention. Félicité's story ('nullement ironique . . . Je veux api-toyer, faire pleurer les âmes sensibles, en étant une moi-même')[14] is allowed to speak for itself—and the fact that Flaubert gives her taxidermist the same name (Fellacher) as the copyist of his youthful work *Par les champs et par les grèves* (i. 498, 1046) is probably no more than a whim. *La Légende de Saint Julien*, too, is on the whole (fictionally) factual, though the hermit's reactions to his occasional descents into the city—'l'air bestial des figures . . . l'indifférence des propos glaçaient son cœur'—remind us that the hermit of Croisset is not far off.

But, for all their perfection, the stories offer less rich nourish-ment than *Madame Bovary*, which will remain the masterpiece in spite of the vagaries of critical fashion, which sometimes point towards *L'Education sentimentale* or even *Bouvard et Pécuchet*. The long germination, agony for Flaubert, is responsible for that richness, going as it does with a long rumination on cliché and authenticity, passion and posture. 'Ménage tes pauvres nerfs, soigne-toi mieux,' Flaubert writes to Louise Colet in October 1853 (ii. 454); and then, catching himself in the expression of an *idée reçue*, he adds: 'Conseil bourgeois, plus facile à donner qu'à suivre.' Later Homais, 'les larmes aux yeux', is to use the same terms in his parting advice to Léon: 'Prenez garde au froid! Soignez-vous! Ménagez-vous!' Flaubert is perhaps unfair in reserving for himself the italics and disclaimers which preserve him from the charge of platitude. Yet he may sense that he is not all that different from his characters ('La bêtise n'est pas d'un côté et l'Esprit de l'autre. C'est comme le Vice et la Vertu. Malin qui les distingue'—ii.585–6); and that curious mixture of closeness and detachment is what gives its power to *Madame Bovary*. Flaubert constantly curses the prose-writer's lot, by comparison with the freedom of the poet (e.g. ii.457).

---

[14] *Correspondance*, vii (Paris, 1930), 307.

But he is also the born novelist and (to use an old compliment) 'creator of characters'. Long coexistence makes them so real for him that he frequently quotes them in his letters ('*chouette*, comme dirait Homais'—ii.586), and indeed in the novel itself (Lheureux was constantly dropping in on Emma, 's'inféodant, comme eût dit Homais'). Far from rejecting traditional notions of the novel Flaubert has an almost mystical belief in the novelist's need—and power—to 'enter into' his characters. There is the well-known claim that, when describing Emma's suicide, he could taste the arsenic in his own mouth; and of Rodolphe's and Emma's fatal ride he writes:

Aujourd'hui, par exemple, homme et femme ensemble, amant et maîtresse à la fois, je me suis promené à cheval dans une forêt, par un après-midi d'automne, sous des feuilles jaunes, et j'étais les chevaux, les feuilles, le vent, les paroles qu'ils se disaient et le soleil rouge qui faisait s'entre-fermer leurs paupières noyées d'amour.   (ii.483–4)

'Madame Bovary, c'est moi' was perhaps an ill-considered aside. '*Madame Bovary*, c'est moi' would have been completely uncontentious.

6

Echo and Self-Knowledge

GABRIEL JOSIPOVICI

ECHO AND NARCISSUS

FROM the start the fates of Echo and Narcissus seem to be inseparable. If they are not exactly mirror-images of each other then at least, in Ovid's retelling of the story, their fortunes are tantalizingly intertwined.

Narcissus' mother, a naiad of the river called Liriope, asks Tiresias if the boy will ever live to a ripe old age, and the seer answers: 'Yes, if he never knows himself.' The meaning of the mysterious prophecy is made clear in what follows. The nymph Echo, who cannot speak except to repeat the last words said to her, falls in love with Narcissus, but he spurns her and she wastes away until she is only a voice. Meanwhile, Narcissus falls in love with his own image, seen in the water:

> Poor boy,
> He wants himself; the loved becomes the lover,
> The seeker sought, the kindler burns. How often
> He tries to kiss the image in the water,
> Dips in his arms to embrace the boy he sees there,
> And finds the boy, himself, elusive always,
> Not knowing what he sees, but burning for it,
> The same delusion mocking his eyes and teasing.
> Why try to catch an always fleeing image,
> Poor credulous youngster? What you seek is nowhere,
> And if you turn away, you will take with you
> The boy you love.[1]

But it is not only the boy's beauty that seduces Narcissus. It is the promise of something more, the hint that what he is seeing can give him what no one else can, understands him better than anyone else in the whole world:

---

[1] This and subsequent quotations are from Ovid, *Metamorphoses*, iii. 338–511, trans. Rolphe Humphries (Bloomington and London, 1955).

> You promise,
> I think, some hope with a look of more than friendship.
> You reach your arms when I do, and your smile
> Follows my smiling; and I have seen your tears
> When I was tearful; you nod and beckon when I do;
> Your lips, it seems, answer when I am talking
> Though what you say I cannot hear.

But there is of course a price to pay for such perfect reciprocity, as Narcissus himself suddenly understands:

> What I want is with me,
> My riches make me poor. If I could only
> Escape from my own body! If I could only—
> How curious a prayer from any lover—
> Be parted from my love! And now my sorrow
> Is taking all my strength away; I know
> I have not long to live, I shall die early,
> And death is not so terrible, since it takes
> My troubles from me; I am sorry only
> The boy I love must die; we die together.

To love myself and find myself another—that is the impossible desire. Since that cannot be it is better to die. That at least will release me from an intolerable existence. The one sadness is that it will also mean the death of the one I love. But then another way of looking at it is that at least we will both die together.

So Narcissus kills himself, and Echo, now only a voice, mourns him in the only way she can:

> you could hear her
> Answer 'Alas!' in pity, when Narcissus
> Cried out 'Alas!' You could hear her own hands beating
> Her breast when he beat his. 'Farewell, dear boy,
> Beloved in vain!' were his last words, and Echo
> Cried the same words to him.

As the water reflects his image so Echo reflects his words. As he is forever separated from himself, so she is forever separated from him. It is as though once that narcissistic duplication had taken place it is designed to go on splitting into two unsatisfied halves for ever and ever. Or perhaps one could say that once an echo is heard it is designed to go on repeating the same words for ever and ever.

Yet Ovid, for all that he touched, in this brief story, the very heart of Romanticism and its discontents, was a man of the first and not of the nineteenth century. So his story ends not with death but with a flower and a bit of traditional lore:

> But when they sought his body, they found nothing,
> Only a flower with a yellow centre
> Surrounded with white petals.

THE WORLD'S ECHO

Wordsworth wrote 'The Boy of Winander' in 1798, and then, as he did with so much of his early poetry, he incorporated it virtually unchanged in *The Prelude* (ll. 364–97). There it becomes an example of those special childhood experiences which can never be recovered in later life, but which the poet, through his art, brings back for us intact.

The poem opens abruptly:[2]

> There was a Boy; ye knew him well, ye cliffs
> And islands of Winander!

There *was* a boy. Presumably he no longer exists. The poem, though, does not go on to tell us his story, but glides instead into the iterative mode:

> —many a time,
> At evening, when the earliest stars began
> To move along the edges of the hills,
> Rising or setting, would he stand alone,
> Beneath the trees, or by the glimmering lake;
> And there, with fingers interwoven, both hands
> Pressed closely palm to palm and to his mouth
> Uplifted, he, as through an instrument,
> Blew mimic hootings to the silent owls,
> That they might answer him . . .

The almost aggressive narrative opening has miraculously changed into a cradling rhythm which seems able to dispense with a main verb for far longer than we would have thought possible, while not noticeably distorting the natural rhythms of the spoken language: 'many a time, at evening, when the earliest stars began to move . . .

---

[2] Wordsworth has changed the punctuation here and there in the *Prelude* version. I quote here from the earlier version, as printed in *William Wordsworth: The Poems*, 2 vols, ed. John O. Hayden (Penguin English Poets, 1977), 362–3.

rising or setting, would he stand . . .'. This is Wordsworth's special
magic, the totally new element he brought into English (and into
European) literature.

But even here the sentence is not done. The Boy stands 'Beneath
the trees, or by the glimmering lake' (the adjective, we sense, is
more than merely formulaic; soon we will see just how it earns its
keep); and now, typically, Wordsworth extends the period with a
breathtakingly simple 'and', allowing us to keep our balance yet
propelling us forward. The second half of the sentence tells us what
the boy does. In contrast to Robinson Crusoe on his island, this
activity on the part of the boy is not directed outwards, towards the
improvement of his position in the wilderness, but rather towards
the merging of himself in his surroundings by means of echo and
imitation: interweaving his fingers, he blows *mimic* hootings to the
silent owls, to get them to respond. 'Uplifted', in line 9, seems to
float free of reference. Analysing it after the event we see that it
must refer to the hands. But is this a purely physical description? Is
there not a sense of the boy himself being uplifted by what is going
on?

The mouth and fingers—indeed, the whole boy—become an
instrument for those imitations of the owls' hootings, which seem
to succeed in calling forth an answer; for, the poem goes on to say,

> they would shout
> Across the watery vale, and shout again
> Responsive to his call . . .

How much less sense we would have of the owls as *responsive* to
the boy's call, were that sentence not folded in on itself already,
with its 'they would shout . . . and shout again . . . '. Even then
the cry is not allowed to vanish but is once again extended by the
poet through the naïve but effective use of the dash:

> . . . Responsive to his call—with quivering peals,
> And long halloos, and screams, and echoes loud
> Redoubled and redoubled . . .

This brings us to the heart of the little poem, as echo gives way to
silence:

> And, when there came a pause
> Of silence such as baffled his best skill:
> Then, sometimes, in that silence, while he hung

> Listening, a gentle shock of mild surprise
> Has carried far into his heart the voice
> Of mountain-torrents . . .

Wordsworth here deploys one of his favourite devices, the tension between a breath pause at the end of a verse line and the enjambement required by the sense. The voice, like the boy, '*hangs* . . . Listening', just as earlier there is a 'pause . . . Of silence', and the silence is somehow confirmed by the word's almost immediate repetition.

As he hangs, then, listening, 'a gentle shock' carries not just 'into his heart' but '*far* into his heart' the voice of mountain torrents. As so often in early Wordsworth the inner, affective self is somehow expanded, and given contours, by the very breath of the verse, so that we too, as readers, come to feel that the silence after the echoes goes deep inside us, travelling through our bodies rather as the torrents themselves travel through the Lakeland landscape, and carrying with it a rich and complex geology which now speaks within us and through us, but in its own voice and not in either the poet's or ours.

Still the great period has not ended, for now, in the stately climax, the aural echo, which played such a crucial role, as we have seen, in both the poetry and the fiction, is expanded to include a triple *visual* echo (Narcissus is never very far away from Echo):

> or the visible scene
> Would enter unawares into his mind
> With all its solemn imagery, its rocks,
> Its woods, and that uncertain heaven received
> Into the bosom of the steady lake.

'Uncertain' is brilliant here, another non-formulaic adjective, which sends us back to the 'glimmering lake', and sets up the uncertainty in our own minds that is the sign of those last lines: the echo or reflection is in the Boy's mind *and* in the lake *and* in the mind of the reader. Yet if the lake is glimmering it is also steady, and these two adjectives could also be seen as accurate descriptions of the poem. Each would seem to rule out the other, but Wordsworth's distinctive genius consists precisely in making each an index of the other.

Echo and reflection function here not to divide, as in Ovid, but to unite. Through his mimic hootings the boy is bound fast to the owls, the hills, the woods, the mountain torrents and the lake, as the seemingly ponderous iterations of the poem bind us to the boy. We are reminded of the climax of so many early Wordsworth poems, notably the most compressed of the Lucy poems, 'A Slumber did my Spirit Seal', where both girl and poem end 'rolled round in earth's diurnal course /With rocks and stones and trees!' The overt meaning is that Lucy is dead. But death has taken on a new meaning as a result of the poem, neither Christian resurrection nor Romantic annihilation but a mysterious combination of the two.

The boy of Winander too is, of course, now dead. We grasped that with the opening phrase, and the poem, in a concluding section, returns to it:

> This boy was taken from his mates, and died
> In childhood, ere he was full twelve years old.

But the poet does not tell us this as would a novelist, from some position outside and above the orbit of his creature. Wordsworth, in his final section, depicts him wandering through the very landscape the Boy had inhabited and the churchyard where he is buried. 'And through the churchyard when my way has led', he tells us, conveying by this the sense of passivity, of responsiveness, which is so typical of the boy as well. There, on summer evenings,

> A long half-hour together I have stood
> Mute-looking at the grave in which he lies!

The poet is excluded, apart, yet meditating on the past, as we find him in *Tintern Abbey*. Wordsworth wrote an essay on epitaphs which is, in a sense, the last document in European culture to assert the continuity of past and present, the ability of the simple epitaph to sum up a life satisfactorily. Since his day writers have tended to contemplate epitaphs ironically, suggesting that the pious words inscribed on tombstones can tell us nothing about the person buried beneath.[3]

But if the essay is the last of its kind, a poem such as 'The Boy of Winander' is surely the first of another kind. For the poem, unlike those inscribed on tombstones, does not rest content with tradi-

---

[3] See John Mepham, 'Mourning and Modernism', in *Virginia Woolf: New Critical Essays*, ed. Patricia Clements and Isobel Grundy (London, 1983), and John Kerrigan, 'Knowing the Dead', *Essays in Criticism*, 37 (Jan. 1987), 11–42.

tional pieties, but seeks to bring the Boy back to life. The poet may stand mute before the grave, but the result of that silence, we sense, is the poem we have before us, and which allows us to enter the very being of the Boy. That being is summed up in his hooting to the owls, which calls forth an answer from them, and then in that silence which allows the geology of the place to enter into him *unawares*, until he becomes the world in which he stands. He is like Lucy, yet alive. On the other hand, he dies before he can reach adolescence and it is left to the poet, through a radically new use of language, to make him live for us—and, of course, for himself.

It is as though Wordsworth, accepting that a poem will only ever be an echo of reality, turns the tables by revealing how reality itself is, in its essential being, echo, but echo as the assertion of a generous reciprocity.

THE MIND'S ECHO

Edgar Allan Poe wrote a number of essays and meditations on landscape. Though these are ostensibly written to celebrate the wonders of man's ability to imitate nature in the creation of elaborate gardens and the like, their effect is chilling. For instead of the communion with landscape leading the mind out of itself and so healing its self-divisions and anxieties, that communion only leads man back to himself. Though Poe talks of *Kabbala* and the discerning of the secret languages of God in nature, the effect is only to throw us back on ourselves: we had thought it was other and find it the same. At the same time these essays and meditations also seem to reveal the final bankruptcy of the American dream: instead of infinite spaces to colonize and chart, infinite adventures to recount, there is, in the end, only the sense that we have been here before.

This is also the subject of the tales. 'The Fall of the House of Usher' is particularly interesting in this context, because it is in some ways so close to Wordsworth's 'Boy of Winander', yet almost its polar opposite in the feeling it conveys. As with Wordsworth's poem, the setting is evening and the central image is that of a reflection in a lake. But where one brought renewal and a feeling of life, this brings only a sense of dreariness and death:

During the whole of a dull, dark, and soundless day in the autumn of the year, when the clouds hung oppressively low in the heavens, I had been passing alone, on horseback, through a singularly dreary tract of country, and at length found myself, as the shades of the evening drew on, within view of the melancholy House of Usher.

Without understanding why, the traveller's soul is filled 'with a sense of insufferable gloom'. It seems to him that his feelings can only be compared to the 'bitter lapse into every-day life—the hideous dropping off of the veil' of the opium addict. Here, he suggests, we have reached reality itself, a reality unredeemed by any 'goading of the imagination'. Trying to grasp the reason for this,

I reined my horse to the precipitous brink of a black and lurid tarn that lay in unruffled lustre by the dwelling, and gazed down—but with a shudder even more thrilling than before—upon the remodelled and inverted images of the grey sedge, and the ghastly tree-stems, and the vacant and eye-like window.

It is as though the reduplication of the house has robbed it of its life. Those windows like eyes through which no spirit shines have already been referred to in the opening lines, and they are later to be made explicit in the poem sung by Roderick Usher and entitled 'The Haunted House':

> In the greenest of our valleys,
>> By good angels tenanted,
> Once a fair and stately palace—
>> Radiant palace—reared its head.
> In the monarch Thought's dominion—
>> It stood there!
> Never seraph spread a pinion
>> Over fabric half so fair.

But alas, 'evil things, in robes of sorrow,/Assailed the monarch's high estate',

> And travellers now within that valley
>> Through the red-litten windows, see
> Vast forms that move fantastically
>> To a discordant melody;
> While, like a rapid ghastly river,
>> Through the pale door,
> A hideous throng rush out forever,
>> And laugh—but smile no more.

The mountain torrents, which in the pause between the hootings of the owls had seemed to enter the very being of the Boy of

Winander, here become merely a dead image for the madman's loss of his grip on language.

What has led to the deterioration? It is hinted that there is something about the house and its grounds which has affected Roderick Usher's mind—'above all', the narrator says, 'the long undisturbed endurance of this arrangement, and . . . its reduplication in the still waters of the tarn.' But there is a further, secret mirroring at work in this haunted house: the suggested incest between Roderick and his sister, who has recently died and been buried.

The denouement is both horrific and expected. The dead sister turns out to have been put living in the tomb, and she now, at the climax of the story, appears at the door of the room in which Roderick and the narrator have been talking:

There was blood upon her white robes, and the evidence of some bitter struggle upon every portion of her emaciated frame. For a moment she remained trembling and reeling to and fro upon the threshold, then, with a low moaning cry, fell heavily inwards upon the person of her brother, and in her violent and now final death-agonies, bore him to the floor a corpse, and a victim to the terrors he had anticipated.

The narrator flees in horror. A wild storm is beating about the house and grounds. A terrifying light flares in his path, and as he turns to look back he sees that the long zig-zag crack, which had been barely discernible in the façade of the house, has now widened and is letting through the gleam of a blood-red moon:

While I gazed this fissure rapidly widened—there came a fierce breath of the whirlwind—the entire orb of the satellite burst at once upon my sight—my brain reeled as I saw the mighty walls rushing asunder—there was a long tumultuous shouting sound like the voice of a thousand waters—and the deep and dank tarn at my feet closed sullenly and silently over the fragments of 'The House of Usher'.

The whole narrative, like so many post-Romantic fictions, exists between the moment in the opening lines, when the narrator senses that something is dreadfully wrong, and the eruption of that wrong into the light of day.[4] There is relief, as well as horror, in Roderick Usher's finally succumbing 'to the horrors he had anticipated'—and it is worth contrasting that anticipation in our minds with

---

[4] See ch. 6, 'Hawthorne: Allegory and Compulsion', of my *The World and the Book* (2nd edn, London, 1979).

Wordsworth's 'gentle shock of mild surprise' which forms the climax to *his* narrative. In the Poe it is as though the story cannot exist without a sense of a fatal flaw, a primal guilt, and cannot go on once that flaw has emerged into the light of day. That emergence is quite literal here, as the only apparently dead sister rises from her grave in order to die properly by bringing down her *alter ego*, her brother, and the entire scenery that contained the two of them.

At one level this is a psychological tale, with its themes of incest, madness and repression. But its springs lie elsewhere. Like Beckett, Poe makes use of what lies to hand, the banalities filling the popular reader's mind. In his case it is the trappings of Gothic. But, like Wordsworth and Beckett, he is concerned with the point at which the literary and the psychological mesh. It is as though such writing cannot go on pretending to be innocent. To do so, to write a story of adventure in the style of Fenimore Cooper, say, would be forcing the living world into the tomb of letters. Once this is recognized the story itself finds its theme: the revenge of life upon letters. Reduplication, echo, is the sign of writing, yet it is also that which writing itself must annihilate, destroying doubleness, leaving the lake empty of reflection.

This is brought out equally clearly in 'William Wilson', Poe's richest tale of doubles. This time there is no narrator distinct from the action. The story opens: 'Let me call myself, for the present, William Wilson. The fair page now lying before me need not be sullied with my real appellation.' Who the narrator is, and what his relation is to his name is what is in question. As usual, Poe turns the clichés of Gothic to his own rather different ends. The fair page should not be sullied with his real name because that name is too dreadful to write down; but also because to put the 'real name' down would so sully any page that that would be the end of all writing. In other words, to go on writing at all, a false name has to be substituted for a real one.

But a false name is, precisely, one that can be precisely imitated. With that opening sentence, therefore, we are at once in a world that refuses the falsehood of an unthinking transposition of life into literature, *and* a world condemned to infinite reduplication. That, however, is left in abeyance as Poe moves easily within the parameters of his chosen genre, describing 'my' ancestry, childhood and schooling. It is the school and its over-symmetrical appearance which he pauses on longest:

But the house!—how quaint an old building was this!—to me how veritably a palace of enchantment! There was really no end to its windings—to its incomprehensible subdivisions. It was difficult, at any given time, to say with certainty upon which of its two stories one happened to be ...

And as the house reduplicates the maze-like grounds, so the schoolroom reduplicates the house, for

Interspersed about the room, crossing and recrossing in endless irregularity, were innumerable benches and desks, black, ancient, and time-worn, piled desperately with much-bethumbed books, and so beseamed with initial letters, names at full length, grotesque figures, and other multiplied efforts of the knife, as to have entirely lost what little of original form might have been their portion in days long departed.

It is here, in this palimpsest of a building, that he meets the boy who is to play such a central role in his life. No relation, but bearing the same name as himself, born on the same day, like him in appearance, this *alter ego* seems to take pleasure in imitating him, though no one else, surprisingly, seems to notice either this or any other of the coincidences. Most horrible of all to Wilson is the fact that his rival, as he calls him, 'had a weakness of the faucial or guttural organs, which precluded him from raising his voice at any time *above* a very low whisper' (author's stress).

The horror engendered by this 'twofold repetition', as he calls it, gives the narrator no rest. One night he creeps up to his rival's bed:

I looked;—and a numbness, an iciness of feeling instantly pervaded my frame. My breast heaved, my knees tottered, my whole spirit became possessed with an objectless yet intolerable horror ... Was it, in truth, within the bounds of human possibility, that *what I saw now* was the result, merely, of the habitual practice of [his] sarcastic imitation? Awe-stricken, and with a creeping shudder, I extinguished the lamp, passed silently from the chamber, and left, at once, the halls of that old academy, never to enter them again.

But of course he flees in vain. The other goes on haunting him, and here too, as in 'The Fall of the House of Usher', the end is both horrible and never in doubt. The narrator, driven to distraction, kills his double, then feels that he is looking into a mirror as he sees himself totter towards himself, 'all pale and dabbled in blood'. But it is not himself—or is it?

It was Wilson; but he spoke no longer in a whisper, and I could have fancied that I myself was speaking while he said: 'You have conquered, and I yield. Yet, henceforward art thou also dead—dead to the world, to Heaven and to Hope! In me didst thou exist—and, in my death, see by this image which is thine own, how utterly thou hast murdered thyself.

As in Ovid, the hero and his mirror-image converge, but only in the moment of death. Knowing himself, he has to die; or perhaps it is that death brings a kind of self-knowledge. But death, one could also say, is the only way of stilling forever the horror of the echo.

IN SEARCH OF THE LOST ECHO

It is characteristic of Proust that the climax of his novel of repetition and return should begin with a return that is not a return. At the start of *Le Temps retrouvé*[5] Marcel recounts how he went to stay with Gilberte, now Mme de Saint-Loup, at her country house in Tansonville. The scene had already been prepared for as early as the fourth page of the novel, when Marcel is recalling all the rooms he has ever slept in:

j'étais dans ma chambre chez Mme de Saint-Loup, à la campagne; mon Dieu! il est au moins dix heures, on doit avoir fini de dîner! J'aurai trop prolongé la sieste que je fais tous les soirs, en rentrant de ma promenade avec Mme de Saint-Loup, avant d'endosser mon habit. Car bien des années ont passé depuis Combray, où dans nos retours les plus tardifs c'étaient les reflets rouges du couchant que je voyais sur le vitrage de ma fenêtre. C'est un autre genre de vie qu'on mène à Tansonville, chez Mme de Saint-Loup, un autre genre de plaisir que je trouve à ne sortir qu'à la nuit, à suivre au clair de lune des chemins où je jouais jadis au soleil . . .   (i.6–7)

In the course of their walks Gilberte takes him back over all his childish haunts, for Tansonville is within walking distance of Combray. Aren't you excited? she asks him. But, sadly, the answer is no: 'J'étais désolé de voir combien peu je revivais mes années d'autrefois. Je trouvais la Vivonne mince et laide au bord du chemin de halage' (iii. 692). Even the amazing discovery that the two ways, that of Swann and that of Guermantes, which had seemed to him to belong to quite different universes, can in fact easily be encompassed in a single stroll, fails to move him. 'Elle m'étonna beaucoup', says Marcel, when she reveals this fact to him, as when she shows him the source of the Vivonne, which he had imagined as

[5] All references to *A la recherche du temps perdu*, 3 vols, ed. Pierre Clarac and André Ferré (Pléiade, Paris, 1954).

something rather like the entry into Hades, but which turns out to be 'une espèce de lavoir carré où montaient des bulles'. But 'ce qui me frappa le plus, ce fut combien peu, pendant ce séjour, je revécus mes années d'autrefois, désirai peu revoir Combray, trouvai mince et laide la Vivonne' (693).

And yet the narration of this reaction has a curious effect on the reader, who has, after all, lived through Marcel's childhood in Combray with him. Paradoxically, it makes him feel the mystery of the past, and the joining of the two ways only serves to remind him how they were once fully alive for Marcel and totally distinct; totally distinct *because* fully alive. Unlike Wordsworth, the visit to a once sacred spot does not set feeling and memory in motion; unlike Poe, this meeting with his past self is anything but fatal. And it *is* a meeting with his past, for Gilberte tells him about her side of the encounter in the forest path, her view of him then. But Marcel simply cannot relate past to present. He is no longer in danger, the past cannot hurt him—but only because he is, in a sense, no longer alive. He is in the state recommended by Tiresias: not to know himself.

If we search our minds for a parallel experience to this one we quickly discover it: it is Swann looking back at his love-affair with Odette and wondering how he could have spent the best years of his life on a woman 'qui n'était même pas mon genre' (i. 382).

Tansonville, however, is only a stage, perhaps a necessary stage, in Marcel's progress. For had he remained in this mood he would not have written 'Combray', and we would not have known about the Vivonne in another mode. The fact that we do, that we have already experienced it differently, and can therefore register disappointment at this return which seems to be no return, is a proof (available to our senses but not yet to our consciousness) that matters will not end here.

On his last night in Tansonville Gilberte lends Marcel a copy of the Goncourt *Journals* to read in bed. The next few pages consist of a transcription of a dinner party, described by the Goncourts, at which the guests are those old friends of Marcel's, and thus of ours, the Verdurins, Cottard, Brichot, *et al.* As everyone knows, it is reading about that dinner party that makes Marcel at once thankful that he has in fact never pursued his career as a writer—for who would want to do so if that is the end result?—and sad that he never had the gifts required for such a career. But the way the pastiche ends

has perhaps not been remarked upon enough. It is difficult to quote from the pastiche, for Proust's point is the evenness of the Goncourts' tone, the way everything is seen in the same light, but we can cut into the passage as it nears its end:

Et la suggestive dissertation passe, sur un signe gracieux de la maîtresse de maison, de la salle à manger au fumoir vénitien dans lequel Cottard nous dit avoir assisté à de véritables dédoublements de la personnalité, nous citant ce cas d'un de ses malades, qu'il s'offre aimablement à m'amener chez moi et à qui il suffirait qu'il touche les tempes pour l'éveiller à une seconde vie, vie pendant laquelle il ne se rappellerait rien de la première, si bien que, très honnête homme dans celle-là, il y aurait été plusieurs fois arrêté pour des vols commis dans l'autre où il serait tout simplement un abominable gredin. Sur quoi Mme Verdurin remarque finement que la médecine pourrait fournir des sujets plus vrais à un théâtre où la cocasserie de l'imbroglio reposerait sur des méprises pathologiques, ce qui, de fil en aiguille, amène Mme Cottard à narrer qu'une donnée toute semblable a été mise en œuvre par un conteur qui est le favori des soirées de ses enfants, l'Ecossais Stevenson, un nom qui met dans la bouche de Swann cette affirmation péremptoire: 'Mais c'est tout à fait un grand écrivain, Stevenson, je vous assure . . . ' Et, comme, sur mon émerveillement des plafonds à caissons écussonnés, provenant de l'ancien palazzo Barberini, de la salle où nous fumons, je laisse percer mon regret du noircissement progressif d'une certaine vasque par la cendre de nos 'londres', Swann, ayant raconté que des taches pareilles attestent sur les livres ayant appartenu à Napoléon 1er . . .   (iii. 716–17)

The anecdote about Napoleon goes on for a further twelve lines, when Marcel, who has to get up early the next morning, closes the book. But we have seen enough of the Goncourt style, with its even movement over objects, people, anecdotes and books, to make us sense that it is indeed a kind of death-in-life. Everything is equally important here and nothing has any meaning. We watch a group of reasonably cultivated people taking dinner in town and we are left to wonder what point their lives can have. Time does not exist here, nor do joy or sorrow seem to touch either the writer or the people he so carefully describes.

   That, as all readers of Proust know, forms the turning-point for Marcel. Proust deliberately blurs the passing of time in the next few years, as Marcel goes back and forth from his sanatorium to Paris, and the war destroys the French countryside and the fabric of Parisian social life. But soon he will experience that series of shocks to his system which will alert him to the fact that the Goncourts have got it wrong, and will be led to recognize that art is indeed the central element in his life, but an art which accepts both Echo and Narcissus.

We watch Marcel coming alive in those last pages of the novel, until he reaches the point where, understanding fully what his task is, he is ready to write the book we have been reading. But paradox holds to the end, for that task, which gives new meaning to his life, and which, from one perspective, can be seen as his attempt to join himself once more to his dead mother, condemns him, like Roderick Usher's sister, to be buried alive for the remainder of his days; not, it is true, in the exotic House of Usher, but in the cork-lined room at 102 Boulevard Haussmann.

7

Rilke: Surviving the Self

ANTHONY THORLBY

WER, wenn ich schriee, hörte mich denn aus der Engel
Ordnungen? und gesetzt selbst, es nähme
einer mich plötzlich ans Herz: ich verginge von seinem
stärkeren Dasein. Denn das Schöne ist nichts
als des Schrecklichen Anfang, den wir noch grade ertragen,
und wir bewundern es so, weil es gelassen verschmäht,
uns zu zerstören. Ein jeder Engel ist schrecklich.

[Who, if I cried, would hear me among the angelic
orders? And even if one of them suddenly
pressed me against his heart, I should fade in the strength of his
stronger existence. For Beauty's nothing
but beginning of Terror we're still just able to bear,
and why we adore it so is because it serenely
disdains to destroy us. Every Angel is terrible.]   (p. 225)[1]

The opening lines of Rilke's *Duino Elegies* are justly famous. It is
not hard to believe that Rilke truly heard them, as he declared,
spoken to him on the sea wind. What could sound more in character with the spirit of the age than this declaration of personal solitude in an alien universe? Indeed, the plight of the I who here
speaks—the I of the poet, which becomes in lyrical utterance the I
of the reader, the I of every individual in his subjectivity—is worse
than solitude. He knows not only that no cry of his would ever be
heard, he knows too that were he to be heard and 'clasped to the
bosom of an angel', he would be quite annihilated. But this desperate realization is only half of what came to Rilke in that rush of
inspiration. He continues, as if by way of explanation or conse-
quence: 'For the beautiful is nothing but the beginning of the terrible . . .'. Why does Rilke write 'for'? The connection between the
poet's personal plight and the nature of beauty is far from clear, but

---

[1] Translations of poems are by J. B. Leishman, *Selected Works*, vol. ii (London,
1960). I have modified them slightly in my text.

the rhythm of the lines persuades us that there must be one. We are left wondering whether this is a new theme or a continuation of the first, and in any case what the intended continuity signifies. We notice that the first lines confront the overpowering menace of the angels' universe only hypothetically, indeed negatively—Rilke knows better than to attempt any such thing. The lines which follow are in the indicative, and they seem by contrast to be positively affirmative in what they assert about beauty, 'for' beauty confronts us with no more than the beginning of terror, which we are just able to bear, and in fact admire; we admire beauty precisely because 'it serenely disdains to destroy us.' In beauty, then, we are no less aware of our utter vulnerability, but here the menace is suspended. The function of the final half line is to emphasize the connection again: the terror which threatens to destroy our private individuality in reality is the same terror whose serene aspect we admire in beauty. The further grammatical modification from 'I' to 'we' suggests that the individual shares the experience of beauty with others, whereas he confronts the universe alone.

It is the announcement of these two themes together, almost as though they were one and the same, which makes the lines a magnificent introduction to the sequence of elegies as a whole, for their entire subject-matter will relate to one theme or the other; and it also makes them a memorable, almost archetypal evocation of 'modern' culture—as it used to be called, though that expiring expression is now evidently overripe for renaming. Similar feelings of individual isolation and vulnerability often appear, in Rilke's contemporaries, to have been fundamental to the discovery of a new significance and value in 'the beautiful', which at the same time acquired an aura of metaphysical mystery greater than the more specific, traditional beauty of particular arts. Glimpses of this experience are to be found, in German literature at least, long before Rilke's time, amongst the German Romantics, in Schopenhauer, then in Nietzsche, until eventually it permeates the intellectual sensibility of more than one generation of so-called moderns. In Schopenhauer's philosophical vision, it is the very principle of individuation throughout the whole scale of nature which is called into question: selfhood becomes the centre of a metaphysical agony, in which life's world-creating energy is divided against itself; yet mysteriously, this painful division is seen and heard in art as transcendently beautiful. Nietzsche's first great essay on tragedy

explores precisely this mystery again, in order to explain why there
can be none other than an 'aesthetic justification' of the spectacle of
existence, where life rejoices in the destruction of individuals. Rilke
knew this essay well, and his marginalia show his intuitive sympathy for Nietzsche's (and Schopenhauer's) idea of music, as being
supremely capable of making us feel the destruction of the individual as a 'joy'. It was apparently from reading this essay that Rilke
realized the immense significance of music for poetry—a significance he increasingly sought to exploit. Far from being a merely
mellifluous arrangement of the words (he admits that he used for-
merly to think of it in this way), music should be understood as the
primary inspiration and source of poetry, power latent in the tonality and rhythm of language, which generates the flow of images
and words, and similarly inspires all other forms of art. And in its
audience it 'destroys the individuality within each, and creates a
unity out of hundreds'. In music the force of life's terrible indifference and destructiveness towards human beings is transformed into
a communal experience of beauty.

When Rilke discovered in French literature a comparable
instance of beauty realized through an experience of terror, he
attached great importance to it. He comments on Baudelaire's
poem 'Une Charogne' both in letters and in his largely autobiographical fiction, *The Notebooks of Malte Laurids Brigge*, where he
says Baudelaire had seen 'in this terrible and apparently only repul-
sive thing [Rilke uses the same general term here as in the Duino
Elegy, *das Schreckliche*] that which truly and continuously exists,
the truth which all existence has' (p. 175).[2] In a letter, Rilke associates with this poem Flaubert's tale of *Saint Julien l'hospitalier*,
which he interprets symbolically as a similar test of artistic integ-
rity, of readiness to face and accept existence in all its aspects, to
the point even of lying down with the leper. 'An artist must have
known this in his being at some time, for him to overcome himself
and find his new blessedness' (19 Oct. 1907). Rilke's understanding
of Baudelaire's poem—and perhaps also of Flaubert's story—goes
rather beyond that of the author himself, a fact which Rilke recognized in his comment that Baudelaire 'got it right, except in the last

---

[2] References are to Rainer Maria Rilke, *Sämtliche Werke* (Frankfurt a. M.,
1966), vol. i.

stanza'. He is referring to Baudelaire's final declaration, which defies the terrible mortal decay of the woman he loved:

> Alors, ô ma beauté! dites à la vermine
> Qui vous mangera de baisers,
> Que j'ai gardé la forme et l'essence divine
> De mes amours décomposés!

There is often to be found in Baudelaire's work, which Rilke knew well, evidence like this of a rather diffuse spiritual idealism and even of a vestigial religious belief; it is this which Rilke feels to be out of keeping with the imaginative vision of the rest of the poem. Perhaps the phrase 'form and essence divine' (which might suit a hymn) need only be understood metaphorically, as an expression simply of how imperishable the poet feels his love to be—or perhaps his poem. But behind the phrasing there hovers still the half-thought that there really is an eternal realm of the spirit, safe from the transience of physical nature, and the home of such forms and essences as Plato and Aristotle recognized, perhaps even the heavenly home of all those individual souls the Christian church would save. Reality, as Rilke understands it, lacks any such dimension of transcendence. For him the perspectives of personal feeling have *only* metaphorical significance, with the result that the significance of metaphor itself is called into question; and this has the further result of blurring the distinction between literal and figurative language. Indeed, with the collapse of transcendence, part of the conventional basis of signification in language altogether is called into question, and the possibility emerges of putting it on a new basis. It is in view of this that Rilke came increasingly to regard his life and work as devoted to a single great task, crowned ultimately with success when he completed the Elegies and the Sonnets to Orpheus, and passing through phases of lesser enlightenment and even spiritual darkness, like a religious calling. The task was to come to terms with a new and 'terrible' vision of reality without transcendence, and to re-establish what the significance might then be of poetry, of art generally, and of other aspects of human spirituality, for which there was in existence no longer any metaphysical justification.

The direction which Rilke's work follows in pursuit of this goal is always the same: not to try to save something from the terror of existence (as at the last Baudelaire had attempted to do), nor to seek above and beyond it any consolation from its pain, but completely to accept everything that is, to face it and not hide from it, to assimilate and affirm it—so totally that, he believes, it will look and sound like its own opposite, a vision of beauty, a song of praise. Why on earth this transformation should happen is the central mystery of Rilke's poetry; what makes it appear to happen are the music and magic of his poetic language which seem to transform familiar things into another relationship, playing across opposites and opposition so that they feel like identity. That Rilke believed it had happened is clear from letters he wrote a year after finishing the *Duino Elegies* and the *Sonnets to Orpheus*: 'To presuppose the oneness of life and death', and 'to know the identity of terror and bliss . . . is the essential meaning and idea of my two books.' That is a very abstract way of expressing it, and somewhat misleadingly equates the meaning of his poetry with an idea. What actually happens there feels much less theoretical. Although Rilke's poetry does occasionally rise to such Olympian observations, it is not sustained by them, and should certainly not be systematized into a primarily philosophical speculation. It is part of the persuasive charm of his poetry that it seems to spring from much more than ideas and thoughts about the world; it seems to be grounded in some quite immediate and personal experience, some contact with reality that is deeply felt in every fibre of his being; its authenticity seems indeed to be ultimately almost physical. We have to remind ourselves firmly that this is of course an artistic illusion like any other, and observe how it has been brought about.

Consider, for instance, a passage in *Malte Laurids Brigge* in which Rilke encounters (in Paris) 'the existence of appalling terror in every component of the air' (p. 176). What is in his mind is the memory of 'all the agony and horror that has occurred in places of execution, torture chambers, operating theatres, madhouses'. Rilke does not present this as a thought or a memory, but as something outside himself, something materially enduring, existing in itself, penetrating the present, so that, as he tells himself (in the intimate second person singular) 'thou breathest it in with transparent stuff'; it even becomes deposited as crystals amongst his bodily organs. The imagery here might be thought of traditionally as constituting a rather powerful simile or metaphor to express a sense of solidarity with human suffering: it is as if it had become a part of the air we breathe, it is like a painful deposit in our body, it 'clings' to our world. Rilke has altered the semantic perspective, however, so that the passage no longer sounds like metaphor but like description, like a statement of material fact. The human and spiritual experience of terror is regarded as a thing as much as the air itself (assisted in this by Rilke's favourite use of an adjectival noun, *das Entsetzliche*, on a par with another adjectival noun, *Durchsichtiges*: the two are breathed in together); it lodges in the body as a shape, rather than in the mind as a thought, it is a component part of a reality which is simultaneously and indissolubly spiritual and material. This change of perspective affects particularly the appearance and stature of the human subject; instead of a metaphorical vista surrounding and magnifying the centrality of the sentient self, we see a reality hostile to the self, and immensely bigger. As the passage continues, the self vainly tries to hide 'in its own littleness' from the vastness which rises up all around it, and also inwardly through all its bodily cells and passages. Until finally the self is driven 'out of itself', by its own heart, pursued by the heart—symbol now of a power of 'real' feeling which is no longer self-contained, self-centred: 'And now thou art standing almost outside thyself and thou canst not get back in.' Like a beetle that is stepped on, the self squirts out, and its 'bit of superficial hardness and adaptation is without meaning'.

This must be one of the most striking evocations of the self's anguish, indeed extinction, in modern literature. *Malte Laurids Brigge* is full of similar passages exploring the edges of the self, where it becomes aware—through experiences of illness and fear and death—of its own strangeness and fragility, and of some transformation of all the familiar perspectives of meaning that is just beyond its grasp. 'Just one step further, and my deep wretchedness would be supreme happiness,' Malte writes (p. 156), but this ultimate goal of all Rilke's work is not attained in this book. Rilke regarded Malte as a failure, less as a book perhaps than as a person: 'the ordeal was too much for him . . . the book is nothing but this knowledge, exemplified in one for whom it was too tremendous' (19 Oct 1907). Rilke makes this comment in the same letter in which he writes about Baudelaire and Flaubert, and the knowledge and the ordeal he means are summed up in their vision of decay and their impulse to embrace it. From the point of view of subjectivity, that prospect is annihilating; only from another viewpoint, from which the cares and concerns of subjectivity have disappeared, will

the pain be rediscovered as joy. Malte goes to the very end of the
first, the traditional viewpoint of the individual and independent
mind; he experiences its breakdown, where the distinctions
between physical and spiritual dissolve, and the self feels driven
out; but he can go no further. He anticipates a time when he will—
as was to be the case with Rilke in later years—write in a different
way, words which will not be expressions simply of his personal
understanding; he already feels that he is 'being written . . . I am the
impression which is being transformed' (p. 156)—but he still
phrases this thought in the first person singular. Perhaps no other
form of expression is possible in a fiction about a person? The book
ends with yet another parable of a self dispossessed, which refuses
to be the person others know and love, refuses all personal relationship in fact—and waits now for a greater relationship to begin.

We may gain some insight into the mysterious process whereby
personal pain is transformed into supra-personal joy—that further
positive step into spiritual happiness which Malte could not take—
by looking at another letter of Rilke's on the subject of *Malte Laurids Brigge*. 'What is expressed there, what is suffered there, is
nothing but this question: How is it possible to live when the fundamentals of our life are so incomprehensible?' (8 Nov. 1915). The
fundamentals he means are love and death, and the spectacle of
men's 'terror and evasion' before them have driven him into amaze-
ment, confusion, 'and then into a sort of horror. But behind the
horror there is something else.' In order to explain what this something else is, Rilke continues:

Once, years ago, I tried to tell someone whom this book had frightened,
how I myself sometimes regarded it as a negative, as an empty form, the
hollows and depressions of which were all pain, despair and saddest
insight, but whose cast, were it possible to produce one (like the positive
figure obtained with bronzes), might perhaps be happiness, the most defi-
nite and certain serenity.

Rilke's thought here is probably inspired by memories of working
with Rodin, whose work he enthusiastically admired, learned from,
and wrote about. Sculpture impressed him above all because it
transformed life into a thing: 'It gives more than words and images,
more than likenesses and illusions: human longings and anxieties
[are here in the process] purely and simply of becoming a thing'
(p. 355). No matter what the ostensible subject-matter in real life,

sculpture 'translates it into something matter-of-fact and nameless: in this manual language, meanings relate entirely to performance in solid material' (p. 386). Rilke explores the same thought again with regard to surface values, for sculpture can be seen equally as an art of surfaces; it expresses everything through modulations of surface, 'it does not go beyond the surface, it nowhere goes into the inside of things' (p. 422). Does it not make us see that 'all that we call mind and soul and love is only a slight change on the small surface of a face that is near to us? . . . Would not someone who could see and render all physical shapes, render for us (almost without knowing it) all life's intellectual and spiritual meaning?' This might seem to be a rather narrow assessment of sculpture, but Rilke goes on to enthuse no less about other aspects of the sculptor's medium, such as movement, volume and light, on to which the significance of the subject is similarly transferred.

In all of these reflections Rilke is elaborating the same idea: namely, that in the sculptor's medium a subjective vision of life is translated into its apparent opposite: into the solidity of a thing, into the materiality of stone or bronze, into physical contours and surfaces. He elaborates the idea still further in his letters about Cézanne's paintings, in which he perceived a kinship with his own work, and an ideal he wished to follow. An ideal of work, in the first place, of dogged devotion to the activity itself of painting, to the exclusion of all other interest or feeling. In Cézanne's case the medium into which experience is translated is colour: 'So incorruptibly did he concentrate living things into their colour components, that they began a new life in another world, a Hereafter, of colour, without memories of their previous existence' (18 Oct. 1907). Cézanne's still-lifes and portraits and landscapes have a quality which Rilke praises as 'matter-of-factness' (*Sachlichkeit*), a word he used also of Rodin's sculptures, associating it there also with namelessness, which suggests that things become so entirely transformed into the substance of their new medium that they even lose their name. Rilke says that this matter-of-fact rendering into colour excludes any other kind of 'alien unity', by which he appears to mean any attempt to unify the picture in more conventional ways: 'apples, onions, oranges are represented by colour alone . . . there is no interpretation, no judgement, no conceptual superiority' (18 Oct. 1907). The entire canvas is organized in terms of colour, 'as though every place knew of all the others'; the subject-matter's

'bourgeois reality loses all its gravity in a total picture-existence,'
(22 Oct. 1907). Rilke perceives a most striking instance of this
matter-of-factness in the eyes of Cézanne's self-portrait, two
unblinking patches of dark colour whose pure gaze is without
expression or personal interpretation of any kind. Whatever feelings Cézanne may have experienced for his subject-matter have
become absorbed completely into the paint-work; and this lack of
subjective perspective permits a new *réalisation* (Rilke borrows this
word from Cézanne) of the objective world also—it ceases to be the
world usually recognized as realistic (from a subjectivist viewpoint)
and becomes a new artistic reality in its own right. Rilke imagines
the spirit in which Cézanne painted objects as follows:

One sees . . . how necessary it was to get beyond even love. It's natural
enough to love each of these things, if you are making them yourself; but if
you show it, you make them less well: you judge them instead of *saying*
them. You cease being impartial; and love, the best thing of all, remains
outside your work, does not enter into it, is left over untransposed beside it.
This is how the school of mood painting came into being (which is no
better than the realist school). They painted 'I love this' instead of painting
'Here it is'. In the latter case everyone must look carefully for himself to see
whether I loved it or not. It is not shown at all, and many people will even
assert that there is no question of love there at all. So utterly has it been
consumed in the act of making. This consuming of love in anonymous
work, from which such pure things arise, has probably been achieved by no
one so successfully as by old Cézanne.   (13 Oct. 1907)

Apart from his admiration for Cézanne's canvases, Rilke cherished
the thought that the French painter knew Baudelaire's 'Une
Charogne' by heart and could still recite it in old age. Did Cézanne
share his own sensibility with regard also to life's terrors, did the
supra-personal matter-of-factness of his work proceed from a similar crisis of self-consciousness? There is little further evidence, but
Rilke is sure from his own experience that 'one would find amongst
his early works some in which he had violently overcome himself to
reach other extremest possibilities of love'; that this was 'a love
which had passed through the fire'; and that 'true work, fullness of
task, all this begins on the far side of the ordeal of self-overcoming'
(19 Oct. 1907). He attributed to Cézanne a kind of blessedness,
indeed saintliness, in his unselfconscious acceptance of the world
through work; work which consumes personal life entirely, becoming part of the blood, offered the only—but certain—way of salva-

tion to the individual soul in its solitude and despair. Rilke develops this thought more fully in a beautiful requiem poem which he wrote for a young German poet, Wolf Graf von Kalckreuth, who had translated poems of Baudelaire; he committed suicide at the age of nineteen. With a beguiling lyricism, Rilke first suggests the kind of romantic illusions which might have prompted the young man to seek in death the joy he could not find in life— oneness with nature and oneness in love. And then, by means of a dialectical reversal which is a constant source of persuasive power in his poetry, Rilke suggests the opposite: the joy von Kalckreuth wanted lay already within him, in the darkest intuitions of his despair, like a promise of salvation. The first half of the poem elaborates this theme that all that was needed was already there, only the young poet could not see it, he rejected the materials life offered, became increasingly isolated and cut off, and for that reason lacked the light to decipher his own impressions. The dialectical emphasis falls increasingly on the self-enclosure of the young poet, who by an act of violent destruction has stopped life's potential for transformation. The second half of the poem takes the dialectic a decisive step further, to reveal the positive significance of what von Kalckreuth had assumed to be purely negative and painful experiences: of heartache and renunciation and mortification. Here in fact lie the positive resources of the artistic spirit: the first 'makes room' for feeling, the second is necessary to creative contemplation, while the third is the death of self, which is the condition of all good work. The argument is highly metaphorical: to show how this positive conclusion may be got out of such negative premisses, Rilke employs the image he used in the letter about *Malte*: the pain of personal experience is the hollow mould from which the solid cast of art is taken. How mistaken, then, to complain that in itself the mould—one's personal life—is empty! In the much quoted lines which follow, Rilke sums up his most fundamental aesthetic principle:

> O alter Fluch der Dichter,
> die sich beklagen, wo sie sagen sollten,
> die immer urteiln über ihr Gefühl,
> statt es zu bilden; die immer noch meinen,
> was traurig ist in ihnen oder froh,
> das wüssten sie und dürftens im Gedicht
> bedauern oder rühmen.

> [O ancient curse of poets!
> Being sorry for themselves instead of saying,
> for ever passing judgement on their feeling
> instead of shaping it; for ever thinking
> that what is sad or joyful in themselves
> is what they know and what in poems may fitly
> be mourned or celebrated]   (p. 209)

The force of these lines depends, as so often in Rilke, on their dialectical energy, their rhetoric of not this but that. We are all familiar
with personal feelings, and see well enough how poetry might be
said to praise or lament them: so the thought of poetry doing something like the opposite of that seems to suggest a clearer, more defi-
nite alternative than is in fact stated by the two words 'sagen' and
'bilden'. Rilke typically employs them without explanation or overt
show of metaphor, as though his meaning were quite matter-of-
fact. He illustrates it by means of two further images borrowed
from the plastic arts; these are more obviously metaphorical, and
they brilliantly convey the relationship Rilke believed should exist
between the poet's self and the poetic work. The poet should transform what is in him into words in the same 'hard' way that a cathedral mason 'grimly puts himself into the serenity of stone'. Then,
once his personal story has truly entered a poem, and become an
image there, 'it will not return'; it is independent of its author, who
can look back on it as at the portrait of an ancestor on the wall.

The despair of subjectivity, which Rilke believed it was necessary
to overcome through a new objectivity in art, can be understood
also as being partly due to the lack in the present day of an agreed
symbolism—objects and places and events which visibly embody
the emotional and spiritual concerns of all. It is a familiar problem
amongst modern artists, and Rilke voices it often in letters and
poems. His requiem for Kalckreuth ends by acknowledging it:

> Die grossen Worte aus den Zeiten, da
> Geschehn noch sichtbar war, sind nicht für uns.
> Wer spricht von Siegen? überstehn ist alles.
>
> [The big words from those ages when as yet
> happening was visible are not for us.
> Who talks of victory? To endure is all.]
>
>   (p. 210)

Malte's plight can likewise be described in these terms: 'Life was everlastingly slipping back into the invisible, and he struggled to keep a hold on it by means of phantoms and images, finding these in memories of his own childhood, in his Parisian surroundings, in things he had read' (10 Nov. 1925). Rilke idealized periods in the past which had been in this respect 'the opposite of our own, where increasingly everything internal remains internal . . . without any prospect of finding external equivalents for its various states' (1 Mar. 1912). And when he found a place which matched his inner feeling, his excitement knew no bounds:

[In] the Spanish landscape . . . the outward things themselves—tower, mountain, bridge—instantly possessed the unparalleled, unsurpassable intensity of the inner equivalents through which one would have wished to portray them. Appearance and vision everywhere merged in the object, in each a whole interior world was revealed, as though an angel who encompassed all space were blind and gazing into himself. This, a world no longer seen from the standpoint of people, but in the angel, is perhaps my real task, at least all my previous endeavours would be united in it.

(27 Oct. 1915)

The angels Rilke alludes to here—they are the same angels with which we began and which we saw to be so indifferent to the person of the poet—are symbols of a more-than-human reality, one in which existence and meaning ('appearance and vision') merge, as they never do in subjective experience. Rilke is seeking to remedy the dilemma of subjectivism, in fact, by creating a new symbolism having a supra-personal focus; as with many modern writers and artists who have attempted something similar, the attempt is inevitably somewhat paradoxical, because the symbolism remains essentially private (Rilke's angels are not those of religious tradition). However, Rilke handles this dilemma more successfully than many of his contemporaries who merely transform the subjective into the inscrutable; Rilke's symbolism preserves for the most part a broadly comprehensible relationship with familiar experience— even his most exalted symbolic declarations have an intimate appeal. In this letter, for instance, Rilke is appealing to the intense response many people feel towards a place or a landscape; but instead of thinking of this intensity as something in the person responding, he thinks of it as something the object possesses in itself. The result is a world 'no longer seen from the standpoint of people' but—and here Rilke establishes a meaning for his symbol by simple contrast, by that dialectical reversal we have observed before—'in the angel'. To reveal the familiar world in this symbolically more-than-human context is indeed one aspect of that great 'task' to which Rilke felt that his life's work, and especially the Elegies and the Sonnets, was devoted.

Rilke certainly found some traditional symbolism in the legend of Orpheus most suitable for his purpose, and in rather less need of private adaptation than in the case of the angels. The death of the poet could scarcely be symbolized more vividly—or with more obviously Nietzschean implications—than by the story of Orpheus, whose head still sang after his violent death at the hands of the Maenadic women. Rilke makes use mainly of the Orphic poet's ability to enter the underworld, and he doubtless knew also of the Orphic cults' reputation for affording guidance to the afterlife. From the beginning, Rilke's poetry is infiltrated by the theme of death, by awareness of death as a permanent presence within life, together with intuitions of the dead and of the realm they inhabit. Orpheus shares with the angels their remarkable characteristic of being able to move through both realms of the living and the dead, and of not drawing a sharp distinction between them, as lesser mortals 'all make the mistake of doing':

> Engel (sagt man) wüssten oft nicht, ob sie unter
> Lebenden gehn oder Toten. Die ewige Strömung
> reisst durch beide Bereiche alle Alter
> immer mit sich und übertönt sie in beiden.

> [Angels (it's said) would often be unable to tell
> Whether they've moved among living or dead. The eternal
> torrent whirls all the ages through either realm
> for ever, and sounds above their voices in both.]

(p. 226)

Orpheus is characterized in the same terms:

> Ist er ein Hiesiger? Nein, aus beiden
> Bereichen erwuchs seine weite Natur.

> [Does he belong here? No, his spreading
> nature from either domain has sprung.]

(p. 255)

Given the dialectical structure of Rilke's poetic thinking, we notice a further parallelism between the absence of any opposition between 'appearance and vision' in the greater reality known to the angels, and the absence either for them or for Orpheus of any opposition between life and death. Evidently there is some essential connection between knowledge of the underworld and the voice of poetry—an idea which Rilke expresses in many beautiful variations:

> Nur wer die Leier schon hob
> auch unter Schatten,
> darf das unendliche Lob
> ahnend erstatten . . .
>
> Erst in dem Doppelbereich
> werden die Stimmen
> ewig und mild.
>
> [Only by him by whose lays
> shades were enraptured
> may the celestial praise
> faintly be captured . . .
>
> Not till both here and beyond
> voices are rendered
> lasting and pure]
>
> (p. 257)

The sonnets are addressed to Orpheus, but the legendary figure himself does not appear in them; in a much longer poem, which Rilke wrote earlier about the legend of Orpheus's attempt to bring Eurydice back from the dead, Orpheus does appear in person, only to become the subject of a personal defeat. Rilke evokes very strikingly the impossibility and even the undesirability of what Orpheus attempts. The focus of the poem falls first on Orpheus with Eurydice unseen behind him, he impatient to reach the light of day, his senses divided between what lies ahead and what lies behind (which he is not allowed to turn and look at); the focus is then transferred to Eurydice and stays with her to the end, when Orpheus is a mere nameless figure seen against the light, 'whose face was not to be recognized'. The entire second half of the poem is an extravagantly lyrical evocation of Eurydice's condition in death:

> Sie war in sich, wie Eine hoher Hoffnung . . .
> Sie war in sich. Und ihr Gestorbensein
> erfüllte sie wie Fülle.

> Wie eine Frucht von Süssigkeit und Dunkel,
> so war sie voll von ihrem grossen Tode . . .
>
> Sie war in einem neuen Mädchentum
> und unberührbar; ihr Geschlecht war zu
> wie eine junge Blume gegen Abend . . .
>
> [Wrapt in herself, like one whose time is near . . .
> Wrapt in herself she wandered. And her deadness
> was filling her like fullness.
> Full as a fruit with sweetness and with darkness
> was she with her great death . . .
>
> She had attained a new virginity
> And was intangible; her sex had closed
> like a young flower at the approach of evening.]
>
> (p. 190)

Rilke's lyricism here is not entirely successful; something between silliness and bad taste clings to it, and the reason seems to be that the distinction between metaphorical and literal meaning does not entirely disappear—the reader catches hints of out-of-place literalness in the midst of the similes. Eurydice's new condition is more successfully stated in plain negative terms: she is no longer the person she was:

> Sie war schon nicht mehr diese blonde Frau,
> die in des Dichters Liedern manchmal anklang,
> nicht mehr des breiten Bettes Duft und Eiland
> und jenes Mannes Eigentum nicht mehr.
>
> [Even now she was no longer that blonde woman
> who'd sometimes echoed in the poet's poems,
> no longer the broad couch's scent and island,
> nor yonder man's possession any longer.]
>
> (p. 190)

And having established this supra-personal ground quite firmly, Rilke returns to a metaphorical mode of expression with more confidence; the images succeed one another more fluently, whatever reality this is it is imagined to be forever changing, and there is no time to reflect on what in all this is literal and what metaphorical. The effect of the imagery is not unlike rapid description—except that what it 'describes' is a reality which simply becomes the way it is imagined:

Sie war schon aufgelöst wie langes Haar
und hingegeben wie gefallner Regen
und ausgeteilt wie hundertfacher Vorrat.

Sie war schon Wurzel.

[She was already loosened like long hair,
and given far and wide like fallen rain,
and dealt out like a manifold supply.

She was already root.]

(p. 190)

With this last image, Rilke recalls the imagery of the opening lines, which describe, again by means of metaphors indistinguishable from literals, the underworld landscape; here souls are embedded like shining ore, here are the roots, between which the blood goes forth to men. The poem takes place entirely in this underground world, in which it feels right and inevitable that Eurydice should remain. There is only one place outside it in which she might be expected to find another existence: this is the world re-created by Orpheus in his poetry, a duplicate world in which 'everything exists once again: woods and valleys, paths and places, field and river and beast.' The inspiration which led Orpheus to create this art-world was his love for Eurydice, or rather his sorrow at losing her; yet the one thing which is not here, where everything else under the sun is to be found, indeed another sun and stars, is Eurydice herself, or Orpheus either, or his feelings. Orpheus is obviously an adept at Rilke's art of transforming personal feelings into an objective artefact; there is no vestige of the personal in his poems, there are only things, an entire universe of things, possessing that symbolic intensity which comes from their being the objective equivalents of feeling. The lyrical mode in which Rilke designates these symbolic things—'field and river and beast'—is the counterpart of his highly metaphorical mode. Both modes can be observed frequently in his poems, though not always in such clearly contrasting examples as here; their rhythm and style are basically very different, and so is their semantic structure. Where one generates metaphors which (at their best) come to be read as objective statements, the other states objective things which—like the 'tower, mountain, bridge' Rilke saw in Spain—have the resonance of symbols. What the two modes have in common is made memorably clear by the narrative of this poem: there is no place for the person in either of them. Eurydice exists in two ways for Rilke, as sexuality and as universal ideal, and in neither is she a person; in one realm she is dissolved in all the beauty and fecundity of nature, in the other she sustains a whole universe of artistic creation—but again from the experience of her being utterly lost to the lamenting poet. When he turns to look at her in person, when he tries to bring her person back from the dead to be with him in life, he loses her for ever.

The most memorable affirmation of the connection between personal vulnerability and loss and the achievement of poetry is to be found at the climax of the *Duino Elegies*, whose central problem it resolves. As we might expect from the twin themes of the opening lines, the condition of man's existential otherness and separateness from nature is also the condition under which he discovers the saving word. Rilke does not explain the connection in the Ninth Elegy any more than in the First; poetry does not proceed or persuade by explanation, but by qualities of imaginative vision which evoke belief. And of these there is abundance, beginning with the beautiful contrast worked out in the Eighth Elegy between the way human beings see the world and the way animals do; man distances himself from what he sees by his conscious understanding of it, he takes leave of the immediate present in every instant. Each instant also becomes unique and irrevocable, and as the Ninth Elegy develops, Rilke briefly explores this uniqueness as a possible source of distinction by which the human individual might justify his fragile existence; but the thought remains inconclusive at this stage. For the litany continues of man's futile attempts to achieve significance: how intensely he feels, how much he learns, and suffers, and loves—and yet it all amounts to nothing in Rilke's estimation, because it is all of it 'unsayable', *unsäglich*. Much hangs on the meaning of this one word, which has to be understood in the context of Rilke's poetic thinking as a whole. The standard by which he is judging what cannot be said is the angel, or the greater reality symbolized by the angels; they, we recall, do not even notice a difference between the existence of the living and of the dead, let alone hear the voice of an actual individual. Obviously, human beings can speak subjectively of their experiences, and to one another; but just this kind of subjective utterance we have already heard Rilke dismiss as bad poetry—for the reason, we now discover, that the degree of reality such poetry boasts of is lightweight by comparison with the fullness of the reality in which the angels exist, the truly infinite reality of the stars (for instance), which are 'much more unsayable' (*besser unsäglich*). There is evidently no point in trying to make our poetry compete with reality, which already is so much more than we can possibly feel, think or say:

> *ihm*
> kannst du nicht grosstun mit herrlich Erfühltem; im Weltall
> wo er fühlender fühlt, bist du ein Neuling.

> [you
> can't impress *him* with the splendours you've felt; in the cosmos
> where he more feelingly feels you're only a novice.]

> (p. 245)

Faced with this overwhelming and annihilating prospect, there would seem to be nothing left to say. And yet with the word 'unsayable' Rilke conjures up one last possibility: namely, that there may be something else altogether that words are able to say. This clearly cannot be any of the subjective stuff of personal experience, neither thoughts nor feelings, but perhaps it might be simple objective things, objects, of which Rilke now gives a short list: 'Are we perhaps here just to say: House, bridge, well, gate, jug, fruit-tree, window—and at most: pillar, tower . . .'

It is hard to tell whether this is supposed to be poetry as it stands, or simply a list of subjects for poetry. And what does Rilke mean by 'saying', *sagen*, a word he repeats three times and italicizes? Presumably something more than this bare statement of proper nouns. He stressed the same verb in the Requiem poem, where it also acquired its meaning largely by contrast with the subjective utterances and personal responses of the kind of poets he rejected; true saying he likened to carving in stone. Here in the Ninth Elegy, the whole weight of what has gone before in evocation of the evanescent human condition, the alienation from reality of human consciousness, and the inadequacy by angelic standards of any subjective experience, bears down by contrast with the offered alternative of these simple things, and seems to lift them up as symbols of enduring worth. They are things, we notice, which belong in a human environment, are the work of human hands, and the embodiment of human values. Rilke adds one further name, that of 'threshold', and shows that he is thinking of what *it* becomes in the experience of successive generations of lovers who wear it ever-so-gradually away. Is not Nature's secret and cunning intention, he asks, in inspiring sexual love, to allow things to know delight through lovers' feelings? Similarly, through human saying, things become something more than 'inwardly they ever thought themselves to be'. These slightly fanciful thoughts might not carry much conviction without the rhetorical force, and especially the imaginative dialectic, of the preceding preparatory and contrasting passages. The reversal of perspective from human-centred to thing-centred is also most beautifully introduced by the image in which Rilke realizes that something quite different (from all the unsayable ingredients of personal experience) has to be looked for: 'Yet the mountain wanderer brings back to the valley from the precipice-edge not a handful of earth, which is the common unsayable stuff of all men's lives, but a word, pure, and patiently acquired, the yellow and blue enzian.' The images of earth and flower illumine the distance between personal experience and poetic word, which Rilke's inspiration has finally leapt across in order to affirm his faith in things. The suggestion in these lines, first, of moving beyond the annihilating opposition between man's subjectivity and angelic reality, and secondly, that there may be something much more beautiful to be unearthed, gives the passage a feeling of triumphant resolution. It is not in fact a new idea in Rilke's writing; we find something very similar, for instance, in Malte's reflections on what poetry should and should not be. But like so many of Rilke's poetic ideas, which recur more than once in his work, this renewed expression of it raises it to a higher level of intensity and effectiveness; its truth resides in its artistic realization.

Nor is this at all the end of the idea; as the passage develops, Rilke gradually comes to a still further, complementary, and in a sense opposite realization. His attention is focused at first on the concrete object as a visible image of human activity and concern (we remember his excitement at seeing such symbolic things in the Spanish landscape). He regrets in passing that so much of modern life is lived without symbols—so much 'action without image'—and turns to the ancient artefacts produced by a ropemaker and a potter, in order to hold them up to the angel in praise of the world human beings have made. The angel remains an emblem of life's absolute totality and power, beside which man's ephemeral self is reduced to nothing; but the things man makes can apparently withstand the angelic test. For the 'saying' of things is directed ultimately at the angel ('a world no longer seen from the standpoint of people, but in the angel, is perhaps my real task'). Even suffering, even complaining of suffering, can resolve itself into a shape, a form (*Gestalt*), and 'serve as a thing, or die in a thing—and pass blissfully on beyond the violin'. Rilke evidently regards music too as one of the all important 'things' men make, into which human feelings are absorbed and through which they are transformed; (there is a hint of something like transcendence in the phrase 'pass blissfully on beyond the violin'—*und jenseits selig der Geige entgeht*—though transcendence only in an artistic sense, for Rilke knows no other kind.) And with this extension of man-made things from visible objects to the invisible forms of music, Rilke arrives at the completion of his thought: the things man makes, no matter how materially solid they may be, all become invisible when they are 'said', when they are taken into the human heart, and praised (in poetry) to the angel. It is human beings who introduce on earth this dimension of spiritual invisibility, articulating it through language, and Rilke imagines that it is the deep desire and dream of earth to become invisible 'in us'. Man's difference from Nature, which left him before so unaccommodated in life, becomes now the grounds for a new, almost passionate relationship; ecstatically, Rilke accepts and endorses earth's will to be transformed. Above all, human transience and insubstantiality of person (which appeared at first to be man's primary weakness) turn out now to be closely associated with this capacity to render invisible and transform. Rilke characterizes 'us' as the most transient of all things on earth, for we are aware of change in every instant, as the brief earlier passage on this theme urgently insisted (but without reaching there any conclusion). And because we are in this condition, things are able to find in us their desired transformation into the invisible state— almost as if they were being 'raised up': *unsichtbar in uns erstehen* suggests a kind of redemption.

As Rilke feels his way beyond the impasse of personal life, the first hesitant tone of his question: Are we perhaps here just to say, gives place to an increasingly joyful declaration of confidence in life as a whole—the life of the earth, whose inmost will he has discovered, and now embraces as his own. *Erde, du liebe, ich will.* He feels the surge of springtime in his blood, is totally won over to it, and endorses as right the whole living process, including death which he calls earth's 'holy inspiration'. This ecstatic surrender of self (*Namenlos bin ich zu dir entschlossen*), this rejoicing in the infinite plenitude of existence (*Ueberzähliges Dasein entspringt mir im*

Herzen), sounds more like a Dionysian rapture as described by Nietzsche than a new kind of saying, let alone any kind of poetry. Has Rilke been talking about more than just poetry and poets, does he mean that 'we'—truly all men—are here in order that we may 'say', and praise things, and transform the earth, and rejoice in earth's invisible and impersonal will? As he extends and explores the idea of saying beyond the confines of the 'pure' word, beyond the word as pure image of a thing, so he reveals how much more he has in mind than a specifically literary or even artistic activity. The phrase he adds to the first fundamental commandment of his now articulate creed shows that it is not just addressed to poets: 'We will, we must transform things utterly in the unseen heart, transform them in—O, infinitely in us! No matter who we may be.'

What does it mean to expand the lesson of poetry in this fashion, and to regard the call to joyful transformation as valid for all men? The prosaic mind sees an obvious difference between poetry and life, and prefers to avoid any blurring of the common-sense distinction between them. Such a mind, the mind of modern civilized society, which keeps every form of imagination and spirituality well away from its 'real' concerns, is consistently and frequently condemned by Rilke, as it was by Nietzsche. For Nietzsche, there should ideally not be any difference between Dionysian rapture and the new kind of saying which he too imagined. His was an ideal compounded of ideas drawn from Wagnerian music, German philosophy and Greek tragedy; it was a thoroughly intellectual, artistic, indeed poetic inspiration, based upon a profound understanding of art and language—and yet he certainly intended it to be true for all men, and lamented the passing, when modern civilization was born, of a culture in which he believed his ideal had been realized by a community as a whole. Rilke also looks back to ages and places with a better sense not just of poetry but of the spirit, and his high prophetic style, with its oracular declarations and imperatives, is intended to be a gospel for living, not just for writing. The truth of his message is undoubtedly rooted in his experience of writing poetry; this had for him all the seriousness of a spiritual calling, and he felt his life to be fulfilled and justified when it transformed itself into poetry—or else not justified, and desperately without meaning, when no transformation took place and it could not be 'said'. For him there was ideally no distinction between poetry and existence, though he was well enough aware of all the civilized common sense which forced them apart. The modern self was a creature of that mistaken common sense; the elegiac note of the Elegies is inspired by its fate and by the need to come to terms with the truth that the self has no place in the real order of things. This could only be done perhaps, not by cultivating its unhappy subjectivity, for that only aggravates an already sick sense of alienation from the world, but by reaching beyond the boundaries of the self altogether. Might it not be possible for language to voice again the undivided reality of things without invoking a distinction between what is real and what is only thought, what is literal and what is metaphorical? Is not language an imaging of things that is also a total inward transformation of them? Only a self-conscious mind, which insists on the difference between what is inside itself and what is outside, will keep these two aspects of language apart.

Thus, the process of redemptive transformation which Rilke discovers in the spirituality of the creative mind, he goes on to treat as a transformation desired and willed and realized in the total reality of the earth. Man's spiritual activity he can feel at last to be an integral part of the entire process of existence, even though man's personal individuality has to be accepted—quite joyfully—as a casualty of this metaphysical reunion. The same ambiguity and the same individual cost can be observed in the case of Nietzsche's Dionysian rapture: it is both an artistic and cultural experience and also a participation in nature's organic process, and the two are seen to merge where the individual is destroyed—in personal tragedy (which Nietzsche similarly regards joyfully). Both writers assimilate the structure of reality to the structure of art, and particularly to the structure of language; art for them is not about reality, it is reality. And both consequently cultivate a visionary expectation of a new art, a new language, which will renew the face of the earth, liberating it from all the fictions of subjective identity and objective fact with which civilization has vainly overlaid it. Whether either of them ever achieves such art or speaks such language, as distinct from speaking about its possibility and desirability, it is hard to tell. The Sonnets to Orpheus play undoubtedly very beautiful variations on themes present already in the Elegies (and still earlier poems), in particular the passage from thing to inner transformation, from simple name to shifting metaphor. These two modes of Rilke's poetry, which we have already

observed, express two contrary and complementary aspects of
language on the one hand, and of existence on the other: lexical
fixity and semantic fluidity, being and becoming, the Apollonian
and the Dionysian. In the Sonnets they merge; one tells us

> Mag auch die Spieglung im Teich
> oft uns verschwimmen:
> *Wisse das Bild* . . .
> Denn wir leben wahrhaft in Figuren.
>
> [No matter if the reflection in the pond
> is often blurred for us:
> *let us know the image* . . .
> For we live truly in figurations.][3]

And the other says:

> Wolle die Wandlung . . .
> Alles Vollendete fällt
> heim zum Uralten.
>
> [Choose transformation and change . . .
> All that is finished and perfect
> falls back home to the primal.]

The most remarkable moments in Rilke's poetry occur, as we have
seen, when the distinction between these two modes fades, and the
metaphorical and the literal constitute a single reality. As the
sonnet—the third of the first cycle—reminds us, with its fusion of
'song' with 'existence' (*Gesang ist Dasein*), these moments unfold
when the perspective of personal concerns, and even of personal
syntax, is put aside:

> . . . lerne
> vergessen, dass du aufsangst. Das verrinnt.
> In Wahrheit singen, ist ein andrer Hauch.
> Ein Hauch um nichts. Ein Wehn im Gott. Ein Wind.
>
> [Learn to forget that it was you who sang out. That all dissolves away,
> To sing in reality is a far different breath of air,
> A breath about nothing. A breathing in the god. A wind.][4]

---

[3] My translation, cf. p. 257 in Leishman.
[4] My translation, cf. p. 254 in Leishman.

8

Proust's Narrative Selves

MALCOLM BOWIE

Let the milky way be split into the milky way of inventor/explorers and the
milky way of investor/exploiters

Velimir Khlebnikov

MODERN computational scholarship has revealed that the word
moi, as noun or pronoun, occurs on average 1.1996 times per page
in Proust's *A la recherche du temps perdu*. Few readers, of course,
will be surprised by this scrap of statistical information, for the
novel is still widely thought of as being concerned above all else
with the splendours and miseries of the self-absorbed human individual. Even those who dislike the notion of 'self', and think of it as
the sign of a dangerously unhistorical attitude to the study of the
human mind, are likely to grant Proust's vast and intricate discussion of the notion an important historical place: the modern,
secular, psychological *moi*, launched upon its spectacular European
career in the sixteenth century, reaches in Proust a moment of
extraordinary power and authority. For a moment, indeed, the
human self and its vicissitudes become the essential subject-matter
of art. And even if Proust's novel, in its insistent and sometimes de-
ranged talk of the *moi*, contains the seeds of the self's decay, his
achievement is none the less a splendid one. His account of the self,
however antiquated the notion itself may nowadays seem, is grand,
generous and endlessly hospitable to experience.

The narrator wonders at the beginning of *Le Côté de Guermantes* how the self acquires its improbable power of endurance.
How is it that, having once fallen into deep sleep, one is able to
become again the individual one once was?

On appelle cela un sommeil de plomb; il semble qu'on soit, même pendant quelques instants après qu'un tel sommeil a cessé, un simple bonhomme de plomb. On n'est plus personne. Comment, alors, cherchant sa
pensée, sa personnalité comme on cherche un objet perdu, finit-on par

retrouver son propre 'moi' plutôt que tout autre? Pourquoi, quand on se remet à penser, n'est-ce pas alors une autre personnalité que l'antérieure qui s'incarne en nous? On ne voit pas ce qui dicte le choix et pourquoi, entre les millions d'êtres humains qu'on pourrait être, c'est sur celui qu'on était la veille qu'on met juste la main.   (ii. 88)[1]

Seeking the self as one might seek a lost object is here submitted to one limitation only, but that is a daunting one. The object cannot not be found. Still baffled by sleep, still dispersed and nebulous, the newly awake individual homes in upon, and efficiently reassumes, his accustomed form. He cannot do otherwise. Descriptions of this kind are not unfamiliar in Proust's book, and they offer an optimistic allegory of its overall ontological project. After bafflement, understanding; after dispersal, concentration and self-knowledge.

Le Temps retrouvé fulfils the promise of passages like this. It sets forth a *tableau vivant* in which the evanescent multitude of the narrator's previous selves at last finds anchorage; in which every lost object is found; in which the conflicting dispositions of the human individual, and the endless varieties and sub-varieties of human passion, are assigned their place in an inclusive artistic design ('comme une église . . . comme un régime . . . comme un monde' — iii. 1032); and in which the narrator, speaking on behalf of all men and women from the vantage-point of that design, can at last affirm as a source of certainty and clear moral vision the very self that had previously been so mobile and dispersed. *Le Temps retrouvé* describes a simple chain reaction: involuntary memory reveals the temporal architecture of the self, the invariant substratum that until then had been present but unrecognized beneath its fluid and accidental surface forms; this ontological discovery triggers an artistic one, which in turn creates an exhilarating sense of moral purpose. And this culminating sequence of mental events can easily be thought of as providing the reader with a global answer to countless earlier riddles that may have teased him. In the slow unfolding of the book, he will have noticed a bewildering plurality of narrating selves, and may well have wondered what authorization Proust had, what strange dispensation from the ordinary requirements of verisimilitude, when he brought together, in his portrayal of a supposed single individual, saint and scoundrel, eagle

---

[1] I have used the first Pléiade edition of *A la recherche du temps perdu*, 3 vols, ed. Pierre Clarac and André Ferré (Paris, 1954), and refer to it by vol. number and page in my main text.

and dove, liar and truth-telling paragon. The narrator in his last triumphantly stable form becomes a capacious container for all the waywardness, inconsistency and self-division that have marked his passage through the text.

There seems to me something unsatisfactory about any reading of the book that does not resist as well as endorse *Le Temps retrouvé* in the performance of its harmonizing and integrating role. I can see that Proust's last volume is a guide for the perplexed and that it illuminates many corners left dark by earlier volumes. I can see too that the supremely accommodating selfhood of *Le Temps retrouvé*, far from merely altering retroactively what has gone before, confirms and blazons forth a notion that has already made many premonitory appearances. We need a guiding, stabilizing notion of human individuality with which to battle our way through the intricacies of Proust's text, and, late in the book but also earlier, Proust provides us with one. But what do we lose when we adhere too closely to the ontological *telos* of the book? We lose, I shall be suggesting in what follows, a whole range of paradoxes, dissonances and unusual consonances, and with them a vein of disturbing moral speculation. The reader who has felt his or her perplexities dissolve as the general teleological pattern of the book emerges is invited to look again, and more fondly, at certain of its perplexing details. It could be that Proust was in need of a resonant exit-speech when he promoted involuntary memory to its crowning role, and that his narrator's celebrated 'quest' in fact gives no more than a lightweight intellectual superstructure and an air of righteous striving to a mental adventure of a less than public-spirited kind.

The strangeness of this adventure, and the extravagant expenditure of time and ingenuity into which it periodically leads the narrator, may be observed with special clarity in *Le Côté de Guermantes*. Among many passages in which the supposedly overriding structural idea of the novel is not only absent but unthinkable, I have chosen the scenes of jealousy and recrimination between Saint-Loup and Rachel in which the narrator figures as a singularly elastic *terzo incòmodo* (ii. 155–83). The psychological drama here belongs quite as much to the narrator as to the enraged and acrimonious lovers whom he observes. Indeed his monologue is punctuated by silences on the one hand and by cascading repetitions on the other, and in each case displays the symptoms of an urgent undeclared passion. When a chance encounter with two of Rachel's former fellow-prostitutes threatens to reveal to Saint-Loup more of her past than she would care to have him know, it is the anxiously repetitious narrator rather than either of his companions who dominates the scene:

Il ne fit pas qu'entrevoir cette vie, mais aussi, au milieu, une Rachel tout autre que celle qu'il connaissait, une Rachel pareille à ces deux petites poules, une Rachel à vingt francs. En somme Rachel s'était un instant dédoublée pour lui, il avait aperçu à quelque distance de sa Rachel la Rachel petite poule, la Rachel réelle, si toutefois l'on peut dire que la Rachel poule fût plus réelle que l'autre. Robert eut peut-être l'idée alors que cet enfer où il vivait, avec la perspective et la nécessité d'un mariage riche, d'une vente de son nom, pour pouvoir continuer à donner cent mille francs par an à Rachel, il aurait peut-être pu s'en arracher aisément, et avoir les faveurs de sa maîtresse, comme ces calicots celles de leurs grues, pour peu de chose. Mais comment faire? (ii. 162)

In a sense of course the narrator is simply adopting Saint-Loup's uncertainties in the act of describing them, and allowing his own eloquence to be dulled by a passion that can do no more than impotently repeat the beloved's name. But there is too much writing of this kind for such an explanation to be fully satisfactory. The economic dimension of this passage has already been set forth, and in similarly stammering terms: the 'Rachel . . . Rachel' refrain to be found here continues a lengthy 'vingt francs . . .vingt francs' refrain from a few pages earlier (ii. 159), and this trifling amount— Rachel's prostitutional price—has been insistently played off against the excessive amounts that her lover must now expect to pay in order to keep her, or that he might now be tempted to pay in order to uncover her secrets. These calculations in francs proliferate in the text at this point and acquire a fantasmatic life of their own. And while it is not surprising to be told that passion has a price-structure and is subject to market forces, it is perfectly alarming to find these home truths reiterated and rephrased over several pages. A delirious monetary system has invaded the text and is busily translating its characteristic psychological idiom into cash terms. Why?

On the face of it, this is an elaborate Proustian conceit on the familiar themes of duplication and duplicity. Rachel is not what she seems. Or rather, like her namesake in *La Juive*, the Halévy–Scribe opera from which the narrator extracts for her the nickname 'Rachel quand du Seigneur' (i. 576–7), she is two people at once and bears two different prices. Scribe's Rachel is both Jew and Christian, Proust's is both sexual commodity and an idolized lady 'of great price'. But the social and financial *dédoublement* exhaustively attributed to Rachel prefigures another play of alternating perspectives, and one with which the novel is henceforth to be hugely preoccupied: the play between heterosexuality and homosexuality. And the martyrdom that awaits Scribe's heroine in the closing scene of *La Juive* is to be assumed not by the modern Rachel of *A la recherche* but by the narrator himself, whose path towards knowledge of human sexuality is to be, in its later stages, slow, cruel and disconsolate. The disarray of the narrative during this episode, and its feverish fluctuations of tone, are so marked yet so little explained that we read on 'for the plot', demanding to know more.

The revelation that Saint-Loup is a homosexual prompts, it will be remembered, the long, melancholy coda of *La Fugitive*. At the end of a volume in which an immitigable sense of loss has become the ground of consciousness—in which Albertine's flight and death bring uncontrollably to the narrator's mind the absences with which she had tormented him when present and alive—the discovery that Saint-Loup is 'comme ça' provides consciousness with its culminating loss, its final unthinkable extremity. At the very moment when it was impossible to imagine things worse, worse they became. The vulgar monosyllabic 'comme ça' rings out as a portent and a malediction. And in the last sentence of *La Fugitive*,[2] the narrator's memory of himself, Saint-Loup and Rachel at a restaurant table moves him to tears that the ratiocinative texture of his monologue can do nothing to explain.

In a novel that is plotted and paced with astonishing skill throughout, the Saint-Loup sub-plot stands out as a particularly ingenious tale of mystery and suspense. In part, the beauty of its denouement lies simply in the light that the narrator's banal discovery sheds upon earlier incidents in the novel, and in the outrageous expanse of text that separates behavioural effect from psychological cause. Saint-Loup behaves oddly during the restaurant scene and those that follow—he is by turns craven and defiant

---

[2] The last sentence, that is to say, of *La Fugitive* as it appears in the first Pléiade edition. On the problem of locating the exact dividing-line between *La Fugitive* and *Le Temps retrouvé*, see Jean-Yves Tadié's introduction to the first volume of his new Pléiade edition (Paris, 1987) and Jean Milly's introduction to the Garnier–Flammarion edition of *La Fugitive* (1986), 34–6.

towards Rachel, and twice resorts to fisticuffs in her company—and
it is only after 1,500 pages that this behaviour is at last seen as
coherently motivated. This is architectonic plotting of a kind that
Tristram Shandy and *Tom Jones* made familiar, although Proust's
edifice contains cantilevers, suspensions and buttresses still more
audacious than those of Sterne or Fielding.

But this denouement is fine and imposing in another way too.
The withheld weeping upon which *La Fugitive* ends is reminiscent
of Tennyson's

> Tears, idle tears, I know not what they mean.
> Tears from the depth of some divine despair
> Rise to the heart, and gather to the eyes . . .

The narrator's tears are a symptom without a cause, or with a
cause—a 'divine despair', as one might indeed call it—that is much
too large to have exact explanatory force. They are *lacrimae rerum*
provoked by the memory not of Priam slain but of a tiff and a street
brawl. At this level, the ending does not so much solve earlier mys-
teries as echo and reinforce the narrator's earlier puzzlement. An
abiding residue of doubt surrounds the Rachel episode. This has to
do not with Saint-Loup's motives but with the narrator's own, and
not with a single sexual discovery but with the anxious speculation
on sexuality for which the narrator is a perpetual vehicle. In the
company of Saint-Loup and Rachel, he cannot say what is going
on, for they kindle in him too many disparate desires. And selfhood, if it is here at all, lies not in a stable, adjudicating narrative
voice but in the versatile play of appetite that the narrator displays.
He is voluble and laconic, intrusive and discreet. He sides with man
against woman and woman against man. He aligns himself both
with the homosexual desire of the 'promeneur passionné' and with
Saint-Loup's seemingly wounded and seemingly heterosexual pride
in refusing unwelcome advances. The 'self' is a vacancy awaiting
substance and structure, a mobile force-field in which the desires of
others meet and are inflected, a rapid sequence of reactive and
imitative gestures.

The relationship between the narrator at the start of *Le Côté de
Guermantes* and the narrator at the end of *La Fugitive* is a strong
one and creates a powerful effect of internal cohesion within the
novel. But this effect is not produced by recreating at the later point
a personality, an identity, a temperament or a pattern of connected

psychological motifs that was already present earlier. It comes from the buttressing of one fragmentary psychological portrait against another of the same kind, and from a sense of perplexity and dispossession that becomes more pronounced as the plot unfolds.

What makes Proust's polymorphous narrator such an improbable textual construction in these central volumes of the novel is the cult of scientific precision that he adheres to even as he records his losses and confusions. Not only is the narrator's mobile and almost self-free consciousness not nebulous, but Proust, in describing its characteristic motions and the behaviour in which they issue, repeatedly returns to the exactitude of the exact sciences. When Saint-Loup unleashes blows upon a shabbily dressed sexual opportunist, the narrator reports having seen not fists but a non-human display of matter and kinetic energy:

tout d'un coup, comme apparaît au ciel un phénomène astral, je vis des corps ovoïdes prendre avec une rapidité vertigineuse toutes les positions qui leur permettaient de composer, devant Saint-Loup, une instable constellation. Lancés comme par une fronde ils me semblèrent être au moins au nombre de sept. Ce n'étaient pourtant que les deux poings de Saint-Loup, multipliés par leur vitesse à changer de place dans cet ensemble en apparence idéal et décoratif. Mais cette pièce d'artifice n'était qu'une roulée qu'administrait Saint-Loup et dont le caractère agressif au lieu d'esthétique me fut d'abord révélé par l'aspect du monsieur médiocrement habillé, lequel parut perdre à la fois toute contenance, une mâchoire, et beaucoup de sang. (ii. 182)

The moment of misrecognition is arrested and lingered over, but not because the mental processes involved are complex ones. Indeed the first goal of this description seems to be that of expelling mind from the scene in favour of a purified behaviourism: muscular movements of the human body become the professional property of the astronomer, the geometer and the arithmetician.

This holding back of concern for the motivation and moral status of human action is of course a mainspring of much Proustian wit, and is often to be seen at work on a large scale. The social performances of the Guermantes clan become a fencing match, in which their cold, steely gaze turns to real steel (ii. 444). During the Doncières episode, Saint-Loup retells the history of human warfare as an exquisite tale of bloodless strategic schemes transmitted from age to age (ii. 109–17). Mme Verdurin, appalled at the mention of an 'ennuyeux', is transformed into a lifeless piece of civic sculpture

(i. 259). Legrandin's sycophancy, as he bows to a local landowner's wife in Combray, is perfectly expressed by, and dissolved into, the 'ondulation de pure matière' that passes through his animated rump (i. 125). In all these cases, the pleasures of scansion, measurement and formal description are rediscovered in the wild regions of social life. The narrator removes himself from the contest of human desires into a handsomely equipped observatory from which greed, lust, ambition, violence and hatred may be viewed as so much matter extended in space. But Proust's countless sudden excursions into natural science, for all the intellectual clarity that each of them individually displays, do not exert an integrative and centralizing force upon his phenomenology of selfhood. His optical expertise is applied in what appears as a conscientiously indiscriminate fashion. This is not Newtonian optics, in which the machinery of vision guarantees the intelligibility of the universe, although Proust's scientific phrasing often has an unmistakably Newtonian ring. It is an impatient, desiring optics, intent upon multiplying the opportunities for human sight and enlarging the field of vision, and readily able to accept that each visual constellation is short-lived. Stars become fists, and fists, once recognized as instruments of aggression, trace for a moment a further, more abstract, astronomical pattern. And then the whole contraption is lost from view.

A la recherche contains innumerable moments of intense vision that pay no ontological dividend. And Proust dramatizes the brevity and singularity of these moments with a succession of images, running through the entire book, in which the eye itself becomes an object of sight. Legrandin's eye receives the first wound when the limits of his social success begin to be revealed:

je vis au milieu des yeux bleus de notre ami se ficher une petite encoche brune comme s'ils venaient d'être percés par une pointe invisible, tandis que le reste de la prunelle réagissait en sécrétant des flots d'azur. (i. 127)

Later in 'Combray', when the narrator's own worldly ambition is at stake, his eye undergoes a similar but more pleasurable violence from the eyes of Mme de Guermantes:

en même temps, sur cette image que le nez proéminent, les yeux perçants épinglaient dans ma vision (peut-être parce que c'était eux qui l'avaient d'abord atteinte, qui y avaient fait la première encoche, au moment où je n'avais pas encore le temps de songer que la femme qui apparaissait devant moi pouvait être Mme de Guermantes), sur cette image toute récente, inchangeable, j'essayais d'appliquer l'idée: 'C'est Mme de Guermantes', sans parvenir qu'à la faire manœuvrer en face de l'image, comme deux disques séparés par un intervalle. (i. 175)

In the scene with Rachel, Saint-Loup's eyes record his sudden switches of mood: 'il était tellement rempli par son indignation contre le danseur, qu'elle venait adhérer exactement à la surface de ses prunelles ... une zone disponible et souple parut dans ses yeux ... ses yeux étincelaient encore de colère' (ii. 181–3). In such cases as these the eyeball is a transmitter rather than a receiver of information, and a new set of hallucinatory anatomical and physiological features are ascribed to it in order to maintain its expressive power: the eye may release coloured secretions, emit or receive arrows or pins, contain notches or unsuspected empty zones, and be coated in an adhesive glaze. The 'speaking' eyes of popular fiction have here been superseded by an entirely reorganized organ of sight. The price to be paid for this varied repertory of more-than-ocular effects, this uncanny ability of the eye to materialize mental states upon its outer surface, is extreme brevity and discontinuity in the messages it emits. For the eye, like the objects of sight, is a moving configuration of planes, volumes and textures, and it has almost no retentive power. Albertine's eyes—'qui ... semblent faits de plusieurs morceaux' (iii. 91)—are an unreadable encyclopedia of fears, impulses, schemes and deceptions, while those of la princesse de Nassau — 'yeux stellaires, semblables à une horloge astronomique' (iii. 979)—are a flickering chronicle of her remembered and half-remembered sexual encounters. This dismantling and reassembling of the visual apparatus is a source of pathos at certain moments in the novel and of creative affirmation at others; the eye is a miniature world that now slips from the perceiver's grasp, now offers him a new speculative adventure. But in either mode, Proust's account speaks of perception without a core, of pattern-making that no higher pattern guides.

During his reverie on the cries of Paris in *La Prisonnière*, the narrator remarks that the local fruit-and-vegetable seller probably knew nothing of the plainsong that her melodious cries resembled. Although Leo Spitzer, in a celebrated essay,[3] has pointed out that her medieval predecessors are indeed likely to have known certain Gregorian cadences well, it is unreasonable to expect a modern

---

[3] 'L'Etymologie d'un "cri de Paris" ', in *Etudes de style* (Paris, 1970), 474–81.

street-trader to have any detailed knowledge of medieval musical theory. Yet this is what the narrator seems for a moment to wish when he speaks of her being ignorant of 'l'antiphonaire et [les] sept tons qui symbolisent, quatre les sciences du quadrivium et trois celles du trivium' (iii. 118). Beneath the seeming condescension of this, an urgent Proustian impulse is finding expression. The cry itself:

> A la tendresse, à la verduresse
> Artichauts tendres et beaux
> Ar-tichauts

is dizzily overdetermined at this point in the novel. Tenderness has begun to retreat from the human to the vegetable world, and artichokes now possess a freshness that the relationship between Albertine and the narrator does not. The intoned phrases rising from the street connect modern Paris to its medieval past, commerce to religious observance, popular song to elevated musical culture, and eating to the arts and sciences of mankind. This is a point at which Proust's text, so richly apparelled in the language-based sciences of the trivium, suddenly becomes aware of the role that the sciences of number and measurement also play in its analytic fabric. His quadrivium is to be found not simply in the scientific imagery of the novel but in the calculating intelligence with which seemingly remote areas of experience are brought into conjunction. But where arithmetic, geometry, music and astronomy were, for the Pythagorean tradition, akin to one another as co-equal and mutually confirming manifestations of Number, for Proust no underlying principle firmer than that of analogy unites them. The 'yeux stellaires' of la princesse de Nassau, like Saint-Loup's constellated fists, promise not an ultimate congruence between the minute and the vast but an endless journey from one moment of resemblance, and one relativistic act of measurement, to the next. And this journey in turn promises not a philosophical emancipation from the passions but a new way of measuring their force. Speaking of his infatuation with Mme de Guermantes, the narrator recalls: 'Pour moi ce n'était plus seulement les étoiles et la brise, mais jusqu'aux divisions arithmétiques du temps qui prenaient quelque chose de douloureux et de poétique' (ii. 120).

Proust's scansions often cross vast distances. They show him to have been a metaphysical wit possessed of a strong liking for physics, and an 'interdisciplinarist' beyond the dreams of the modern university. In this passage from *Le Temps retrouvé*, for example, a future astronomy of social life is sketched:

> si dans ces périodes de vingt ans les conglomérats de coteries se défaisaient et se reformaient selon l'attraction d'astres nouveaux destinés d'ailleurs eux aussi à s'éloigner, puis à reparaître, des cristallisations puis des émiettements suivis de cristallisations nouvelles avaient lieu dans l'âme des êtres.
>
> (iii. 992)

For a moment the natural and human sciences have become intelligible to each other, and a single dynamism—that of alternating dispersal and concentration—is seen to govern the stars in their courses, the growth of crystals, the structure of the human mind, and Mme Verdurin in her successive salons. This is a vision both of order within the cosmos and of the ungovernable plurality of mental worlds. In *La Prisonnière*, this plurality had already received its loftiest encomium, and had been quite disconnected from any principle of order:

> Des ailes, un autre appareil respiratoire, et qui nous permissent de traverser l'immensité, ne nous serviraient à rien, car si nous allions dans Mars et dans Vénus en gardant les mêmes sens, ils revêtiraient du même aspect que les choses de la Terre tout ce que nous pourrions voir. Le seul véritable voyage, le seul bain de Jouvence, ce ne serait pas d'aller vers de nouveaux paysages, mais d'avoir d'autres yeux, de voir l'univers avec les yeux d'un autre, de cent autres, de voir les cent univers que chacun d'eux voit, que chacun d'eux est; et cela nous le pouvons avec un Elstir, avec un Vinteuil, avec leurs pareils, nous volons vraiment d'étoiles en étoiles. (iii. 258)

This interlacing of optics, astronomy and music, which is also an indefinite sequence of displacements between small and vast, not only promises no selfhood to the artist and to those who follow his example, it presents selfhood as an impediment to creative perception. The only conception of self that can usefully remain is that of a discontinuous itinerary, leading towards but never reaching that moment of plenitude at which the entire range of possible forms would stand revealed and realized. When each human being has become a hundred universes, who will then be the gentleman, the liar, the thief or the novelist? Such visions of an ideally dispossessed and characterless human individuality occur often as Proust's novel moves grandly towards the apotheosis of self upon which *Le Temps retrouvé* ends, as if those last moments of potency and moral resolve could be attained only by way of an emptiness within the self resembling that of interstellar space.

The morally resolved artist into whom the narrator is transformed at the end of the novel is himself an improbable construction. He has of course been foreshadowed on numerous earlier occasions, as have the moral principles on which he is to base his critique of social man and woman. That he is eventually to be an altruist, a respecter of individual rights, a truth-teller and a trenchant prosecutor of corruption and folly has already been half-promised by the narrator's elaborately textured social observation. And the narrator has been shown to be capable both of energetic moral commitment and of firm self-criticism for his failures to act virtuously. But as a moralist he has other characteristics too, and these leave us only partially prepared for Proust's exalted final perspectives.

Gilbert Ryle, in his essay on Jane Austen, speaks 'with conscious crudity' of moralists as belonging either to the Calvinist or to the Aristotelian camp. While members of the first group think of human beings 'as either Saved or Damned, either Elect or Reject, either children of Virtue or children of Vice', those of the second pursue distinctions of an altogether more delicate kind:

the Aristotelian pattern of ethical ideas represents people as differing from one another in degree and not in kind, and differing from one another not in respect just of a single generic Sunday attribute, Goodness, say, or else Wickedness, but in respect of a whole spectrum of specific week-day attributes. *A* is a bit more irritable and ambitious than *B*, but less indolent and less sentimental. *C* is meaner and quicker-witted than *D*, and *D* is greedier and more athletic than *C*. And so on. A person is not black or white, but iridescent with all the colours of the rainbow; and he is not a flat plane, but a highly irregular solid.[4]

To some extent this may seem to fit the facts of Proust's narrator's case well. After all, he possesses to a remarkable degree the ability to make contrastive moral judgements, and he deploys his contrasts with such ingenuity that his discourse often seems dedicated to continuity—'iridescence'—rather than discreteness in the handling of moral notions. Besides, few of Proust's admirers would wish to remove him from the company of Aristotle and Jane Austen if this meant handing him over to Ryle's dourly dichotomous Calvin. Yet

---

[4] *Collected Papers*, i (*Critical Essays*) (London, 1971), 284.

a crucial quality of the moral life as lived by Proust's narrator is entirely missing from Ryle's paradigm. This is the quality that could be called supererogatory risk-taking. In the pursuit of new knowledge, the narrator must be prepared to traverse uncharted moral territories and to improvise for himself a value-system commensurate with this or that moment of epistemological zeal.

At the simplest level, telling the truth to a truth-resistant audience may involve lying. In *A l'ombre des jeunes filles en fleurs*, the narrator reports having given his parents an unverified account of the origins and the antiquity of the Swanns' staircase. Without doing so, it would have been impossible for him to persuade them of its true worth: '[mon] amour de la vérité était si grand que je n'aurais pas hésité à leur donner ce renseignement même si j'avais su qu'il était faux' (i. 505). In the turbulent world of the child and his family, here is an early intimation of the 'glorieux mensonge' that is art. And once the pursuit of new knowledge has been conceived of as an ethical imperative, lying itself—workaday lying, not the superior mendacities of art—may begin to reveal unsuspected virtues: 'Le mensonge, le mensonge parfait . . . est une des seules choses au monde qui puisse nous ouvrir des perspectives sur du nouveau, sur de l'inconnu, puisse ouvrir en nous des sens endormis pour la contemplation d'univers que nous n'aurions jamais connus' (iii. 216). A new science requires, it seems, a new morality.

Closely related to this, there is another form of supererogation towards which the narrator is continually drawn. Those who are in pursuit of pleasure—and especially those whose pleasures are familiarly thought of as perverse, aberrant or anti-social—are themselves pursued by the narrator's relentless, inquisitive gaze. Sado-masochism, for example, which is discussed and theatricalized in numerous ways, from the Montjouvain episode of 'Combray' (i. 159–65) to the scenes in Jupien's brothel in *Le Temps retrouvé* (iii. 809–40), provides an exacting test for the moralist's powers of discrimination. In each of these extended episodes, which together place an elaborate frame around the many plainer accounts that are to be found in the inner volumes, the narrator's crisp expressions of disapproval free him to enjoy the pleasures of voyeurism guiltlessly. But the achievement of pleasure is no more his main goal than is the defence of rectitude. A grandiose moral experiment is in progress, and the narrator follows a clear experimental principle in conducting it: let my perception of life in, say, Jupien's establishment be as delicately calibrated as that which I would bring to bear upon any other complex scene of social communication and commerce.

His experimental results are presented with relish. Charlus, emerging in considerable discomfort from the flagellation chamber, is still able to inspect Jupien's assembled staff with a discriminating eye and ear:

Bien que son plaisir fût fini et qu'il n'entrât d'ailleurs que pour donner à Maurice l'argent qu'il lui devait, il dirigeait en cercle sur tous ces jeunes gens réunis un regard tendre et curieux et comptait bien avoir avec chacun le plaisir d'un bonjour tout platonique mais amoureusement prolongé . . . Tous semblaient le connaître, et M. de Charlus s'arrêtait longuement à chacun, leur parlant ce qu'il croyait leur langage, à la fois par une affectation prétentieuse de couleur locale et aussi par un plaisir sadique de se mêler à une vie crapuleuse. (iii. 824–5)

And the narrator describes *in propria persona*, and with a similar devotion to piquancy and local colour, the enlarged field of sexual opportunity that the war has created in Paris. Canadians are valued for the charm of their ambiguous accent, but '[à] cause de leur jupon et parce que certains rêves lacustres s'associent souvent à de tels désirs, les Ecossais faisaient prime' (iii. 823). But tracing out this spectrum of libidinal intensities is not a task for the mere voluptuary or tourist, for an equally differentiated value-spectrum crosses it at every turn. Although sado-masochistic transactions of the kind in which Jupien specializes can scarcely be thought of as possessing, in themselves, a complex moral content, the larger social world of the brothel can. Indeed its content is presented as strictly—iridescently—continuous with that of 'society' itself. In this low-life world the narrator finds again the hypocrisies, fidelities, betrayals and occasional unadvertised acts of philanthropy that are the volatile stuff of salon life, and he also finds ample new material with which to extend his discussion of such topics as lying, self-deception and envy. In the moral as in the epistemological domain, the narrator is a seeker after variety and novelty, and urges himself forward to the moment of completion—when the last possible modulation of the moral life will have become audible. He is not only a pluralizing eye, a self constituted from all other selves, but an optimistic surveyor of human conduct—one who expects to discover new notions of virtue and vice at every point of the compass.

Such dreams of plurality and plenitude were of course common among Proust's contemporaries. Busoni—to take a strong but relatively neglected example—lamented in his *Sketch of a New Esthetic of Music* that so much in the Western musical tradition, from tonality itself to the standard notational system and the mechanics of keyboard instruments, seemed to want to substitute discreteness for continuity and avoid hearing the true harmony of nature: 'How strictly we divide "consonances" from "dissonances"—*in a sphere where no dissonances can possibly exist!* . . . Nature created an *infinite gradation—infinite!*'[5] Proust hears the true music of moral judgement and takes the risks appropriate to its pursuit. No act of judging can be final, for the continuous gradations of conduct and character flow on. It is not surprising, therefore, that after an adventure so protracted he should wish to stage an apocalypse in the last pages of his book. One could scarcely imagine a better reward at the end of it all than a single choice to make, a single project to execute, a single self to reassume and single imposing moral value to defend.

But where does the novel end? With the narrator's self-discovery, with the death in battle of Saint-Loup, or with the war-time night sky that each of them contemplates?

Je lui parlai de la beauté des avions qui montaient dans la nuit. 'Et peut-être encore plus de ceux qui descendent, me dit-il. Je reconnais que c'est très beau le moment où ils montent, où ils vont *faire constellation*, et obéissent en cela à des lois tout aussi précises que celles qui régissent les constellations, car ce qui te semble un spectacle est le ralliement des escadrilles, les commandements qu'on leur donne, leur départ en chasse, etc. Mais est-ce que tu n'aimes pas mieux le moment où, définitivement assimilés aux étoiles, ils s'en détachent pour partir en chasse ou rentrer après la berloque, le moment où ils *font apocalypse*, même les étoiles ne gardant plus leur place? Et ces sirènes, était-ce assez wagnérien, ce qui, du reste, était bien naturel pour saluer l'arrivée des Allemands, ça faisait très hymne national, avec le Kronprinz et les princesses dans la loge impériale, *Wacht am Rhein*; c'était à se demander si c'était bien des aviateurs et pas plutôt des Walkyries qui montaient.' Il semblait avoir plaisir à cette assimilation des aviateurs et des Walkyries, et l'expliqua d'ailleurs par des raisons purement musicales: 'Dame, c'est que la musique des sirènes était d'un *Chevauchée*!

⁵ Ferruccio Busoni, *Sketch of a New Esthetic of Music* (*c.*1911), in *Three Classics in the Aesthetic of Music* (New York, 1962), 89.

Il faut décidément l'arrivée des Allemands pour qu'on puisse entendre du Wagner à Paris.' A certains points de vue la comparaison n'était pas fausse.

(iii. 758–9)

From certain points of view the comparison was not false, but from others it was. Proust has here transferred from the narrator to Saint-Loup the task of recapitulating, in a burlesque manner, many of the narrator's own metaphorical habits and, in particular, his inventive play with the quadrivium. A sudden new relationship between music and astronomy is glimpsed—one in which measurement and pattern-making are caught up in the machinery of modern warfare. Saint-Loup is continuing to aestheticize violence as he had during the Doncières episode but he is also prolonging, and recasting in millennial terms, a mode of perception that Proust's narrator has displayed throughout the novel. Aerial combat creates new constellations, new displays of matter and kinetic energy, and these are in direct line of descent from the countless 'astral phenomena' that the narrator had previously recorded. Astral aircraft rise above the mere carnage of war, rather as Halévy's exquisite salon melody in 'Rachel quand du Seigneur' rises above the impending brutality that Scribe's text describes.

In transferring these images to Saint-Loup, Proust is of course preparing the way for the 'real' apocalypse of the book and for the unimpeachable depth and seriousness of perception that the narrator, alone among its central characters, is eventually to acquire. Saint-Loup in becoming the supremely witty artist of scattered selfhood, the inventor of momentary geometries and ever-changing optical effects, leaves the way open for the narrator to become a single self at last. But the clarity and complexity that the book's earlier images of dispersal possess cannot simply be removed from the record by the last fortified version of selfhood upon which the narrator reports. On the contrary, those earlier short-lived configurations have such imaginative authority that they may prove to be the feature of the book that we remember best and cherish most. If so, the centralized and resolved self on which the novel ends may be seen not as a redemption but as one momentary geometry among many others.

9

Self-Image and Self-Disclosure in Sartre's Autobiographical Writings

S. BEYNON JOHN

No French writer since the war has given himself over more freely to photographers and interviewers than Sartre. We have witnessed a torrent of images, private and public, and a selection of them in a glossy anthology like Liliane Syndyk-Siegel's *Sartre: Images d'une vie* (1978) represents an act of public consecration. Here is the infant 'Poulou', with his ringlets still intact, posing behind a boat at the seaside; here in 1928 is the dandified *normalien* in his straw boater; here the flattering studio portrait of him taken in 1939; here Brassaï's photograph of him in 1945, seated at a café table with papers spread out in front of him.

All photographs are a kind of death. They seize on the living moment, freeze it in a posture and convert it into history. These particular photographs of Sartre tell us little except what he once looked like to others. However, when he singles one out for approval, we may properly feel that this is an elective self-image, something in which he either claims to see his 'true' self or else something which he aspires to be. When at the age of twenty-one (in 1926) he sends his current lover 'Camille' (Simone Jollivet) a childhood picture of himself and recommends it as 'Byronic',[1] we suspect, in spite of the light-hearted tone, that he is telling us something about his ambition to be a major writer. So too, when he urges Simone de Beauvoir on 23 December 1939 to seek out the 'study' by Gisèle Freund, he is telling us something about how he would prefer to be seen by her: 'A votre retour ne manquez pas de passer chez Monnier. G. Freund y expose tous les jours ses photos de 2 à 6. Vous y verrez la toute belle de moi où j'ai l'air d'un ange' (*Lettres*, i. 504). Here too the mild self-mockery does

---

[1] J.-P. Sartre, *Lettres au Castor et à quelques autres*, i: *1926–1939* (Paris, 1983), 19.

not entirely mask the anxiety to be seen as handsome, as other than he is.

But these are merely hints of the self. What is disconcerting, even daunting, is the astonishing wealth of self-disclosure which confronts us in Sartre's case. It is hardly an exaggeration to claim that one of his major achievements has been to construct a great autobiographical edifice that occupied a substantial part of his life, though not continuously, and assumed a wide variety of forms. These range from autobiography proper, *Les Mots* (1964); the letters to Simone de Beauvoir and others, mostly written between 1926 and 1940; the notebooks Sartre kept during the 'phoney war' of 1939–40; and the spate of interviews, some very lengthy, given by Sartre in the 1960s and 1970s. Nor can one ignore the vein of self-disclosure that surfaces in Sartre's critical essays on Gide, Nizan, Merleau-Ponty and others, or the way in which he reveals himself indirectly in his major biographies of Baudelaire, Flaubert and Genet. Discriminating among these different modes of self-disclosure in terms of their truth to life, the quality of their moral and psychological insights, or their consistency and vividness of recall, would require a far more ambitious study than is possible here. I propose something more modest: to look at questions of self-image and self-disclosure as exemplified by what Sartre reveals of his sexual sensibility in his autobiographical writings.

I want first to discuss the matter of candour and spontaneity in Sartre's different kinds of self-disclosure. If one contrasts the highly wrought form of Sartre's single excursion into formal autobiography, *Les Mots*, with the texts of his letters, notebooks and late interviews, one inevitably gains the impression that these provide more unguarded moments in which the chance occurs for frank and complete self-disclosure. In the late interviews, for example, this seems like a temptation for him, but an occasional asperity of tone suggests the degree to which the interview is being used by Sartre not to tell all but as a form of self-justification. In addition, an element of self-presentation, of inventing or confirming a public persona, enters into some press interviews and renders them of uncertain value as means of access to the writer's subjectivity. Like his photographs, Sartre's interviews of the 1970s, as also his contributions to the film made about him and released in 1977, must be seen as indicating the extent to which even an honest and well-intentioned writer of eminence enters into complicity with his questioners in the creation of a myth about his own life.

Certainly the interviews are highly informative and revealing, but they are also repetitive and lack the pristine freshness, momentum and recklessness of the early letters and notebooks. Published posthumously in 1983, these bring Sartre back from the dead like Lazarus, which is to say as a challenging and uncomfortable presence who raises more questions than he answers. It is precisely this headlong character of the letters that Sartre recaptures in memory, thirty-five years after they were written, when he observes to Simone de Beauvoir: 'Moi, j'écrivais d'un trait, sans ratures, sans me préoccuper d'un autre lecteur que celui à qui j'envoyais la lettre: donc, ça ne me paraît pas un travail littéraire valable.'[2] But this testimony to the artless spontaneity of the letters does not correspond with Sartre's practice in his notebooks. As he wrote to Simone de Beauvoir on 26 October 1939: 'Ça me fait toute une petite vie secrète au-dessus de l'autre, avec des joies, des inquiétudes, des remords dont je n'aurais pas connu la moitié sans ce petit objet de cuir noir' (*Lettres*, i. 377). In a word, the significance of raw experience can only be grasped when one is at a remove from it, and it is the act of writing in his little black book which effects this remove. It is an insight that he returns to in the notebooks themselves: 'Il y a presque toujours un décalage entre le moment où j'ai senti et le moment où j'écris.'[3] And in the gap between experience and its verbal translation, emotions (shame, self-justification, revenge) may well infiltrate and colour what is to be recorded. As Sartre confesses to Simone de Beauvoir on 2 March 1940, on the subject of making entries into his notebooks about his relations with other people: 'J'en ai écrit, depuis avant-hier *cent* pages, imaginez, et sans épuiser le sujet. C'est d'ailleurs dommage mais il faudrait parler d'Olga, de Bost, de vous, de Tania et alors je devrais indignement truquer. J'ai donc arrêté *avant* l'histoire d'Olga avec quelques phrases sibyllines à l'usage de T. annonçant une transformation totale survenue peu après . . . ' (italics in the text).[4]

---

[2] S. de Beauvoir, *La Cérémonie des adieux, suivi de Entretiens avec Jean-Paul Sartre (août–septembre 1974)* (Paris, 1981).
[3] Sartre, *Les Carnets de la drôle de guerre, novembre 1939–mars 1940* (Paris, 1983), 91.
[4] Sartre, *Lettres au Castor et à quelques autres*, ii: *1940–1963* (Paris, 1983), 112–13.

This suggests neatly the limits of candour but, in general, the letters and notebooks live up to the ideal proposed by Sartre in an interview originally given in 1971: 'Et il ne me viendrait pas à l'esprit d'éliminer des lettres, des documents sur ma vie personnelle. Tout cela sera connu. Tant mieux si cela permet que je sois aussi transparent aux yeux de la posterité — si elle s'intéresse à moi — que Flaubert l'est aux miens.'[5] Flaubert was no doubt rather less transparent to Sartre than he imagined, but, in any event, this does not rule out the possibility that candour in the letters and notebooks is being used as an offensive weapon. The exhaustive descriptions Sartre provides of himself occasionally strike one as guileful attempts to postpone or impede description of himself by others, as if he guessed that the evidence he offered against himself could never be a substitute for the evidence others might bring against him. And here it has to be said that this remorselessly clever man can be naïvely surprised at the view which others have of him, even when he himself has provided them with the evidence. Tania, for example, is scandalized by the contents of his *Carnets* and even the privileged 'Castor' herself, as one can infer from Sartre's letter of 14 December 1939, seems to have felt that the notebooks revealed a different Sartre from her familiar companion: 'puisque ça vous semble un peu l'œuvre d'un étranger, dire avec quel caractère vous apparaît le bonhomme' (*Lettres*, i. 482). Here the idea, familiar to us from *L'Etre et le néant*, of the self as a vacancy waiting to be filled, is given a new twist. In thus expressing uncertainty about the 'true' subject of the notebooks, Simone de Beauvoir confirms that the very act of writing itself produces or creates a 'self'.

Interviewed at seventy in 1975, Sartre conceded that it might be possible to infer something of 'les rapports sexuels et érotiques de ma vie' from his fiction and philosophy, but added rather testily: 'Mais ça ne représente qu'un moment de ma vie sexuelle. Et elle n'y est pas avec suffisamment de détails et de complexité pour qu'on puisse me trouver vraiment.'[6] The letters and notebooks more than fill the gap. In the dazzling array of topics and insights contained in these, sex can fairly claim to be prominent. Dominating everything in the letters is Sartre's inexhaustible appetite for gossip—'ce désir infâme d'historiettes'—sometimes trivial and boring, often sca-

---

[5] Sartre, 'Sur *L'Idiot de la famille*', *Situations X* (Paris, 1976), 105.
[6] Sartre, 'Autoportrait à soixante-dix ans', *Situations X* (Paris, 1976), 147.

brous, and what it reveals of his passionate curiosity about the psychological quirks of friends, lovers and casual acquaintances. Sartre is especially tireless on the subject of his own love-life. The *histoires de coucherie* are maliciously reported in the case of friends while his own sexual conquests are treated in a spirit in which male-chauvinist conceit and self-congratulation are combined with cynical detachment and a rather odious lack of feeling. The calendar of Sartre's conquests is lengthy: from that 'Toulouse' (another nickname for Simone Jollivet) who will become the mistress of the stage director Charles Dullin, and die in madness and squalor; through the tempestuous, drunken and myth-making Tania and the importunate Lucile, to the moody and self-dramatizing Olga Kosakiewicz; Marie Girard, 'la femme lunaire', who had been Sartre's lover in Berlin; and the young student, Martine Bourdin, who had also stirred the passions of Merleau-Ponty and whose physical charms are gloatingly specified by Sartre in a page (*Lettres*, i. 188) reminiscent of the sixteenth-century *poésie de blason*.

From this promiscuous sexual traffic I want to isolate two episodes that are peculiarly revealing of Sartre's attitudes to women. The first concerns a woman referred to as 'Gégé', and is the subject of a letter written by Sartre from Laon during the year 1937:

Je suis remonté avec elle dans ma chambre pour prendre un costume à faire dégraisser (hypocrite petit homme, dira le bon Castor. Bon Castor, j'étais pur, j'en fais le serment) et alors 'Je t'ai été fidèle à ma manière, Cynara.' Comme ça, parce que ça se trouvait, parce que ça se devait. Je l'ai embrassé sur la joue, elle m'a embrassé sur la bouche. Je lui ai ôté son corsage, elle a ôté sa robe et son pantalon. J'ai couché avec elle. Elle m'a dit qu'elle m'aimait et je n'en ai rien cru. Je lui ai dit que je l'aimais bien et elle l'a cru. Elle m'a dit: 'J'ai eu presque du plaisir.' Alors je lui ai fait cadeau d'un exemplaire d'*Erostrate* pour la remercier'.　　(*Lettres*, i. 136)

This letter breathes coldness, calculation and duplicity. So far from being spontaneous and candid, it bears all the signs of a literary exercise. The overriding tone is one of ironic mockery, and whatever sensuality or inwardness might have been part of the experience has been expelled by a narrative technique in which a series of short sentences, each disposed in symmetrical antitheses, each articulated about a verb of action, renders everything from the outside and reinforces the impression of male mastery and detachment in the sexual act. The intertextual allusions to Dowson's poem and to Sartre's own story *Erostrate* enhance the sense of artifice and literary self-consciousness, the sense of an experience that has been undertaken precisely so as to be turned into words. The arch and wheedling disclaimer—'Bon Castor, j'étais pur, j'en fais le serment'—is clearly intended not to be believed and, in this respect, calls for the approving complicity of the reader of the letter. In the same way, the insistence on the absence of pleasure, and on Sartre's refusal to be duped by the lady's declaration of love, is a tactic for disarming the potential jealousy of his reader. The absent reader of this artful and salacious narrative is, of course, Simone de Beauvoir herself, who is thus converted by correspondence into a compliant *voyeuse*. As this is far from being the only occasion on which Simone de Beauvoir is made the witness of what Sartre calls his 'amours contingentes' (a characteristic fusion of the language of feeling and the technical language of philosophy), it suggests that she neither demurs at, nor disapproves of, this sort of confidence, and may even invite it. For example, one notes, in 1974, the indulgent manner in which she recalls the pre-war Sartre reporting his visit to a Naples brothel: 'vous me l'avez raconté avec beaucoup d'amusement quand je suis revenue le lendemain' (*Entretiens*, 233), or the scabrous dream of a dark-skinned prostitute which Sartre recounts to her in another of his letters (*Lettres*, i. 435).

One is forced to conclude that something in 'le Castor' responds to the picture conveyed in the letter about Gégé of a highly manipulative Don Juan using and mocking his sexual partners. She enters into a *louche* complicity with the male seducer and presumably derives a kind of pleasure or boost to her own self-esteem as Sartre's 'fidelity' to her survives yet another sexual involvement. As for Sartre himself, he seeks here in 'le Castor' a mirror that will return to him the self-image he has contrived for himself in the process of composing the letter, which is to say, that of a practised seducer who amuses himself with encounters in which sexual pleasure is conspicuously absent. It is not a pretty picture, though one suspects that in this act of self-disclosure, so knowingly presented, Sartre lacks any true awareness of how squalid his conduct might look to any reader other than Simone de Beauvoir. Essentially, in this episode, his sexual partner has been symbolically reduced to a prostitute by being paid off for her services with a copy of Sartre's story about a sexual pervert who never undresses before the whores whom he pays to parade before him in the nude.[7] The sexual act with a woman is demoted and reduced to something contemptible.

Nor is this an isolated example. Writing to Simone de Beauvoir when he is on holiday with the exacting Tania, Sartre confesses dejectedly: 'Loin de vous je mesure le néant de la chair et je ne m'amuse pas trop bien' (*Lettres*, i. 233). This distaste for physical relations with his lovers casts an equivocal light over his campaigns of seduction and suggests an extremely complicated sexuality that does not emerge in any single moment of self-revelation but which has to be pieced together from disclosures scattered among the letters and notebooks. In the many letters to Simone de Beauvoir in which his sexual experiences with other women arc alluded to, and his own sexual attitudes discussed, there is almost total silence over the specifically sexual or erotic dimension of his relations with her. This implies a further limit to the candour and spontaneity that are claimed for the letters. Yet these letters, like the 'amours contingentes' they often depict, demonstrate graphically how necessary female relationships are to Sartre, how important to his sense of living in the world and to his own image of himself. In this respect, it is difficult to judge whose prisoner is whose, a reflection supported by a curious passage in Sartre's letter of 24 November 1935 to Simone de Beauvoir, in which he refers to his relations with Tania: 'elle me trompera peut-être mais je suis devenu légendaire pour elle, en ce moment, elle me 'salue bien bas' comme vous savez et ça lui fait son petit mythe romanesque et pompeux. Ne me détruisez pas ça, je vous en prie' (*Lettres*, i. 431).

What emerges most clearly from Sartre's self-disclosures is that 'le Castor' functions as both mirror and judge, and that she is placed on an altogether different level from Sartre's other lovers, even those of long standing, like Tania and Olga, who are capable of driving him to desperation. For Sartre, 'le Castor' is in a class of her own, as the language he tends to use about her makes clear. On 6 October 1939 he writes: 'Mon cher amour, vous êtes la plus parfaite, la plus intelligente, la meilleure et la plus passionnée. Vous êtes le petit parangon et je me sens humble devant votre chère petite personne . . .' (*Lettres*, i. 336). Again, on 17 November 1939, he pays tribute to 'l'estime absolue et totale que je porte à votre petite

---

[7] S. Doubrovsky, 'Sartre: retouches à un autoportrait (une autobiographie visqueuse)', in *Lectures de Sartre*, ed. C. Burgelin (Lyons, 1986), 121.

personne...' (ibid. 415), whilst on 24 February 1940, at an especially critical time in his personal life, he praises her in these terms: 'Mon petit, mon cher petit, il n'y a qu'avec vous que je sois propre et cela ne vient pas de moi, cela vient de vous, petit parangon' (*Lettres*, ii. 95). It is respect rather than sexual passion which is the dominant note in these declarations, and elsewhere it is matched by a vein of tenderness which is notably absent from the references he makes to his 'contingent loves', some of whom appear to open up an almost tragically intense world of feeling: 'Il me semble qu'à ce moment je me saisis dans ma structure la plus essentielle, dans cette espèce d'âpreté désolée à me voir sentir, à me voir souffrir, non pour me connaître moi-même, mais pour connaître toutes les "natures", la souffrance, la jouissance, l'être-dans-le-monde... C'est de là que vient cette attraction magique qu'exercent sur moi les femmes obscures et noyées, T., autrefois O...' (*Carnets*, 83). So Sartre, writing towards the end of 1939 in a language quite different from that he applies to his relationship with Simone de Beauvoir, a language that conjures up the spellbound world of romantic fiction.

I shall return to the significance which tenderness comes to have for Sartre, but not before tracing a second episode in his love-life that reflects the polar opposite of the qualities of respect and tenderness, and which is more characteristic of his sexual attitudes before the Second World War. This episode is the subject of a remarkable confessional letter of 24 February 1940 in which he appeals to Simone de Beauvoir as an ethical arbiter. It concerns the collapse of his love-affair with the student Martine Bourdin and a manœuvre in which he involved himself in order to get rid of her while ingratiating himself with Tania. The details do not matter. What matters is the traumatic shock produced on him by the affair. Part of Sartre's scheme for disposing of Martine involves him in writing an irate and insulting letter. In this he protests that their affair was never intended to be more than a passing fancy: 'Je ne t'ai jamais aimée, je t'ai trouvée physiquement plaisante quoique vulgaire, mais j'ai un certain sadisme que ta vulgarité même attirait...', and he adds: 'Mes lettres, qui furent des exercices de littérature passionnée, dont nous avons bien ri, le Castor et moi, ne t'avaient à l'époque pas entièrement dupée...' (*Lettres*, ii. 90–1).

It is difficult to exaggerate the sophistry and moral incoherence of this letter in which the writer's 'sadism' is solemnly advanced as sufficient excuse for his being attracted to a 'vulgar' lover, just as his original love-letters are now dismissed as so transparent that their recipient must have seen they were a joke, the more so as an 'independent' witness ('le Castor') had read them as such. It is a relief to record that the self-serving brutality of this letter brought on a bout of conscience, remorse and self-blame. Sartre recognizes that his entire sexual conduct has been reprehensible: 'Ici ce que j'accuse ce n'est pas tant celui que je fus avec elle mais mon personnage sexuel en général; il me semble que jusqu'ici je me suis conduit en enfant vicieux dans les rapports physiques avec les gens' (ibid. 93). He now declares himself to be disgusted by 'l'atmosphère de canaillerie sadique' which characterized his relations with Martine, and to feel 'soiled' by the affair. In his conclusion he severely condemns himself: 'je n'ai jamais su mener proprement ni ma vie sexuelle ni ma vie sentimentale; je me sens tout profondément et sincèrement un salaud. Et un salaud de petite envergure, par-dessus le marché, une espèce de sadique universitaire et de Don Juan fonctionnaire à faire vomir' (ibid. 94). Nothing could confirm more vividly Sartre's discovery that his physical relations with his 'contingent loves' have proved radically defective, perhaps tainted with perversity and, at the very least, something of an elaborate *game* of seduction in which he himself displayed detachment, lack of reciprocity, an equivocal attitude toward the sexual act and, sometimes, contempt for his partners. This Don Juan does not enjoy women as much as conscript them to his own designs.

I want now to explore how moments of self-disclosure elsewhere in the letters and notebooks help one to understand something of the complicated sexual psychology which underlies the crisis sparked off by the collapse of Sartre's love-affair with Martine Bourdin. The child is father to the man. Through the success of his puppet shows in attracting little 'girl friends' ('fiancées'), Poulou discovered, in the sunlit hours spent in the Jardin du Luxembourg, that acting and story-telling were forms of seduction more potent than personal charm or good looks (*Carnets*, 322).[8] From this period also dates his first excited encounter with Edmond Rostand's dashing rhetorician, Cyrano de Bergerac, and with Jacasse,

[8] As has been acutely said, these charming scenes were probably omitted from *Les Mots* because the childhood bliss they celebrate was still too precious in memory for the adult Sartre to be ready to sacrifice it to the ironies of his autobiography. See P. Lejeune, 'Les enfances de Sartre', in *Moi aussi* (Paris, 1986), 149.

the hunchback with the false hump who, in Miguel Zamacoïs's *Les Bouffons* (1907), wins the hand of a princess.

In the event, two ugly heroes captured the imagination of an ugly small boy, for that is how Poulou saw himself and was seen. To parody a familiar religious figure, one might say that Poulou's infant paradise was brought to an end by two Falls. One was the remarriage of his mother to a superintendent of naval dockyards; but the first was having his hair cut short. The ringlets gone, Poulou was revealed as an ugly child with a bad squint. In old age Sartre affected to play down the importance of his ugliness: 'Si, j'étais laid; mais ça n'aurait pas dû beaucoup me gêner' (*Entretiens*, 369); and again: 'Je veux dire que je ne me suis jamais désolé de ma laideur.'[9] The evidence suggests otherwise: certainly in childhood and adolescence, and probably later, his ugliness was lived out as a psychic wound which had to be transcended. It is no accident that the notebooks reveal such fascination with how Kaiser Wilhelm II overcame the congenital infirmity of a withered arm (*Carnets*, 366–86).[10] Withered arm, wall eye: of course there is a great disproportion between them, but both can be profoundly significant in the creation of self-image: 'Une chose qui demeurait toujours, c'était l'œil qui louche' (*Entretiens*, 394). Equally important in Sartre's case is that his ugliness was revealed to him not by a mirror but through the eyes of women: 'La laideur m'a été découverte par les femmes; on me disait que j'étais laid depuis l'âge de dix ans, mais je n'appréhendais pas ma laideur dans une glace' (*Entretiens*, 394). This was peculiarly painful for a child who, in infancy, had been surrounded by a circle of adoring females. The crucial importance which Sartre's ugliness assumes for him in his inner life, and the acute sense he experienced of the baleful influence of others in providing an image of oneself that cannot be escaped from, can both be gauged from the hyperbolic pages devoted to this in his biography of Flaubert. Here it is not too much to say that ugliness is seen as a curse.[11]

In these perspectives, the innocent readings of childhood take on a new force and meaning. Recalling how he was bowled over by the exploits of the hunchback Jacasse, Sartre comments: 'On dira que

[9] A. Astruc and M. Contat, *Sartre, un film* (Paris, 1977), 21.
[10] A. Buisine, *Laideurs de Sartre* (Lille, 1986), 110.
[11] Sartre, *L'Idiot de la famille. Gustave Flaubert de 1821 à 1857*, i (Paris, 1971), 303–11.

ce sont là des espérances d'homme laid: se rattraper par le bien-dire' (*Carnets*, 322). At this time, Cyrano de Bergerac with his freak nose was Sartre's model of the perfect lover, and one suspects he never quite freed himself from the spell. Cyrano epitomized the triumph of spirit over flesh: 'La grandeur, pour moi, s'élevait sur l'abjection. L'esprit reprenait à son compte les misères du corps, les dominait, les supprimait en quelque sorte et, se manifestant à travers le corps disgracié, ne brillait que davantage' (*Carnets*, 322). In a word, Cyrano also symbolized the power of eloquence, of verbal deftness and inventiveness, to win all hearts. Seduction was accomplished by the word: 'pouvoir séducteur des *paroles*' (ibid. 323, italics in the text). This was particularly attractive to a bookish child ('un infâme petit enfant-roi') who wanted to 'aimer comme dans les livres' (ibid. 324).

One can see at work here the process by which mastery of language, of verbal beauty, can cancel out the deformities of the speaker's body and deliver, almost incidentally, the inaccessible object of desire. There is a naïve and astonishing aesthetic confidence about this, a faith in the power of beauty to transform the world. A striking entry in the notebooks confirms this: 'Ce que je voudrais noter à présent c'est que j'attribuais ce désir âpre et vain de la beauté temporelle à *l'homme*. Au lieu que je le tiens à présent pour ma particularité' (*Carnets*, 343–4, italics in the text). In effect, Sartre connects his love of beauty and his desire to live out beauty in the events of his own life (shades of Roquentin!) with the character of his love-affairs. He admits to entertaining the illusion that 'l'événement amoureux pouvait et devait être cet événement nécessaire et pour tout dire beau que je cherchais' (*Carnets*, 344). Everything was intended to lead inexorably towards an end that was beautiful, by way of a meticulous pattern of seduction, to a confession of love and the final physical consummation (ibid. 344). This end was to be achieved 'par mes paroles et par mes gestes' (ibid. 345). In this sense, love was to be a carefully orchestrated game, in which both partners played out the roles allotted to them, with the female refraining from exhibiting signs of strong physical passion, and adopting a passive role. The fascination lay not in the consummation, but in the process of winning the woman, a process to be accomplished by verbal skills and the whole 'rhythm' of seduction: 'Au fond c'était tout un travail littéraire' (ibid. 346). Sartre admits that, at the actual moment at which he is describing

this technique of seduction, he has already discarded it: 'j'ai ces discours, ces silences et ces grâces en horreur . . .' (ibid. 346), while
recognizing that, in the past, he was guilty of using women as raw
material for an essentially aesthetic exercise: 'Dans cette œuvre
d'art périssable que je tentais de construire, la femme représentait la
matière brute que je devais informer' (ibid. 347). God, it might be
said, breathing life into clay.

This disclosure of Sartre's dream of sexual congress as a kind of
courtly pavane in which he is the master of the dance is quite at
odds with what he himself reveals in his confessional letter about
the coarseness and 'sadism' of his relations with Martine Bourdin,
just as it is at variance with the calculated and joyless seduction of
Gégé. It is, however, wholly consistent with what Sartre was to
write in his celebrated study, *L'Imaginaire* in 1940: beauty can only
exist at the level of the imaginary. To quote his lapidary formula:
'Le réel n'est jamais beau.' It seems strange that a man has to reach
thirty-five before realizing that sexual relations cannot be accom-
modated to a purely aesthetic rule. Is it possible that 'sadism' is
what arises when sexual partners fail to live up to a ritual of beauty
imposed masterfully upon them?

There has been little in the letters and notebooks, except that
which we can infer from what is implicit in Sartre's tributes to
Simone de Beauvoir (and even that relationship is sometimes
marred by a kind of sordid complicity), to suggest that he has
found a role for tenderness in his picture of the relations between
men and women. Yet, before moving on to a consideration of
Sartre's relationship with his mother, which will yield a very different view of the bonds between male and female, I should at least
mention some passages in the notebooks which lightly adumbrate
kinds of feeling that are different both from sex as a branch of aesthetics and sex as a form of contempt. After describing his dislike
of entering into emotional bonds with men, Sartre writes: 'Encore
n'ai-je eu d'amitiés qu'avec ce que j'appellerai des hommes-
femmes, une espèce fort rare, tranchant sur les autres par leur
charme physique et parfois leur beauté et par mille richesses
intimes que le commun des hommes ignorent' (*Carnets*, 336).
Sartre goes on to define these 'inner riches' in terms of a developed
capacity for finding interest and delight in a host of common
experiences: a passing face, a fall of the light, etc. He admits that
he shares this disposition: 'Ainsi suis-je moi-même, je crois, malgré

ma laideur, homme-femme, au moins dans mes principales pré-
occupations' (ibid. 336).

One can detect here Sartre's flight from the analytical dryness
and abstraction which he tends to identify with men and, by the
same token, his propensity for preferring female company: 'Bref,
pour moi il y a une moitié de l'humanité qui existe à peine. L'autre
— eh bien il faut le dire, l'autre est mon unique, mon constant
souci. Je n'ai de plaisir qu'à la compagnie des femmes, je n'ai d'estime, de tendresse, d'amitié que pour des femmes' (ibid. 341). And
he concludes: 'je *m'entends* avec les femmes. J'aime leur façon de
parler, de dire des choses et de les voir, j'aime leur façon de penser,
j'aime les sujets sur quoi elles pensent' (ibid. 341). I shall want
briefly to return to this view of a special feminine sensibility at the
end of this essay. At this point, I will content myself with expressing
some unease about a picture of women that could be seen as an
intellectualized version of that familiar figure, woman as *le repos du
guerrier*.

In turning now to *Les Mots* I want to show how Sartre's
emotional attachment to his mother provides him, in retrospect,
with an alternative conception of love which is richer and more
compelling than the sexual transactions arising out of a ritual of
seduction, and which carries with it something of the specifically
feminine qualities he has touched on in the *Carnets*.

The actual quality of Sartre's mother's relationship with her own
father, the authoritarian and theatrical 'Karl', like the quality of her
intimacy with Jean-Baptiste, the naval officer who was briefly to be
her husband before his premature death, is simply not recoverable
from the pages of *Les Mots*.[12] Indeed, we are sedulously prevented
by the narrator from entering those areas of Anne-Marie's life with
any degree of real understanding and sympathy. Bent on revenging
himself on the pretences and illusions of a childhood which, retrospectively, he blames for having misled him into the religion of art,
the adult Sartre has constructed a brilliant, and often hilarious, fiction of family life against which, as readers, we can have no appeal.
There is no 'evidence', other than that provided by the text, against
which we can test the narrator's picture. Take, for example, this
account of Anne-Marie and her mortally sick husband: 'Anne-
Marie le soignait avec dévouement, mais sans pousser l'indécence

---

[12] Sartre, *Les Mots* (Paris, 1964).

jusqu'à l'aimer' (*Les Mots*, 8), or, a little later: 'Après des noces de sang, c'était une suite infinie de sacrifices, coupée de trivialités nocturnes' (ibid.).

What can be said of this lethal dismissal of conjugal relations, by one who could not have witnessed them, except that it is an *invention* that articulates the narrator's jealousy of the father he had never known, a jealousy still sufficiently alive in 1963 to inspire these caustic phrases? What is revealed here is a continuing resentment against even the possibility that a normal sexual bond had existed between his parents. The long dead father has still to be dispatched as a serious rival for the mother's affection and intimacy. And to make quite sure that we do not dwell on this dead father as one who might also have been a lover, he is killed off a second time with jokes and converted into a legendary and anonymous figure, rather like the Man in the Iron Mask or, more significantly, the sexually ambiguous Chevalier d'Eon (*Les Mots*, 12). With the early death of Jean-Baptiste, Anne-Marie and Poulou are converted by the narrator into storybook orphans of the storm, drawn ever closer together in an intimacy conveyed with delicacy and tenderness, even if through a veil of badinage. Fondness and delight attach to a number of these remembered incidents: days in the Jardin du Luxembourg, surreptitious outings with Anne-Marie to the silent films, Schumann and Chopin played on the piano at home. The detail lavished on the closed world of this couple, like the language that transmits it, constantly suggests the force of the emotional ties which unite mother and little boy. In a family circle retrospectively viewed as a centre of play-acting, in which the child must embark on one impersonation after another in order to ingratiate himself with adults—'Un seul mandat: plaire . . . ' (*Les Mots*, 22)—Anne-Marie alone seems uninfected by pretence. The one solid, genuine thing which stands out in memory for the narrator is the way in which Anne-Marie constantly devotes herself to others, and to him: 'Quand j'y pense, aujourd'hui, ce dévouement seul me semble vrai . . . ' (ibid. 23).

This sober avowal seems to me to break out of the web of irony of which *Les Mots* is composed. It exemplifies a true moment of self-disclosure: the expression of filial gratitude by the adult Sartre for the enveloping maternal love and solicitude that had helped to ground his being as a child. It is a moment quite different in character from the more equivocal expressions of this mother/son relationship to which I will shortly turn. It represents a groping toward a position which Sartre will elaborate later, and which has an important bearing on how a child is enabled to affirm him- or herself as an individual. The significance that this idea of the devotion implicit in maternal love will come to enjoy in Sartre's thinking can be specifically gauged from the way in which he, as biographer, will treat Flaubert's infancy. Paradoxically, he achieves this by inverting his own experience as a child and showing what happens when an infant is denied love. In this sense, the young Gustave's experience is shown to be the *negative* of his own. This technique confused the critics who asked whether the hostile picture of Flaubert's mother, Caroline, contained in the first volume of Sartre's monumental study, *L'Idiot de la famille* (1971), was an oblique attack on his own. He was quick to dismiss this: 'Ma mère était non seulement dévouée mais aussi totalement pleine de tendresse . . . ', and he went on to contrast Gustave's infancy with his own happy childhood: 'ce petit garçon sûr de lui, qui a des certitudes profondes parce qu'il a eu dans ses premières années tout l'amour dont un enfant a besoin pour s'individualiser et se constituer un moi qui ose affirmer, ce petit garçon c'est moi.'[13]

The language in which Sartre works out the predicament of the infant Gustave is striking testimony, if indirect, to the power of his feelings for his own mother, and philosophically, the picture of maternal solicitude he presents, marks a serious advance on earlier attempts to account for how individuals gain a sense of their own 'selves'. Sartre begins on a highly speculative note. Caroline, he asserts, wanted a girl, was bitterly disappointed to give birth to a boy, and this deeply affected her attitude to Gustave as a child: 'Si mon hypothèse est juste, la jeune mère vit en lui une bête étrange: elle avait trop espéré se reproduire — au sens littéral du mot — pour ne pas ressentir qu'un usurpateur s'était incarné sans visa dans la chair de sa chair . . . '.[14] Sartre dismisses her motherly care as merely conscientious: 'Excellente mère, mais non pas délicieuse' (*L'Idiot*, i. 136). This is an unexpected phrase, more revealing of Sartre than of Gustave. It implies that Caroline is not neglectful but lacking in some maternal quality which the biographer thinks vital. 'Delicious' would seem to suggest playfulness, complicity, perhaps

---

[13] Sartre, 'Sur *L'Idiot de la famille*', 97.
[14] Sartre, *L'Idiot*, 133.

even flirtatiousness. Nothing could be clearer. Caroline is blamed for not being Anne-Marie and for failing to provide Gustave with that peculiarly intimate and charming relationship which Sartre himself had enjoyed in infancy. As a result, Gustave is portrayed as emotionally frustrated, lacking the spontaneous and unconditional love which is essential if the young child is to have a secure sense of his own individuality.

Here Sartre spells out the precise nature of this maternal love in terms that make it even more apparent that he is talking of Poulou and not Gustave. It provides a passage of poetic intensity, fusing once again the language of feeling and the technical language of philosophy:

La valorisation du nourrisson par les soins l'atteindra d'autant plus profondément que la tendresse sera plus manifeste: si la mère lui parle, il saisit l'*intention* avant le langage; qu'elle lui sourie, il reconnaît l'*expression* avant le visage même. Son petit monde est traversé d'étoiles filantes qui lui *font signe* et dont l'importance est avant tout de lui *dédier* les conduites maternelles. Ce monstre est monarque absolu, toujours fin, jamais moyen. Qu'un enfant puisse une fois dans sa vie, à trois mois, à six, goûter ce bonheur d'orgueil, il est homme: il ne pourra de toute son existence ni ressusciter la volupté suprême de régner ni l'oublier.

(L'Idiot, i. 136, note 1, italics in the text)

Shooting stars, absolute monarch, the supreme thrill of reigning: such is the extravagant language that discloses at least as much about Poulou's childhood world as it tells us about Gustave's. Of course, Sartre confesses, it is just an idea: 'Je l'avoue: c'est une fable. Rien ne prouve qu'il en fut ainsi' (ibid. 139). But however it happened, Sartre insists that Gustave's psychological development was conditioned by his mother's veiled indifference. It produced in him a profound passivity, though things might have turned out otherwise had the bonds between mother and child been different:

S'il a vraiment reçu dans leur plénitude les premiers soins, dédiés par les sourires épars du monde, s'il s'est senti absolument souverain aux temps archaïques de l'allaitement, les choses iront plus loin: cette fin suprême acceptera de devenir l'unique moyen de combler ceux qui l'idolâtrent et dont elle est précisément la raison d'être; vivre sera la *passion*, au sens religieux, qui transformera l'égocentrisme en don; le vécu sera ressenti comme *libre exercice d'une générosité*.

(ibid. 141, italics in the text)

In a word, the truly loving mother will serve as the model who will make it possible for the child to act positively and generously in the world. Through mother-love the child will come to feel that he is 'mandated' to take his place in the world: 'il faut se tromper d'abord, se croire mandaté, confondre but et raison dans l'unité de l'amour maternel . . . ' (ibid. 143).

This striking philosophical excursion is an eloquent tribute to Anne-Marie from the Poulou who has turned into Sartre, and prompts one to wonder why images of maternal solicitude are virtually absent from Sartre's fiction and drama, with the exception of Sarah Gomez in *Les Chemins de la liberté*. The power of the maternal bond, interpreted so positively in the pages of *L'Idiot de la famille*, is echoed in Sartre's late interviews but in such a way as to draw attention to what might be construed as its excessive closeness. Here, in 1974, is Sartre speaking to Simone de Beauvoir about what he felt like as a child before and after his mother's remarriage: 'Avant, j'étais un prince par rapport à ma mère, maintenant je n'étais qu'un prince d'un second ordre' (*Entretiens*, 444). He returns to the subject in the film of his life released in 1977, when he emphasizes the 'perfect' nature of his relations with his mother before she remarried: 'ma mère qui était jusque-là entièrement dévouée à ma cause, et que je considérais un peu comme une grande sœur, ma mère a introduit quelqu'un dans ma vie . . . ' (*Sartre, un Film*, 15–16). The result was to displace him from the centre of her life and to 'me faire faire une rupture intérieure avec ma mère' (ibid. 17). Prompted by a question about the painful nature of this break, Sartre insists defensively: 'Je n'ai jamais imaginé quelque chose de sexuel, ce qui tient à ce qu'ils se tenaient très bien et que par ailleurs ma mère était plutôt une mère qu'une femme' (ibid. 17–18). No doubt this was true but it does less than justice to the intensity of the relationship. Indeed, the fact that this break, and the supplanting male who had precipitated it (and whom he cannot even bring himself to refer to as 'step-father'), still had the power to move him in old age is confirmed by an attentive spectator of the film: 'on voit en effet Sartre mimer avec son corps la scène de rupture et se livrer à un exercice *de dénegation* qui semble fait pour illustrer l'analyse freudienne' (italics in the text).[15]

Whatever is involuntarily revealed here tends to be supported by the discreet self-disclosure operating within the text of *Les Mots*. In

---

[15] P. Lejeune. 'Sartre et l'autobiographie parlée', in *Je est un autre: l'Autobiographie, de la littérature aux médias* (Paris, 1980), 201.

this, the picture of the intimacy shared by Anne-Marie and Poulou is so tenaciously remembered, so charged with veiled emotion, so *rapt* at moments, that the semi-incestuous nature of Sartre's feelings is laid bare. I think of an incident recalled by the narrator in which Poulou as a child seeks to protect Anne-Marie from what he thinks are the dark designs of a passing stranger: 'je surpris son regard maniaque et nous ne fîmes plus, Anne-Marie et moi, qu'une seule jeune fille effarouchée qui bondit en arrière . . . ' (*Les Mots*, 182). Though ignorant of the ways of men, Poulou has sniffed out sexual desire: 'Ce désir, je l'avais ressenti à travers Anne-Marie; à travers elle, j'appris à flairer le mâle, à le craindre, à le détester' (ibid. 182). This is a passage particularly rich in implication, and its obliquity makes it more persuasive than other moments, which I will look at next, in which the theme of incest is made explicit. For what we have here is a son impersonating a husband, an imagined rape fore-stalled (as evidenced by the excited hyperbole of 'regard mani-aque'), a symbolic union of Poulou and Anne-Marie and finally, Poulou's repudiation of the male in himself.

Elsewhere the intimations of incestuous feeling are more self-consciously handled. Here, for example, Karl is humming some ditty about brothers and sisters. Poulou, the narrator insinuates, is disturbed:

Ça me troublait: si l'on m'eût donné, par chance, une sœur, m'eût-elle été plus proche qu'Anne-Marie? Que Karlémami? Alors c'eût été mon amante. Amante n'était encore qu'un mot ténébreux que je rencontrais souvent dans les tragédies de Corneille. Des amants s'embrassent et se promettent de dormir dans le même lit (l'étrange coutume: pourquoi pas dans des lits jumeaux comme nous faisions ma mère et moi) . . . Frère, en tout cas, j'eusse été incestueux. J'y rêvais. Dérivation? Camouflage de sentiments interdits? C'est bien possible. J'avais une sœur aînée, ma mère, et je souhaitais une sœur cadette. Aujourd'hui encore — 1963 — c'est bien le seul lien de parenté qui m'émeuve.	(*Les Mots*, 41).

The rather too insistently 'knowing' tone of this passage, the shift from Poulou's voice to the narrator's, and the unsuccessful attempt to mimic the child's voice as he thinks of lovers in the same bed, all suggest the author's uncertainty about how to handle the poten-tially explosive subject of incest. The jokey manner seems to me a way of distancing an emotion that is still disturbing for the narrator as he tries to recapture a lost childhood, and my reaction is reinforced by the note that follows this passage. In this, Sartre spells out the fascination which the subject of incest has long had for him:

J'ai longtemps rêvé d'écrire un conte sur deux enfants perdus et discrètement incestueux. On trouverait dans mes écrits des traces de ce fantasme: Oreste et Electre dans *Les Mouches*, Boris et Ivich dans *Les Chemins de la liberté*, Frantz et Leni dans *Les Séquestrés d'Altona*. Ce dernier couple est le seul à passer aux actes. Ce qui me séduisait dans ce lien de famille, c'était moins la tentation amoureuse que l'interdiction de faire l'amour: feu et glace, délices et frustrations mêlées, l'inceste me plaisait s'il restait platonique.   (*Les Mots*, 42, note).

Here again the source of incestuous desire has to be attributed to literature, to the imaginary world of books, in order that it can be distanced from the desiring agent himself.

If I have given special attention to the exact character of Sartre's affective bond with his mother, it is because it may hold the key to understanding something of that feminine dimension within himself which Sartre hinted at in the *Carnets* and which he reverts to in his late interviews. In the passages I have just discussed, I would wish to identify a single emotional quality as being common to them all: it is a kind of *tenderness*. The word surfaces already in that, admittedly untypical, passage of the notebooks that I have referred to. Tenderness, too, is the feeling which pervades a well-known page of Sartre's 1947 study of Baudelaire, in which the bonds between poet and mother are seen through the lens of the biographer's own experience:

Lorsque son père mourut, Baudelaire avait six ans, il vivait dans l'adoration de sa mère; fasciné, entouré d'égards et de soin, il ne savait pas encore qu'il existât comme une personne, mais il se sentait uni au corps et au cœur de sa mère par une sorte de participation primitive et mystique; il se perdait dans la douce tiédeur de leur amour réciproque; il n'y avait là qu'un foyer, qu'une famille, qu'un couple incestueux.[16]

The premium Sartre places on 'tendresse' seems to me to arise from the fact that it is rooted in his own experience of maternal love. But, in spite of what he writes about the preciousness of maternal love in his study of Flaubert, he never, in the *Carnets* or his late interviews, seeks to relate women's tenderness to those

[16] Sartre, *Baudelaire* (Paris, 1947), 18.

maternal qualities of nurturing, protection and concern in which tenderness has its roots. In what he says in his interviews, these fundamental and life-enhancing virtues are passed over in favour of notions of feminine charm and sensibility which effectively reinforce sexual stereotypes.

It must be a source of regret that someone whose thinking on a whole range of aesthetic, philosophical and social–political problems proved so very stimulating over forty years failed to connect satisfactorily the deepest insights yielded to him by his exceptionally intimate relationship with his mother and the affectionate and admiring, but superficial, images of women which recur in the interviews he gave in his last years. The personal reflections on women disclosed to Simone de Beauvoir, Michel Contat and Catherine Chaine between 1974 and 1977 represent no progress on the banalities of the notebooks of 1939–40, where, with unwitting condescension, talking trifles to women is preferred to talking philosophy with Raymond Aron (*Carnets*, 341). In insisting to Michel Contat that his relations with women are markedly 'richer' than those with men, Sartre can only account for this in terms which again suggest elusive qualities of sensibility rather than the more solid values grounded in devotion or solicitude: 'D'abord, il y a un langage qui n'est pas la parole, qui est le langage des mains, le langage des visages. Je ne parle pas du langage sexuel proprement dit . . . ' ('Autoportrait', 197). A variant of this recurs in what he admits to Simone de Beauvoir: 'Ce qui m'intéressait dans le fond, c'est de retremper mon intelligence dans une sensibilité' (*Entretiens*, 383). Here again women are valuable principally in the degree to which they provide Sartre with a refuge from the excessive analytical dryness he finds in himself, rather than for more positive ethical qualities. There is no effort in all this to refine and clarify precisely what the content of this female sensibility is, and this unexamined fondness can lead him to statements that reduce women to the status of a relaxed ambience. As he confesses to Catherine Chaine: 'j'aime toujours ce que dit une femme, ce qu'elle fait. Même si elle est très vilaine et qu'elle dit des sottises, ça m'est égal . . . J'aime leur sensibilité, leur manière d'être . . . '.[17]

To the extent that, in his last years, Sartre increasingly lends himself to these public forms of self-disclosure, he betrays his

---

[17] C. Chaine, 'Sartre et les femmes, entretiens avec Catherine Chaine (2)', *Le Nouvel Observateur* 639 (7–13 février 1977), 76.

conviction that the detail of his life is intrinsically interesting and valuable, and that though it may not be exemplary, in the edifying sense, it may none the less come to be seen as having a period, as well as a personal, significance.

10

André Frénaud: the Quest for Self

ROGER LITTLE

Deus escreve direito por linhas tortas.

Portuguese proverb[1]

La pensée approximative est seule génératrice du réel.

Albert Camus[2]

Only bullets
Travel straight lines. Bird flights
Are a better guide to truth.

Patrick O'Brien[3]

THE quest for self mediated through literary expression is clearly not coincidental with that of the psyche, since individuation is overlaid by considerations of individual style. The reader may metaphorically psychoanalyse the writing, unravelling fascinating patterns of awareness and response to life and language, but he must stop short of supposing that his conclusions coincide with what might emerge from a potential study of the author on the couch. The epigraphs to this study are designed not only to suggest that we might, Polonius-like, 'by indirections find directions out', but also to register a shift away from a world in which God is the measure of everything and towards that of our own century, that of 'the disinherited mind'.[4] Self-definition implies the Other, and so the literary critic's excursions beyond the modern text, justified of course by that text alone rather than by any extrinsic considerations, include an endeavour to reconstitute the writer's sense of a *ganz andere* no longer predetermined by Christian convention.

André Frénaud, born in 1907 and profoundly affected by the great social and intellectual movements of his time, is typical of his

---

[1] Cited by Paul Claudel as the first epigraph to *Le Soulier de satin*, in *Théâtre*, 2 vols (Pléiade, Paris, 1959), ii. 647.

[2] Camus, *L'Homme révolté*, in *Essais* (Pléiade, Paris, 1965), 698.

[3] Patrick O'Brien, *A Book of Genesis* (Dublin, 1988), 49.

[4] I borrow the phrase from Erich Heller's title: *The Disinherited Mind: essays in modern German literature and thought* (London, 1975, first pub. 1952).

generation. In common with other modern artists, he attempts 'to find a form that accommodates the mess'.[5] That, in turn, is the critic's task: he too will prefer birds to bullets, avoid the constraints of a methodological grid and seek to establish a sensitive body of utterances which illuminate rather than obscure. He will sympathize with the narrator of Dostoyevsky's *Notes from Underground* in his rejection of simple arithmetic in favour of $2 \times 2 = 5$, which is, as Malcolm Jones observes, 'a better approximation to experienced reality than the more usual equation'.[6]

This cue from arithmetic invites us to turn to Frénaud's celebrated first poem:

EPITAPHE

Quand je remettrai mon ardoise au néant
un de ces prochains jours,
il ne me ricanera pas à la gueule.
Mes chiffres ne sont pas faux,
ils font un zéro pur.
Viens mon fils, dira-t-il de ses dents froides,
dans le sein dont tu es digne.
Je m'étendrai dans sa douceur.

mai–septembre 1938[7]

The reference to 'le néant' and 'zéro' allows two simultaneous readings, one at the level of the café slate which is to be wiped clean

---

[5] Samuel Beckett, commenting on *Comment c'est*, observed: 'What I am saying does not mean that there will henceforth be no form in art. It only means that there will be a new form, and that this form will be of such a type that it admits the chaos, and does not try to say that the chaos is really something else . . . To find a form that accommodates the mess, that is the task of the artist now.' Quoted by J. P. Little, *Beckett: 'En attendant Godot' and 'Fin de partie'*, Critical Guides to French Texts 6 (London, 1981), 78.

[6] Malcolm V. Jones, *Dostoyevsky: the novel of discord* (London, 1976), 45.

[7] In *Les Rois mages*, Collection Poésie (Paris, 1987), 15 (first pub. 1943 with slight textual differences). References to this volume will henceforth be abbreviated as *RM*. Other abbreviations of Frénaud's works in the present text are as follows: *DTD: Depuis toujours déjà* in *La Sorcière de Rome suivi de Depuis toujours déjà*, Coll. Poésie (Paris, 1984; *DTD* first pub. 1970). *IPP: Il n'y a pas de paradis: poèmes (1943–1960)*, Coll. Poésie (Paris, 1967, first pub. 1962). *NIF: Notre inhabileté fatale: entretiens avec Bernard Pingaud* (Paris, 1979). *SF: La Sainte Face*, Coll. Poésie (Paris, 1985, first pub. 1968).

There are few critical writings on Frénaud in English, but in this respect C. A. Hackett was a pioneer. Having included Frénaud in his *Anthology of Modern French Poetry from Baudelaire to the Present Day* (Oxford, 1952), he published

when full payment is made, the other at a metaphysical level implying absorption of the self into the infinite void, and they interact
inseparably. Modesty and pride relate no less intimately: the 'zéro
pur' seems to imply the former, but the certain knowledge of the
accuracy of the calculation bespeaks the latter. The *homo humilis*
of Christianity ('Domine non sum dignus . . . ') has given way to the
homo dignus ('tu es digne') who believes he can survive perfectly
well without belief. We are clearly in a post-Nietzschean world
without God, yet the preoccupation with metaphysics apparent in
Frénaud's personification of 'le néant' tells of a continuing quest,
fundamentally religious in nature, though rigorously, even aggres-
sively, non-denominational. It might be construed in traditional
terms as a quest for a surrogate God but is, in Frénaud's atheistic
universe, a quest for the construction—or reconstruction—of the
self.

In a long poem written in captivity in 1941 and 1942, 'Agonie du
général Krivitski', Frénaud returns to the arithmetic of negation
and to the expression of an ineradicable desire to 'fare forward' (in
T. S. Eliot's phrase) towards a welcoming death which is seen as a
culmination:

> Ma vie, je t'aurai passée comme une torche,
> me brûlant à mon feu en ricanant.
> Et il n'en reste plus: zéro, c'est le bon compte!
> Et il ne reste plus que l'appétit toujours vorace
> que la douce va combler ô ma vie . . . la mort
> qui est l'ouverture de l'être total
> ou du néant.   (*SF*, 114)

Although there is an evident echo here, as elsewhere in Frénaud's

---

'André Frénaud and the Theme of the Quest' in *Modern Miscellany*, ed. T. E. Law-
renson, F. E. Sutcliffe and G. F. A. Gadoffre (Manchester, 1969), 126–36. Serge
Gavronsky presented an interview with Frénaud in an English version in *Poems and
Texts: an anthology of French poems, translations and interviews* (New York,
1969), 97–103. Michael Bishop published 'Maximum and Minimum: the poetics of.
AF' in *French Forum* (Lexington, Ky) 5: 2 (May 1980), 141–55.
  The principal volumes in French on Frénaud (apart from *NIF* which is essential
reading for anyone wanting to find out more about him) are, chronologically, as fol-
lows: G.-E. Clancier, *André Frénaud*, Poètes d'aujourd'hui (Paris, 1953, rev. edn.
1963). *Sud* (Marseilles) 39–40: *André Frénaud* (1981). *Sud* 50–1: *Frénaud/Tar-
dieu* (Colloques Poésie-Cerisy, vol. 2, 1984). *Lire Frénaud*, ed. J.-Y. Debreuille
(Lyons, 1985). Peter Broome, *André Frénaud* (Amsterdam, 1986). Roger Little,
André Frénaud entre l'interrogation et le vide, Marseilles, *Sud* (1989). There

earlier writings, of the poetry of Apollinaire, the more profound influence seems to be that of Dostoyevsky.[8] Apart from the Underground Man's arithmetic rejecting logical, social and philosophical assumptions of order, there are characters elsewhere, in the novels, who express a position with remarkable resonances in Frénaud. One comment which strikes a special chord is that of Shatov in *The Devils* during his philosophical discussion with Stavrogin. His extreme Slavophilia finds, of course, no echo, its weakness being exposed by caricature in the novel itself,[9] but here he seems to attach value to intuition, so developing the Underground Man's view:

Socialism is by its very nature bound to be atheistic because it has proclaimed from the very first that it is an atheistic institution and that it intends to organize itself exclusively on the principles of science and reason. Reason and science have always, today and from the beginning of time, played a secondary and a subordinate part; and so they will to the end of time. Peoples are formed and moved by quite a different force, a force that dominates and exercises its authority over them, the origin of which, however, is unknown and inexplicable. *That force is the force of an unquenchable desire to go on to the end and, at the same time, to deny the existence of an end.* It is the force of an incessant and persistent affirmation of its existence and a denial of death. It is the spirit of life, as the Scripture says, 'rivers of living water', the running dry of which is threatened in Revelation. It is the aesthetic principle, as the philosophers call it, an ethical

are also two major articles by Roger Munier: 'La Clairière et l'ombre', *Critique* 389 (Oct. 1979), 882–9 and 'L'Etre et son poème', *Revue de Métaphysique et de Morale* 87: 4 (Oct. 1982) 436–49.

[8] Cf. for example 'Le Brasier' in *Alcools*, in *Œuvres poétiques* (Pléiade, Paris, 1965), 109:

> Je flambe dans le brasier de l'ardeur adorable . . .
> Je suffis pour l'éternité à entretenir le feu de mes délices . . .
> Il n'y a plus rien de commun entre moi
> Et ceux qui craignent les brûlures

In his book on Dostoyevsky, Malcolm Jones writes (p. 59): 'The Underground Man's ideals are not holy to him any more; he delights in desecrating them. Near-contemporaries, among them Kierkegaard and Nietzsche, discerned similar trends in the intellectual and emotional life of modern man. Problems akin to those of the Man from Underground became the stock-in-trade of the Decadents and, on a more serious level, of twentieth-century existentialist writers of fiction, including Hesse, Unamuno, Sartre and Camus. The cult of the inappropriate finds later and more exaggerated expression, moreover, in Surrealism and the cult of the Absurd.'

[9] I take my cue here from comments made by Richard Peace, *Dostoyevsky: an examination of the major novels* (Cambridge, 1971), 156.

principle, with which they identify it, the 'seeking of God', as I call it much more simply. (Italics added)[10]

The sentence which I have italicized could stand as an epigraph to the whole of Frénaud's output. It is what Sartre characterized, on the basis of his familiarity with *Les Rois mages*, as the principle of *non-espoir*.[11] In this we detect a simultaneous rejection of both hope (either philosophical *espoir* or Christian *espérance*) and despair. Whereas the traditional saying has it that to travel hopefully is better than to arrive, Frénaud dispenses with the hope, considering it a pernicious delusion. In this he is directly in line with early existentialist thought, which has pervaded the literature and thinking of our time.[12] Both optimism and pessimism are set aside in favour of that 'unquenchable desire to go on to the end and, at the same time, to deny the existence of an end.' Its recent expression is most familiar to us, no doubt, through Beckett's work, summed up in the closing words of his trilogy:

You must go on, I can't go on, you must go on, I'll go on, you must say words, as long as there are any, until they find me, until they say me, strange pain, strange sin, you must go on, perhaps it's done already, perhaps they have said me already, perhaps they have carried me to the threshold of my story, before the door that opens on my own story, that would surprise me, if it opens, it will be I, it will be the silence, where I am, I don't

---

[10] Fyodor Dostoyevsky, *The Devils* (Part 2, ch. 1, 'Night' §7), trans. David Magarshack (Penguin, 1953), 256. In the epilogue to *Les Thibault* (1940), Roger Martin du Gard writes in the same vein and characterizes the agnostic *entre-deux-guerres* generation: 'Plutôt les angoisses de l'incertitude que le paresseux bien-être moral offert à tout adhérent par les doctrinaires! Tâtonner seul, dans le noir, ça n'est pas drôle; mais c'est un moindre mal', *Œuvres complétes*, 2 vols (Pléiade, Paris, 1955) ii. 982.

[11] Sartre is credited by Frénaud as having coined the term in 1945 in respect of the latter's poetry: see André Frénaud, 'L'Essence de la poésie', in *Lire Frénaud*, 23.

[12] Sartre's major philosophical work of the period, *L'Etre et le néant* (Paris, 1943), deals with ontology rather than with ethics, but touches on the question. His *L'Existentialisme est un humanisme* of 1946 presents his moral philosophy, and existentialism is there seen as a basically hopeful system of thought. However, Sartre was subsequently to repudiate the work and regret its publication. It is Camus who is more directly concerned with the problem of hope (as well as being profoundly influenced by Dostoyevsky) in *Le Mythe de Sisyphe* (1942) and *L'Homme révolté* (1951): cf. 'Etre privé d'espoir, ce n'est pas désespérer. Les flammes de la terre valent bien les parfums célestes' (*Le Mythe de Sisyphe* in *Essais*, 169). Anyone familiar with Camus's essays will find many similarities of preoccupation in Frénaud.
One recalls also Anouilh's Antigone (in the play of that name, first produced in Feb. 1944) confronting Créon with her rejection of the principle of hope: 'Nous

know, I'll never know, in the silence you don't know, you must go on, I
can't go on, I'll go on.[13]

Persistence in spite of everything is closely akin to the practice of
the Stoics, of whom it has been said: 'le stoïcien n'éprouve pas un
sentiment de révolte devant un monde absurde, mais il ne se con-
tente pas d'accepter passivement le destin, il adopte une attitude
active.'[14] Yet not only do we find very different responses to the
unacceptability of the world in different people: in Frénaud, reactions vary from moment to moment. Underlying all of them, however, is the central recognition that he is unacceptable to himself,
and his poem 'Séparé' leads to this inescapable and brutal conclusion:

> Regards qui m'accueillez en vain,
> je ne suis pas des vôtres, assis à votre table,
> partageant le pain et le vin.
> Je ne sais plus mentir avec vos mensonges.
> Je suis de l'autre côté de votre paix,
> éternellement acceptée.
>
> Ils ont chuchoté: *Un fou, c'est un fou.*
> *Il n'aime pas être heureux.* Ils ont ri.
>
> Je vais ouvrir mon secret, hommes assis:
> Je me suis inacceptable.
>   (*RM*, 34; Frénaud's italics)

Taking his distance from the 'hommes assis', the people around him
who seem to be immured in bourgeois self-satisfaction, Frénaud
shares his ultimately unsurprising secret. His is the legacy of the
Underground Man, his the tradition of Baudelaire's anguished

---

sommes de ceux qui posent les questions jusqu'au bout. Jusqu'à ce qu'il ne reste vraiment plus la petite chance d'espoir vivante, la plus petite chance d'espoir à étrangler.
Nous sommes de ceux qui lui sautent dessus quand nous le rencontrons, votre
espoir, votre cher espoir, votre sale espoir!' Camus too sees the pernicious quality of
hope: 'De la boîte de Pandore où grouillaient les maux de l'humanité, les Grecs firent
sortir l'espoir après tous les autres, comme le plus terrible de tous' ('L'Eté à Alger',
Noces, in *Essais*, 76). The most sustained literary treatment of the paradoxical hope-
lessness of hope in the human condition is nevertheless to be found in Beckett.
[13] Beckett, *The Unnamable*, in *The Beckett Trilogy* (London, 1979) 381–2 (first
pub. as a trilogy in English 1959). The text was written and first published in French
(Paris, 1952).
[14] P.-M. Schuhl, introduction to *Les Stoïciens* (Pléiade, Paris, 1962), lv.

shuttling between 'deux postulations simultanées'.[15] Where Epictetus adumbrated a relationship between self and self, psychiatrists
like R. D. Laing have followed. Language itself seems to contain an
awareness of the dialogue with self that is possible in solitude: as
Hannah Arendt records, 'In solitude, I am "by myself"', together
with myself, and therefore two-in-one ... '.[16] The French
expression 'à part soi' is similar to the English 'by oneself' in reflecting the separation of self into two protagonists, speaker and hearer
taking turns in the endless inner dialogue.

Although outwardly participating in a sociable communion with
others, 'partageant le pain et le vin' in a clear echo of the eucharistic
ritual, the poet-narrator is keenly aware of his difference from those
around him, and refuses to continue their lies or their unthinking
peace. Happiness is not for him a valid goal: more than that, it is
not a possible goal for him, given that he is unacceptable to himself.
That he is also self-engrossed seems apparent in the very formulation of his last line, where the first three words are intimately iden-
tified with the first person singular. The poem makes a firm
statement through its clear narrative components and stark opposition of the insistent lyric 'je' and an unspecified 'vous' which gives
way to 'ils'. The phonetic repetition in the title, where the first and
last vowels are identical, alerts the readers to similar repetitions in
the text.[17] The rhyming of 'vain' and 'vin' seems to suggest a pattern of *rimes embrassées* which is not sustained: instead it draws
attention to other occasional rhymes which are highlighted because
of their irregularity. So 'ri' and 'assis' bridge the gap between the
closing couplets, and the final key word, 'inacceptable', contains
the very word which, at the end of line 2, symbolizes sociability:
'table'. Internal echoes also mirror the phonetic shape of the title:

[15] Charles Baudelaire, 'Mon cœur mis à nu', in *Œuvres complètes*, ed. Claude
Pichois, 2 vols (Pléiade, Paris, 1975), i. 682.

[16] Hannah Arendt, *The Origins of Totalitarianism* (London, 1986), 476 (first
pub. 1951). Nietzsche once wrote: 'I and Me are always too earnestly in conversation with one another' (*Thus Spoke Zarathustra*, Penguin, 1961, 82). Epictetus
(*Dissertationes*, iii. 13, cited by Arendt), Laing (*The Divided Self*, Penguin, 1965)
and most powerfully Arendt herself all make the distinction between solitude and
loneliness, the former being creative, the latter sterile and even destructive. I have
used this distinction in respect of another poet on an earlier occasion: see Roger
Little, *Saint-John Perse*, Athlone French Poets (London, 1973), 104.

[17] Compare Mallarmé's title 'Brise marine' and the far more tightly organized
resonances and reversals of the vocalic pattern i – a – i in the poem (e.g. most
obviously '*La* chair est tr*i*ste, hélas!' and 'F*ui*r! là-b*a*s f*ui*r!').

vôtres/votre (l. 2), pain/vin (l. 3), mentir/mensonges (l. 4), l'autre/ votre (l. 5), éternellement accep*tée* (l. 6), *chuch*oté (l. 7), fou/fou (l. 7), ils ont/ils ont (lines 6–7). It is as if, by working with such doublets, Frénaud re-enacts in the texture of the poem his emotional separation not simply from others but, more importantly, from himself.

While necessarily incomplete, such a reading appears justified by the published text and by the general context of that tortured (and often tortuous) self-consciousness so characteristic of the modern mind. Frénaud insists privately, however, that the others at table are his parents, not other companions of any sort.[18] The experiential circumstances of composition no doubt legitimate such a restriction for the poet: he cannot fail to remember the relationship uppermost in his mind at the time. For him, therefore, the poem is an exploration of self as rebellious adolescent, a portrait of the artist as an angry young man. This might appear to the reader, however, to be a regrettable restriction to impose on a text susceptible of interpretation as an expression of the human condition in modern man, the adolescent's *Angst* and rebelliousness being sustained throughout a lifetime in certain cases, deepening and finding clearer articulation in the mature being. Try as I may, I cannot persuade Frénaud of the validity of this argument, and this is all the more curious because he wrote the poem not as an adolescent but at the age of thirty-one. No parent is mentioned in the text, no limitation is suggested to the family table. I am bound to assume that there is some nuance I have missed, some figure of Frénaud's self patterned in the poem to which I am insensitive. What then is the true self that emerges here? Is it the sum of multiple readings by myself and others or the poet's own recollection? If the latter, is the earlier self not coloured by the remembering self? Even if a time-gap were not involved, is it not imperative to recognize the crucial distinction which Proust made when he wrote that 'un livre est le

---

[18] In a letter to me dated 5 Aug. 1986, Frénaud writes: 'En ce qui concerne le sens de *Séparé* quand j'ai écrit *Je ne s[ui]s p[a]s des votres [sic] assis à votre table*, j'avais en tête les Assis de Rimbaud c['est-] à [-] d[ire] une bourgeoisie bienpensante [*sic*] et bien consentante à laquelle ma famille appartenait et qui aurait voulu me faire acquiescer à ses valeurs. Ce sont mes parents que j'aimais mais contre qui je me suis révolté, auxquels je fais allusion d[an]s ce poème et non à mes camarades d'études et de boisson qui n'étaient pas tous philosophes et poètes contestataires mais, en tout cas, n'étaient pas offusqués de mon "inacceptabilité", transgressant l'ordre, eux-même[s], à leur façon, pour le moins à boire et à courir les filles . . . '.

produit d'un autre *moi* que celui que nous manifestons dans nos habitudes, dans la société, dans nos vices'?[19] Since we can place no absolute reliance on any attempt to bring a poem and a person simultaneously into focus, we are trapped, as so often happens, in a circle of resonant tautology.

Attempts at communication also involve the 'other' at a level less exalted than the numinous, and Frénaud defines himself, as we all do, in relation to society. Coming of age as he did in the late 1920s, he was fascinated by the phenomenon of communism, but never joined the party. By the time he came to write his first poem in 1938, news of Stalin's show trials and purges had cured any *engouement*, but his natural Burgundian conviviality joined forces with his residual sense of fraternity to lead to a number of poems presenting simple folk going about their business. One of the most appealing and instructive is 'Le Souvenir vivant de Joseph F. pêcheur de Collioure':

> En revenant de Collioure le plus long jour de l'année,
> tellement insuffisant pour s'épancher avec l'ami nouveau.
> Malhabiles nous sommes à nous atteindre, les hommes,
> malgré la promesse entrevue dans l'eau du regard.
> La pêche est à portée, mais on prend toujours si peu.
> Richesses furtives qui ne parviennent pas à s'échanger.
> Cœurs obscurcis par trop de navigations douloureuses.
> Cœurs secrets, plus difficiles à gagner que les poissons.
>
> En vain le clapotis figé par la nuit s'efforce de retenir
> le train qui s'allonge dans le matin lent.
> Nous sommes si loin déjà de la lueur de la rencontre,
> emportés dans le quotidien, sans certitude de retour.
> Mais à jamais le souvenir de cet homme comme un fer obstiné,
> dans un coin inaperçu du cœur me blessera
> d'une blessure, comme est la droiture, merveilleuse.
>
> *(IPP*, 92–3)

The expansiveness of simple friendship is restricted into the sharp inadequacy of memory, and the key word of the title, 'souvenir', governs both semantically and vocalically the tightening movement of the poem. The biblical miracle, bathetically reversed in the meagre haul of 'si peu' (here applied to fish but elsewhere in Frénaud denoting the inadequacy both of human existence and,

---

[19] Marcel Proust, *Contre Sainte-Beuve* (Pléiade, Paris, 1971), 221–2.

very specifically, that of poetry),[20] is transferred, in the last line, to the painful recollection of lost fraternity. The longest day gives way to night, meeting to separation, the back vowels of *Collioure, jour* and *nouveau* to the front ones of the second stanza, pointedly grouped in its opening line: *clapotis figé, nuit, retenir,* and continuing in the tightness of *certitude, obstiné, inaperçu, blessure, droiture,* a tightness anticipated in certain key words of disappointment and frustration in the opening stanza: *insuffisant, malhabiles, si peu, furtives, obscurcis, difficiles.*

What emerges from such considerations is that the self is multiple no less for the poet than for his reader on whose subliminal consciousness his phonology and rhythms work their subtle magic. Frénaud's search for self takes him through a quite exceptional range of projections from Stalin to God the Father and include among others Hitler, a Nazi executioner, an anonymous 'little old man', a prostitute and other female voices, a pedlar, a horseman, one of the Magi and Jesus Christ.[21] His poetic voice flexes to include moods and manners from the vulgar to the delicately refined, from the heavily sarcastic to the trippingly witty, from the laboriously philosophical to the sensitively sympathetic. Only on one occasion, however, did the circumstances of war impinge sufficiently for him to mask the signatory André Frénaud behind a pseudonym, and he chose one which was patently improbable as a real name: Benjamin Phélisse.[22] Occasional pseudonyms are often thus. More permanent twentieth-century French pseudonyms show either total assimilation of the name (Guillaume Apollinaire, Paul Eluard, Lionel Ray, Yves Broussard . . .), the use of forename or, more usually, surname alone as a flag of convenience (Colette,

---

[20] More than mere self-denigration or aesthetic modesty, the objective recognition of the inadequacy of poetry is a cornerstone of Frénaud's persistent metaphysical quest. This has, however, led to some misunderstanding among critics: the 'pauvre fête', 'machine inutile' or 'murmure misérable du poème' (see *IPP*, 83, 85) remains the best approximation to the ever-receding ideal and, by its very inadequacy, a spur to pursuing that goal.

[21] I deal summarily with this feature here because I have treated it at length in 'André Frénaud's Plural Voice', *Studies in Twentieth-century Literature*, winter 1989: *Contemporary French Poetry*.

[22] See *L'Honneur des poètes* (Paris, 1943), cited by J. -Y. Debreuille in *Lire Frénaud*, 219. The name Benjamin Phélisse suggests, in the forename, the biblical favourite son and, in the surname, the Latin *felix* (cf. French *félicité*); as such it seems, in the circumstances, a paradoxical choice, brimming with ironies worthy of further exploration.

Aragon, Etiemble, a host of painters . . .), or a more complex distancing as in the case of Saint-John Perse.[23]

Frénaud's poetry is a multiple arena echoing with the projected voices of his central rumination; one could cite many episodes 'tirés du remâchement sans fin dont [s]es poèmes donnent des représentations fragmentaires sur un théâtre intermittent' (*NIF*, 93). Yet he has never shown an interest in writing for the stage, and while it would be an exaggeration to suggest that Dostoyevsky alone furnished his model, it is worth reflecting on ways in which this might have been the case, given that Dostoyevsky had such a profound influence on him. Mikhail Bakhtin has drawn attention to the polyphony, both of structure and of characters, in Dostoyevsky: '*A plurality of independent and unmerged voices and consciousness, a genuine polyphony of fully valid voices is in fact the chief characteristic of Dostoyevsky's novels.*'[24] Low life is amply represented, both as a result of inner faults and as capable of redeeming itself (as in the case of the prostitute Sonia in *Crime and Punishment*), yet in *The Brothers Karamazov* we find both the saintly Zossima and the celebrated chapter showing the Grand Inquisitor, with Christ figuring almost as at Emmaus. It is not by chance, one feels, that the root of Raskolnikov's name, *raskol*, means schism, since the self divides into schizoid factions which represent the inner tensions and argu-

[23] The case of Aragon is complicated by his adoption of occasional pseudonyms, particularly during the Second World War: B. d'Ambérieux, Pierre Cèpe, Jacques Destaing, Germain Dubourg, François La Colère, Georges Meyzargues, Albert de Routisie, Arnaud de Saint-Roman and Paul Wattelet, not to mention Le Paysan de Paris and Le Témoin des Martyrs. The case of Alexis Leger (Just-Alexis Leger, Saint-Leger Leger, Saint-leger Leger, Archibald Persse, St-J. Perse, Saint-John Perse, Allan, Diego, Douglas . . .) is investigated most recently by Roger Little, 'Nom caché, nom savane: réflexions sur les pseudonymes de Saint-John Perse', *Textes, Etudes, Documents* Saint-Leger Leger, Saintleger Leger, 6, in *Pour Saint-John Perse* (Paris, 1988), 27–31. See also my 'Alexis Leger et Saint-John Perse: le masque et la plume', *Actes du colloque de Pau (mars 1987)*, forthcoming, and 'Alexis Leger et Saint-John Perse: le masque et la plume (II)', *Actes du colloque de Pointe-à-Pitre (mai–juin 1987)*, Editions Caribéennes, forthcoming. Probably the most extraordinary sustained use of multiple pseudonyms in modern literature is that made by the Portuguese poet, Fernando Pessoa (alias Alberto Caeiro, alias Alvaro de Campos, alias Antonio Mora, alias C. Pacheco, alias Ricardo Reis, alias Bernardo Soares), though the case of the French novelist Romain Gary/Emile Ajar made quite a stir when it was revealed recently that they were one and the same man.

[24] Mikhail Bakhtin, *Problems of Dostoyevsky's Poetics*, ed. and trans. Caryl Emerson, Theory and History of Literature 8 (Manchester, 1984), 6 (author's italics). Bakhtin's seminal book first appeared as *Problemy tvorchestva Dostoevskogo* (Leningrad, 1929) and was expanded for the second edition, entitled *Problemy poetiki Dostoevskogo*, in 1963.

ments. It is he who most clearly recognizes that he contains within himself his own executioner, rather as Baudelaire, in 'L'Héautontimorouménos', exclaims:

> Je suis la plaie et le couteau!
> Je suis le soufflet et la joue!
> Je suis les membres et la roue,
> Et la victime et le bourreau![25]

In a time of ideological fragmentation, when the Western world 'lacks a spiritual consensus or unity of vision; an age which finds a place for ideological fanaticism, intellectual non-commitment, cynicism, existential despair and cults of intensity',[26] such fragmentation, transferred to poetry, shatters any remaining illusions we may have about a healing unity. It has been well said of Frénaud's work that it becomes

le champ clos où il donne forme, de façon saisissante, à ce combat en lui de voix antagonistes, à la fois 'proies innocentes' et 'bêtes cruelles' [the reference is to the poem 'La Mort d'Actéon', *DTD*, 123] qui disent et dénoncent l'ambiguïté du je. Polyphonie contradictoire, à vif, où Frénaud disparaît et s'affirme sans cesse, dans un balancement antinomique, un mouvement autocritique sans pareil, à ma connaissance, dans l'histoire de la poésie (parent, mais distinct des projections d'un Pessoa).[27]

At the beginning of this century, Apollinaire represented in French poetry a clear case of fragmentation. I have written of him (if I might be permitted a moment of self-quotation such as Frénaud indulges in so often in his endeavour to totalize an identity) as 'a broken mirror, precariously held together in its frame, longing to be resilvered and made whole'.[28] If Frénaud's first collection seems particularly indebted to Apollinaire, it is partly perhaps because of this affinity. Yet Frénaud, like Dostoyevsky, is far more coherent in his aesthetic, philosophical and socio-political stances: the multiplication of voices orchestrating the self serves a single—and single-minded—purpose: that of the quest for self. 'Reality', says the narrator of *Notes from the House of the Dead*, 'strives towards

---

[25] Baudelaire, *Les Fleurs du Mal*, op. cit. 79. Camus, echoing Dostoyevsky, writes: 'Pour que l'homme devienne dieu, il faut que la victime s'abaisse à devenir bourreau' (*L'Homme révolté*, in *Essais*, 581).

[26] M. V. Jones, *Dostoyevsky*, 7.

[27] Alain Lévêque, 'L'Appelant', *Sud* 39–40 (1981), 213.

[28] Roger Little, *Guillaume Apollinaire*, Athlone French Poets (London 1976), 117.

fragmentation.' Exile and captivity, experienced both by Dostoyevsky and by Frénaud, are powerful vectors in the search for ways to approach and express the core of selfhood, offering as they do both the time and circumstances for careful reflection. Distance lends disenchantment. 'Counterpoint becomes a principle of individual consciousness and self-expression,' writes Malcolm Jones, who, in another excellent phrase entirely applicable to Frénaud, refers to Dostoyevsky's 'balance of disharmony'.[29]

William James, to represent what he calls 'the hot place in a man's consciousness, the group of ideas to which he devotes himself', uses the phrase *'the habitual centre of his personal energy'*.[30] Those centres in Dostoyevsky and Frénaud overlap, as we have seen, in many respects. Both are attracted to fundamentally religious considerations, however much one is drawn by contextual circumstance towards the expressions of Russian Orthodoxy and the other to those of Roman Catholicism. As Frénaud observed in conversation with Bernard Pingaud, 'Il est vrai que le christianisme s'est donné sur moi un terrible avantage d'avoir pendant de si longues années contribué à me former, avant que je le reconnaisse pour être "une formation mythique" . . . , privilégié dans mon cas, mais rien de plus.'[31] What emerges, even for the professed atheist, is a profound sense of 'la difficulté de tenir dans la durée une attitude morale exigeante, la nécessité d'une auto-critique sans cesse reprise pour éviter les pièges d'une trop haute conscience de soi' (*NIF*, 59–60).

It has indeed been argued that 'faced with two people who have no experience of God, the one who denies His existence is probably

---

[29] M. V. Jones, *Dostoyevsky*, 64, 194: 'The essential thing to understand is that Dostoyevsky in his imaginative fiction foresees no ultimate harmony on earth. The best that is available to man is equilibrium, a balance of disharmony.' He cites 'Reality strives towards fragmentation' on p. 9.

[30] William James, *The Varieties of Religious Experience* (London, 1902), 196 (author's italics).

[31] *NIF*, 47–8. As Frénaud tells Pingaud, he had attended a Catholic college at Dijon: much of the second chapter of *Notre inhabileté fatale*, 'L'Ombre du père', is devoted to the formative influence of religion and Frénaud's vigorous affirmation of his atheism, e.g. p. 50: 'le sacré, je peux le retrouver, le réintroduire sans dommage à travers ma réinvention des mythes d'origine chrétienne, étant très assuré de ne pas courir le danger de tomber à genoux.' Recognition that Frénaud's stance is non-denominational and atheistic is by no means incompatible with awareness of his moral and fundamentally religious impulse.

closer to the truth.'[32] To be self-engrossed is a dubious replacement for faith, however, if it is not accompanied, as Frénaud indicates, by vigilant self-criticism. Yet the very prefix of this last word betokens a kind of preoccupation with the self, and consequently, while it may not be as patently unhealthy as self-indulgence, self-satisfaction or other self-orientated attitudes, it allows no place for an absolute, objective yardstick by which to judge human action. Frénaud's self-questioning cannot escape from the perils of moral relativity, and the very lack of an absolute means that he cannot avoid a continuation of his persistent search: he is impelled to continue because the lack of an answer is built into his questions, and that, in an entirely modern, almost masochistic way, is how he wants it.

Again, the affinities with Dostoyevsky are apparent. Even in details of metaphor there are coincidences, to say nothing of direct borrowings such as the title for Frénaud's *Poèmes de dessous le plancher*.[33] Vermin abound in both *œuvres*. They are both a threat to and an image of ourselves. One recalls the powerful episode in *Crime and Punishment* (Book v, ch. 4) where Raskolnikov reveals his culpability to Sonia and where first his victim (he is thinking of Alyona Ivanovna rather than her sister Lisaveta, it would seem) and then her murderer, Raskolnikov himself, are seen as lice: 'But I only killed a louse, Sonia. A useless, nasty, harmful louse. . . . If I'd not been a louse, would I have come to you?'[34] Elsewhere, rats pullulate, as they do in Frénaud's poetry, where they embody a gnawing menace to his precarious constructions, provisional castles which are the very metaphor of his poems (as becomes abundantly clear in the significant text 'Le Château et la quête de poème': *IPP*, 233–4). Frénaud talks of the 'grouillement intérieur des pulsions hostiles, qui se trouve symbolisé tout naturellement . . . par ce déboulé d'animaux courant de tous côtés' (*NIF*, 37). A poem such as 'Le

---

[32] J. P. Little, *Simone Weil* (Oxford, 1988), 58. Simone Weil notes: 'Entre deux hommes qui n'ont pas l'expérience de Dieu, celui qui le nie en est peut-être le plus près' (*Cahiers*, new revised edn. Paris, 1970, 1972, 1975, ii. 19). Elsewhere she writes: 'Il y a deux athéismes, dont l'un est une purification de la notion de Dieu' (ibid. i. 257) and again: 'Un mode de purification: prier Dieu, non seulement en secret par rapport aux hommes, mais en pensant que Dieu n'existe pas' (ibid. 268).

[33] A collection was published by Gallimard under this title in 1949, subsequently regrouped in part in *SF*.

[34] Dostoyevsky, *Crime and Punishment*, trans. David Magarshack (Penguin, 1951), 430, 433.

Miroir de l'homme par les bêtes' seethes with the monstrous and verminous creatures of Bosch's paintings—or of Dostoyevsky's underground—and presents the poet himself as a 'fomentateur des odeurs fétides!' (*SF*, 209).[35]

Yet for all this stirring of the miasmal self, with the consequent muddying of the image, there is an important difference between Dostoyevsky and Frénaud. As Bakhtin observes (p. 5): 'For some scholars Dostoyevsky's voice merges with the voices of one or another of his characters; for others, it is a peculiar synthesis of all these ideological voices; for yet others, Dostoyevsky's voice is simply drowned out by all those other voices.' To this list it must be added that some characters, in both Dostoyevsky and Frénaud, are manifestly set up as foils for use in the author's dramatization of an argument. It is also pertinent to remember Erich Heller's observation in respect of the imaginative writer generally: 'the wider the scope of his imagination, the less evidence will he leave behind to show what he himself thought about this or that controversial issue.'[36] This seems to be Dostoyevsky's case. With Frénaud it is different. While his voice merges on occasion with that of some of his characters, at no point in his work does there seem to be any drowning of his voice by other voices, nor could his view be represented simply as a synthesis of his dramatic projections, nor again, ultimately, are we left in any doubt as to his own philosophical stance. He has views which militate against self-effacement. He is most certainly not, in Heller's pithy words (p. 155), 'prepared to betray [his] beliefs for the sake of occasional heresies offering a more felicitous phrase.'

Dostoyevsky has been seen as 'bringing a particular form of unbelief to a consciousness of itself'[37] and Frénaud might well be seen as following in his footsteps. The 'manque essentiel' or 'absence de fondement' (*NIF*, 57) which he designates as the (non-) replacement for God becomes the aim of his ontological quest and is the major preoccupation of all his writings. That 'unquenchable

---

[35] For further comments on Frénaud's bestiary, a version of Baudelaire's 'ménagerie infâme de nos vices' ('Au lecteur', *Les Fleurs du Mal,* op. cit. 82), see Daniel Leuwers, 'Le Bestiaire inquiet d'André Frénaud', *Sud* 39–40: *André Frénaud* (May 1981), 188–200.

[36] Heller, *The Disinherited Mind,* 125.

[37] Stewart R. Sutherland, *Atheism and the Rejection of God: contemporary philosophy and 'The Brothers Karamazov'* (Oxford, 1977), 37.

desire to go on to the end and, at the same time, to deny the existence of an end' which we have already noted in *The Devils* is sufficient motivation for persistence in Frénaud despite its apparently negative focus. In common with many other modern writers, Frénaud gives the void a positive connotation familiar enough to Taoist thinkers but largely unfamiliar in the West until recently except in the context of apophatic or negative theology. This last, which defines the nature of God by spelling out what He is not, is inappropriate to Frénaud's case in so far as its theocentricity is concerned, but relevant in that it reaches towards the positive through the negative, Arguments, however subtle, such as those of Roger Munier, which make of Frénaud an entirely negative quantity by seeing him too exclusively from the viewpoint of the philosopher, ignore at their peril the positive traces left by the poet. We have to accept not merely the arithmetic of $2 \times 2 = 5$, but also the mathematics of $- \times - = +$: minus times minus equals plus.[38]

On an ethical plane, Frénaud claims: 'en préférant une vérité négative à une illusion consolatrice, je me suis fondé en dignité' (*NIF*, 51). *Homo dignus* is thus given higher moral status than *homo humilis*, since he has striven to assume the responsibility which had previously been considered God's prerogative. The modern atheistic position may be arrogant, but it cannot be said that this arrogance is lightly won. As Henri Michaux has written, '*Nous ne sommes pas un siècle à paradis.*'[39] The pursuit of scientific proof into a domain where science has no purchase stems from an attitude which our century applauds. The complex continuum from

[38] I have made my case elsewhere against the attractions of Munier's view and in favour of the double negative applied to Frénaud's position. See 'La Négativité conquérante: réflexion sur l'usage des préfixes privatifs chez André Frénaud', in *Lire Frénaud*, 63–81. Even logically, as Camus remarks, 'toute philosophie de la non-signification vit sur une contradiction du fait même qu'elle s'exprime' (*L'Homme révolté*, in *Essais*, 418). The same paradox lies at the heart of surrealism, another principle rejected by Frénaud. However, it is going too far to say of Frénaud that he radiates joy and that, thanks to him, we can more readily imagine Sisyphus to be happy, as Peter Broome suggests at the conclusion of his recent book (op. cit. 205). Camus may have noted that 'une certaine continuité dans le désespoir finit par engendrer la joie' (*Carnets mai 1935–février 1942* (Paris, 1962), 77), but Frénaud's position is characterized not by despair but, as we have seen, by *non-espoir*, and the pendulum therefore has less far to swing. What is more, Sisyphus's joy was *silent* (cf. *Le Mythe de Sisyphe*, in *Essais*, 197): 'une littérature désespérée est une contradiction dans les termes,' declares Camus elsewhere ('L'Enigme', *L'Eté*, in *Essais*, 865).
[39] Henri Michaux, *Connaissance par les gouffres*, Coll. Poésie (Paris, 1988), 9 (first pub. 1961). Michaux's italics.

louse to man to God which Dostoyevsky explored in the wake of that span of two infinites in Pascal, from 'ciron' to 'espaces infinis', continues to be probed and reiterated.[40]

Yet Frénaud is a poet. Neither ethical nor scientific considerations can be the sole criteria by which the literary critic judges his acts. Were his poems nothing more than transparent vehicles for his philosophy, they would be unlikely to detain us long, since he makes no pretence to being a systematic philosopher. The poems themselves are his acts. While functioning to some extent as a heuristic means for the poet's own self-exploration, they are for the reader the products of those explorations, recognizably provisional, no doubt, but none the less to be explored in turn for the poetic values they embody. One recalls Baudelaire's awareness of the paradox of 'l'horrible' becoming 'beauté' through the very dragomanic power of artistic expression.[41] It is of course important to distinguish these positive manifestations of the quest from the metaphysically positive void which is its aim. When the quest itself is so absorbing, the metaphors of its realization are revealed as the vital expression of the desire to 'fare forward': the end can, as it were, take care of itself, indeed must do so since by definition it can never be attained. Zeno's 'Stadium' argument comes to mind, the attempt to reach the other side being logically impossible because of the infinite divisibility of the space–time continuum.[42] The intellectual interest lies in the journey, not in the arrival. Just so for Frénaud it is life not death, the quest not the end, that engages his being in a monologue for many voices.[43]

After naming several of his long poems—'Enorme figure de la déesse Raison' (*IPP*, 37–46), 'Les Paysans' (*IPP*, 71–9), 'Tombeau

---

[40] For instance in the surgeon-poet Lorand Gaspar's *Approche de la parole* (Paris, 1978). For a sensitive commentary on Pascal's presentation of the human dilemma in the context of Christian apologetics, see John Cruickshank, *Pascal: 'Pensées'*, Critical Guides to French Texts 24 (London, 1983), esp. ch. 4.

[41] Baudelaire, 'Théophile Gautier', op. cit. ii. 123.

[42] 'It is impossible to traverse the stadium; because before you reach the far end you must first reach the half-way point; before you reach the half-way point you must reach the point half way to it; and so on *ad infinitum*.' Quoted in G. S. Kirk and J. E. Raven, *The Presocratic Philosophers: a critical history with a selection of texts* (Cambridge, 1962), 293 (first pub. 1957). Compare Beckett's fascination (at the opening of *Endgame*) with the 'impossible heap' of a life which will be completed only when it is too late to be recognized as a totality by the person concerned.

[43] Cf. Baudelaire's prose poem 'Déjà!': ' . . . quand chacun de mes compagnons dit: "Enfin!" je ne pus crier que: "*Déjà!*" ', *Le Spleen de Paris*, op. cit. 338.

de mon père' (*IPP*, 193–200), 'Agonie du général Krivitski' (*SF*, 93–115)—Frénaud goes on to say:

> quels que soient les pronoms employés — l'Enorme dit *je*, le père est apostrophé, les paysans sont *ils*, et il y a des *il* et des *je* dans le *Krivitski* — , le héros du discours n'est pas le poète, mais un personnage précisément désigné: le prolétaire ou le peuple, le paysan, le père, appréhendé par le fils, enfin Krivitski. Et bien sûr, le poète est derrière chacun, mais du moins s'est-il efforcé que le personnage en question ne soit pas assujetti aux exigences d'une subjectivité étrangère qui le fausserait. Si le seul sujet–objet de la poésie, c'est à la fois le poète lui-même et c'est l'homme-même [*sic*], je voudrais que chacun de ceux que je fais parler s'exprime selon sa vérité propre. (*NIF*, 144–5).

Thus in the case of Krivitski, for example, Frénaud writes elsewhere: 'j'ai attribué à Krivitski une conception — et une justification — de la Révolution dont je ne sais pas dans quelle mesure elle a bien été la sienne. (Elle n'a jamais été la mienne en tout cas.)' (*SF*, 118–19). The imaginative projection into a character clearly involves in Frénaud's mind a simultaneous awareness of the need to distance himself from that character so as to leave him his full independence. The case of General Krivitski is particularly instructive because he is not fiction but fact: he was head of the Soviet counterespionage service for Europe until, in 1937, he rebelled against Stalin's atrocities. Frénaud met him on several occasions after this but appears not to have known his memoirs, first published in 1940, shortly before his assassination, probably at the hands of Soviet secret service agents.[44] Whatever the circumstances presented in the poem, Frénaud's main concern is rather the lesson he draws from his presentation: 'il est possible au poète et à l'artiste de transformer le désespoir d'être, sinon toujours en un espoir, du moins en un non-espoir où il peut vivre, lucide, courageux peut-être, se fiant à un amour des hommes difficile et naïf qui, à la limite, n'a pas d'autre fondement qu'en lui-même' (*SF*, 122). While underlining his moral stance, Frénaud seems to recognize here the possibility of solipsism, an epistemological equivalent perhaps of that critical tautology mentioned earlier.

---

[44] See Frénaud's account, *SF*, 117–22, W[alter] G. Krivitsky, *I was Stalin's Agent* (London, 1939), and Roger Little, 'André Frénaud entre Krivitsky et Krivitski', *Europe* 707 (Mar. 1988), 175–83.

Certainly the difficulties inherent in the poet's projective task are plainly noted in the important 'Note sur l'expérience poétique' (*IPP*, 237–45). It is a text that makes repeated reference, more or less overtly, to Rimbaud's celebrated 'Lettres du Voyant' and to that most famous of affirmations applicable to the distinction between social self and poetic other: 'JE est un autre.'[45] Thus Frénaud writes:

Si Je est devenu un autre, le poète n'a la chance de l'incarner qu'à partir du moment où il commence à redevenir lui-même; la possibilité d'exprimer ce qui le dépasse lui est donnée alors qu'il renaît aussi comme obstacle. C'est le paradoxe et la contradiction fondamentale de l'action poétique.

(*IPP*, 238; Frénaud's emphasis)

This subtle argument takes us to the profoundest level of awareness of the creative act, where the most delicate balance between transparency and opacity is maintained. The 'other' is seen to be not only projected characters or voices, but also any reality which the poet attempts to represent in his work. He does so with any truth only by absorbing it into himself while remaining entirely himself, changed and yet unchanged by the experience of the other. Changed, since otherwise he would have 'had the experience but missed the meaning' as Eliot observed in 'The Dry Salvages'; unchanged, or else, if we apply Yeats's words to the realm of psychology, 'things fall apart; the centre cannot hold.'[46] This 'unité-dans-l'antagonisme', as Frénaud calls it (*IPP*, 240), may be suspect to philosophers but for the poet makes the contingent necessary:

Le toi et le moi se tiennent confondus un instant avant de s'opposer à nouveau et derechef de se confondre. Alternance et concomitance d'une décomposition et d'une réinvention de monde et de l'homme mêlés, le poème s'avance comme une bataille de San Romano tissée d'éclats hostiles et singulièrement accordés.

(*IPP*, 241; the reference is to Paolo Uccello's famous *Rout of San Romano* in the Uffizi, Florence)

A page later, he writes:

---

[45] Arthur Rimbaud, *Œuvres complètes*, ed. Antoine Adam (Pléiade, Paris, 1972), 249, 250.
[46] T. S. Eliot, in *Four Quartets*, in *The Complete Poems and Plays* (London, 1969), 186; W. B. Yeats, 'The Second Coming' in *Collected Poems* (London, second edn, 1950), 211.

Cette 'inhabileté fatale',[47] d'être éprouvée dans l'exaltation même qui lui donne un pouvoir inouï, aggrave chez le poète son habituelle insatisfaction, elle active pathétiquement ce pouvoir et, en le menaçant, l'impatiente. Précipité de glace et de feu, c'est l'*ironie* qui fait tourner le poème et accroît sa déflagration. Elle traduit et surmonte assez désespérément la dérision de l'entreprise. Dans le souvenir encore actif de l'interférence du *Même et de l'Autre*, moment culminant de l'expérience, elle est présente, ambiguë, comme la conscience terrible et souriante de nos limites à l'extrême de notre espoir de les franchir . . .

(IPP, 242; Frénaud's emphasis)

A single sentence of this major essay sums up the key features of the debate and puts in a nutshell the nature of the quest and of its aim: 'L'aventure de la création se poursuit avec des arrêts et des reprises, entre l'interrogation et le vide, dans une tension passionnée' (*IPP*, 244). Implicit in this are all the ironies which we have been exploring and which seem to be so central to our age. The tension and thrust are forces in a balancing act, that dance on the imaginary high wire which Rimbaud encapsulated so brilliantly in one of his 'Phrases': 'J'ai tendu des cordes de clocher à clocher; des guirlandes de fenêtre à fenêtre; des chaînes d'or d'étoile à étoile, et je danse.'[48] Inevitably there are times when the balance is seen to be lost, though these moments are likely to be different for different readers; but there are equally times when we can be gripped by the performance and find ourselves both changed and unchanged by it as we too grope our way forward, constantly uncertain yet no less constantly dissatisfied.

---

[47] Here, as for the title of the book made from his conversations with Bernard Pingaud, Frénaud is quoting Rimbaud's 'Angoisse': 'Se peut-il . . . qu'un jour de succès nous endorme sur la honte de notre inhabileté fatale?' (*Illuminations*, op. cit. 143).

[48] Ibid. 132.

11

Perspectives on the Self in Camus's *L'Exil et le royaume*

ROSEMARIE JONES

A LUI faire sentir si souvent qu'elle existait pour lui, il la faisait exister réellement[1]
Savoir qui j'étais[2]
Il ne savait pas alors s'il était heureux, ou s'il avait envie de pleurer[3]
Dans ce désert, personne, ni lui ni son hôte n'étaient rien[4]
Non, je ne suis pas certain d'exister[5]
Tu vois, je n'ai pas trouvé ma place[6]

These formulations are taken from the six stories which make up *L'Exil et le royaume*. Couched in terms of uncertainty and unease, they pose a double problem: in what ways is the self perceived as unfulfilled, and under what conditions, if at all, can it accede to affirmation, *bien-être*, *plénitude*? The emphasis in the quotations upon the negative, the imperfect and the verb *exister*, suggests that the search for the definition of the self in this text may best be pursued, not by the analysis of character and attribution, but by a survey of perspectives.[7]

The narrative perspective of each of the stories, in fact, is organized in terms of a common framework: a 'vertical' trajectory is articulated against certain 'horizontal' formations. Not surprisingly, for the Western European reader, the trajectory takes the form of

---

[1] 'La Femme adultère' in Albert Camus, *Théâtre, récits, nouvelles* (Paris, Pléiade, 1962), 1560–1.
[2] 'Le Renégat', 1581.
[3] 'Les Muets', 1598.
[4] 'L'Hôte', 1617.
[5] 'Jonas', 1645.
[6] 'La Pierre qui pousse', 1679.
[7] This reading makes the assumption that a fictional self is as reliable a witness and as likely to tell a truth as, for example, an autobiographical *je*. Hence the unqualified transition from 'the characters' to 'the self'. I have tried to 'keep the characters out of it' and avoid a psychological reading, but a comparison between the two approaches is sometimes called for and there may be residual contamination.

the journey or quest. Three cases are obvious, particularly as they describe present narrative movement within a longer journey: Janine and Marcel travelling between the southern Algerian towns on the business trip that has taken them far from the coast; the renegade in flight from his masters after the failure of his self-appointed mission; and d'Arrast perambulating in Iguape thousands of kilometres from France. However, if one considers that a journey is characterized primarily by the *displacement* of the traveller, the application extends to the other stories: Yvars makes his daily *trajet* between home and work, and the setting-forth of Daru and the Arab is inscribed upon the longer itinerary which takes the latter from El Ameur to Tinguit; and Jonas is displaced from the flat's main room and tries to paint successively in the small room, bedroom, corridor, shower and kitchen before constructing his *soupente*.

Displaced or journeying, the characters are transposed into an environment which is alien. It may be literally foreign ('La Femme adultère', 'Le Renégat', 'La Pierre qui pousse', 'L'Hôte'), where the character—in the last-quoted story, the Arab—encounters representatives of a people *other* in its language, appearance, perspectives. For Yvars, the otherness consists in the patronal outlook, the spaciousness of its domain compared to the exiguity of the lives of the working men; for Jonas, it is the constant exposure to disciples and admirers who do not themselves paint but who create discourses about painting.

The results of these encounters may display a number of negative possibilities. Communication is threatened, disrupted, denied or absent. Janine's only verbal 'exchange' with an Arab is with the nightwatchman: he speaks to her in Arabic, a language she does not understand. The renegade's masters do not speak to him, 'Les Muets' speaks for itself, Daru's reply to the Arab's 'écoute' is 'non, tais-toi.'[8] Jonas is subjected to incessant chatter but this, precisely, inhibits his primary means of communication, through painting. D'Arrast appears to escape inclusion in this category: welcomed with open arms by the officials of Iguape, he communicates in a median language represented by Socrate's approximate French and d'Arrast's own ability to speak Spanish, if not Portuguese. Nevertheless, as the macumba ceremony reaches its climax he is excluded

---

[8] *Théâtre, récits, nouvelles*, 1623.

as spectator and from the previous easy intimacy with the *coq*, and it is clearly acknowledgement from the common people of the town that he most desires.

Deprived of communication, the person becomes an object: contemplated, as Janine and Marcel are by shepherds in whose faces only the eyes can be seen; defined, like Yvars as a *tonnelier*, second-oldest employee, with a set place in the workshop; fixated, like Jonas condemned for ever and ironically to represent the subject of the painting *L'Artiste au travail*. But an object at least is perceived, fills a space: 'des Arabes les croisaient qui se rangeaient sans paraître les voir' (1566), another bears down upon Janine and Marcel 'sans les voir' (1568). Jonas's visitors sprawl on the conjugal bed and place their own work between him and his paintings. The renegade is at first the object of the gaze and blows of his masters, but in cutting out his tongue, they violate even his interior space and thus deny his status as entire object. The self of the characters has become space-less, nothing.

Against these attacks on the self there is seemingly no defence. On this most negative of journeys, vulnerability is increased through being in a state where normal activity is suspended. Janine and Marcel are going out to offer their wares, whereas normally people come to them; the renegade and the Arab are prisoners in a strange hand; 'les muets' have been forced to work 'normally', but their not-speaking is a rebellious substitution of abnormality for normality; Jonas's attention is diverted from painting, and the less he paints, the more he talks; d'Arrast views and encounters, but does not produce. Globally, the scope of movement and activity on this journey has become paradoxically so curtailed, the means of expression so hampered, that the characters can only follow, limp and hobble, metaphorically, but also literally 'pieds [the renegade] et poings [the Arab] liés'. Not only has normal activity ceased, but an 'abnormal' entropic situation appears to be taking its place, where death and sterility are substituted for creation and initiation. This is imaged in Janine's childlessness, the renegade's symbolic castration, Yvars's exercise of an outmoded trade, the Arab's taking of life, Jonas's unproductiveness. Even d'Arrast, in the narrative-time, is shown in the seemingly barren period before a work is produced. The movement of narration has led unfalteringly downward. The journey has taken the characters to a waste land where the self, restricted, rejected and impotent, doubts its selfhood.

Elle attendait, mais elle ne savait quoi[9]
Il y a si longtemps que je patiente[10]
Il n'avait rien à faire qu'à attendre, doucement, sans trop savoir quoi[11]
Daru patientait . . . de longues heures dans sa chambre [12]
Epuisé, il attendait, assis, les mains offertes sur ses genoux [13]
Lui aussi attendait, devant cette grotte, sous la même brume d'eau, et il ne
savait quoi. Il ne cessait d'attendre, en vérité, depuis un mois qu'il était
arrivé dans ce pays[14]

A quest, normally, presupposes a specific end or goal, as in the case
of the archetypal Grail: one may fail to appreciate its true nature,
but one is at least conscious of having embarked upon the quest for
it. The characters in *L'Exil et le royaume* are denied even this
teleological consolation. They are embarked on the journey before
even realizing that much of the travel actually consists of waiting;
even then, while much of the waiting in its turn is experienced/nar-
rated as a 'waste sad time', there is no indication either that 'Godot'
will ever come, or that he/it will be either recognizable or 'worth
waiting for'. Daru is able to name the object of his waiting: he
wants the snow to melt; so is the renegade: he lies in ambush to
'tuer le père', but which one? And the waiting referred to in the
quotation above covers a different time-span to that of 'j'attends le
missionnaire'(1579). The length of time Daru had to wait depends
on factors outside himself; Janine and d'Arrast, although on the
one hand perceiving *themselves* as waiting (as quoted above), on
the other, see themselves as the awaited ones, the *hôtes*, to whom a
revelation may be made: 'quelque chose l'attendait qu'elle avait
ignoré jusqu'à ce jour' (1570); 'une rencontre qu'il n'imaginait
même pas, mais qui l'aurait attendu, patiemment, au bout du
monde' (1668).

The temporal, successional framework of the journey has seemed
to obey a law of descent. The downward movement, however,
traverses certain formations of a spatial, 'horizontal' nature,
connected principally with the antitheses exterior/interior and
superior/inferior, but extending also to include light/darkness and

---

[9] 'La Femme adultère', 1565.
[10] 'Le Renégat', 1579.
[11] 'Les Muets', 1598.
[12] 'L'Hôte', 1612.
[13] 'Jonas', 1653.
[14] 'La Pierre qui pousse', 1668.

dryness/water. These do not function as simple oppositions, but form sets of complex and interweaving relations.

The clearest example of the contrariety of exterior and interior is afforded by the contrast drawn between the external world and the humanly created interior. In all the stories except 'Jonas', if rather less strikingly in 'Les Muets', the presence of the natural world is insistent and pervasive. Frequently in Camus's texts, in *L'Envers et l'endroit* and *Noces*, for example, the emphasis falls upon the immutability of the natural world, its permanence contrasting so sharply with the ephemerality of human existence. The accent here is on the dynamics and motion of elemental life: the diurnal rotation, the alternation between heat and cold, wind and stillness, cloud and sunshine, the movement of water, the rhythm of rain. Nature is heard to speak with her own voice, producing a *continuo* which accompanies the more obtrusive noises of men: 'un grand silence frais tomba sur la piste et sur la forêt. On entendit alors le bruit des eaux' (1657). Even the vibration of the air is audible, making a music: 'l'air illuminé semblait vibrer autour d'eux ... il sembla à Janine que le ciel entier retentissait d'une seule note éclatante et brève dont les échos peu à peu remplirent l'espace au-dessus d'elle' (1569); 'c'est la musique, la vaste musique de midi, vibration d'air et de pierres sur des centaines de kilomètres' (1584).

The metaphor, of course, is a *leurre*, and it is a truism now to state that, in Camus's writings, Nature is represented as indifferent to man in the sense of being impassible, alien, providing no mirror for self-reflection. If the natural world presented in this text is 'cruel à vivre', it is primarily because the climate is one of extremes, oscillating between aridity and impassable snow, blinding heat and incapacitating cold: 'il fait encore très froid, tout à l'heure il fera trop chaud, cette terre rend fou' (1579). Indeed, nature is seen to be indifferent in a second sense: that of in-*difference*: because climate is perceived as being *too* hot or *too* cold, *too* dry or *too* wet, a law of antithesis arises which in turn engenders a 'loi du même': 'it' is always *too*, regardless of what 'it' is. The refutation of the pathetic fallacy is here balanced by the exposure of its counter-tendency, equally delusive if less widespread: basing human behaviour on 'natural' standards. The examples of 'human inhumanity' produced by the text exhibit the workings of this polarity principle: the option facing Lassalle's employees: 'c'était à prendre ou à laisser', Daru's presentation of the choice between the eastern and southern routes, without comment, the renegade's conversion from the service of 'good' to that of 'evil'.

By contrast, the self is characterized by the twin principles of difference—of existing as a particular being—and of differentiation. To illustrate how this is imaged in the text involves considering a second aspect of the outer/inner antithesis, and more especially a distinction established between two different kinds of interior. There is one constellation of interiors which presents a range of human responses to the problem of interpreting and experiencing existence. Janine and Marcel's flat responds to the need to be 'à l'abri' which preoccupies them so greatly, the renegade's *tanière* is the place of domination and submission, and Daru's schoolhouse the locus of education, the *atelier* the precinct of industrial production. To these interiors which the characters occupy may be added others, less integrated, whose function in the narrative is nevertheless similar. 'La Pierre qui pousse' is a particularly abundant source, providing notably the church and the cave of miracles. These are bypassed by d'Arrast, but other interiors are successively entered and left; the hospital, clubhouse, the *case* of the macumba, the house of the judge, the *mairie*. These interiors have two points in common: they are principally public, and, taken together, they make up a large number of the most conventional answers to the question, not 'what am I?' but 'what should I do?',[15] or, re-formulated: 'what perspective should I adopt on life?' Even perspectives which appear intensely personal, such as the election of the private sphere rather than the public ('La Femme adultère') or the forced or voluntary severance from the desires of the self ('Le Renégat') have, by virtue of having become product/producer of discourse, fallen into public (dis)repair.

Alongside these interiors, the stories present, foregrounded in the narrative, certain other sites which for ease of reference will be termed simply 'locations'. Three of these are 'true' interiors: Daru's bedroom, Jonas's *soupente*, and the *case* of the *coq*. The other three — the terrace of 'La Femme adultère', the terrace of Yvars's house and the 'éboulis de rochers' where the renegade lies in wait — have a median character which will be discussed shortly. Now the importance of these locations will be obvious in psychological

---

[15] Kant, *Gesammelte Schriften*, vol. 9, *Introduction to the lectures on logic* (Berlin, 1923), 25.

terms, as they are the places in which the characters either experience some form of 'kingdom' or gain some intimation of an alternative to 'exile'.[16] From another angle, however, these locations may be seen as a representation of the self, and that in three main ways. In the first place, they fulfil a very particular function of interposition between inner and outer, the human and the natural. The terrace at Laghouat, human-constructed but exposed to the elements, mediates between the fort and its surroundings; Yvars's house belongs to the town but the terrace overlooks the sea. Although the renegade's hiding-place is a natural assemblage of stones, he refers to it as 'ma maison de rochers' (1588). Within the isolated schoolhouse, Daru's bedroom stores the sacks of grain that will permit the continuance of human life in the desert of stones. By a curious transsubstantiation Jonas's apartment, flooded with light, has become an aquarium in which the human beings are *perdus* (1635). The *cases* of the poor people of Iguape are a composition of natural and man-made materials: 'les cases de terre, de fer-blanc et de roseaux s'accrochaient si difficilement au sol qu'il avait fallu consolider leur base avec de grosses pierres' (1666). Secondly, the locations occupy a median position spatially: looking over the oasis or the sea, on the side of a hill (the renegade and Daru), suspended between floor and ceiling, situated 'entre le fleuve et un grand talus escarpé' (1665). Placed low enough not to imitate the Babel-structure (with the possible exception of the terrace of 'La Femme adultère'), they are high enough to offer a vantage-point from which the exterior may be observed. Thirdly, these locations are distinct from the 'public' interiors mentioned previously, a feature particularly notable in 'L'Hôte' and 'Jonas', for the bedroom is within the schoolhouse but apart from the classroom, and the *soupente* within, but not of, the conflated living- and working-space. These locations may be chosen by the characters in fear, in flight or in freedom, but always in response to some instinctive urge associated with self-preservation or self-expression.

Now the self, in its most basic definition, constitutes the point at which the inner world articulates with the world external, a point

---

[16] The renegade certainly has little sight of a kingdom, and one could question the importance allotted to this location. However, it is from this place that he fulfils his desire to 'kill the father', and in which he has the opportunity to review his past life. Since he is mutilated in the fetish-house and crucified in the open air, the 'éboulis de rochers' is at least a limbo or place of refuge.

of intersection between that which is perceived and that which is expressed. But although the self is 'placed' temporally and spatially, it is not simply a passive point: it is an active agent which, as it were, works out its own salvation. For to cope with reality, the self needs an intermediary perspective: without such, the 'normal' boundaries between the self and the world are transgressed: 'cette terre était trop grande, le sang et les saisons s'y confondaient, le temps se liquéfiait' (1678). In retrospect, the downward trajectory of the characters may be seen to be connected with a disjunction between inner and outer, itself producing, or produced by, a failure of the perspective to function adequately. In most cases this is due to the pressure of the external world, bringing about a new situation with which the previous perspective is unable to deal. The tendency then is to desire to regress, to reintegrate the previous position, to reverse the situation. But the renegade's story illustrates how the inner vision may strive to compel external reality to conform to it.

Two points are at issue here. The dynamic of the self was already suggested, necessarily, with reference to its journeying: the foregoing gives sufficient reason to suggest that within that original movement, the perspective of the 'normal' self is continually adapting. Not merely because the self is in transit, but because the nature of the world exterior to the self is also fluid. The quotation given above from 'La Pierre qui pousse' may have been used to indicate that one can only live with a perspective that is adequate: it foregrounds, equally, the shifting nature of reality. The fact that a dam is necessary to prevent houses being flooded does not mean that the river will stop flowing. Both these points have appeared earlier, if in less visible form. The constant movement of the natural world, translated in this text not only in visual terms but also—and particularly—with reference to sound, functions as both sign and example: sign of the invisible—winds, currents—which is manifest only in its effects; example of the more general law of the 'turning world'. Secondly, reference has already been made to fixing and defining the self. With hindsight, it would seem that the attempt to fixate the self is a distortion of its reality, and that in similar fashion, the way to madness may lie in the failure of the perspective to take account of reality's perpetual motion.[17]

[17] The terms are over-simplified, since of course the self is part of 'reality'.

If the 'nature' of the self is not to be fixed, how can the self be defined? In this connection the characters, in their despair, may have spoken more aptly than they know, for the response to this question can only be: as no-*thing*. The *je* exists only in terms of the variant, and deviant, verb, forming constantly changing relations of perspectival possibility. This looks at first glance like another rehearsal of 'existence precedes essence', but, although this formula would still be more apposite than its reverse, it is difficult to point to any way in which *L'Exil et le royaume* gives critical foothold to notions of essence, selfhood, ipseity. This will be illustrated further at a later stage, in connection with the problems of articulation and representation, but meanwhile, if there is little more to be said on the self's (lack of) nature, it may still be possible to view it from more than one angle, and to explore more thoroughly the relations it forms.

To return temporarily to the natural world: in the previous discussion mention was made only of its (fictionally) literal place and presence in the narrative. In these texts, and again more overtly than in other earlier writings of Camus, certain features of the physical universe take on a symbolic identity so pronounced as to rival the primary denotation. In 'La Femme adultère' and 'Les Muets' the sun is first of all source of light and heat, but it is associated with youth and pleasurable physical activity: for these middle-aged selves, the sun no longer illumines the perspective, but is seen as a possible cause of its disruption, and the reaction is to avert one's eyes or curtain oneself off. The sun as visible star is excluded from Jonas's interior, but if the source is absent its effects are still almost unbearably manifest in the inundation of the apartment with light through the immense window-spaces, and the intense visibility they afford. Locus initially of creation, the flat becomes a place of sterility as Jonas's star attracts daytime visitors and the reflectibility of the interior permits the circulation of lesser lights. 'Le Renégat' presents an interesting case: whereas in the previous three examples the symbolism has been recuperated, in this narrative it is written out.[18] In the initial stages of the story, the sun is employed as a shifting metaphor: associated successively with Catholicism

---

[18] Other instances could be given: see for example pp. 203–4. The fact that—as I would argue—the renegade reveals rather than occludes does not, unfortunately, make interpretation any easier.

(1580), the renegade himself (1580, 1581) and his masters (1582), it occupies a metaphorical space before reintegrating its henceforwardly fixed narrative space as celestial luminary. And in all these metaphorical integrations, the sun is associated with power and domination.

It is of course a commonplace of psychological (and occult) discourse to speak of the sun as a symbol of the masculine principle, and the question therefore arises whether the text engages with the gender of the self. Luce Irigaray, in a provocative re-reading of Western luminaries, has some interesting lines:

La révolution copernicienne n'a pas encore produit tous ses effets dans l'imaginaire masculin. Et l'excentrement de l'homme à lui-même qui en a résulté est avant tout son exstase dans le (sujet) transcendental. S'élevant à une perspective qui dominerait le tout, au point de vue le plus puissant, ainsi se scinde-t-il de son assise matérielle, de son rapport énigmatique au matriciel, qu'il prétendrait surveiller. Spéculariser, spéculer. S'exilant toujours plus loin (vers) là où serait le plus grand pouvoir, ainsi devient-il 'soleil', si c'est autour de lui que les choses tournent, pôle d'attraction plus fort que la 'terre'.[19]

Reuniting the themes of reflection, power, the sun and exile, Irigaray's text invites one to speculate on whether height or elevation might be significant in the context of *L'Exil et le royaume*.

It does indeed prove to be, particularly because summits, peaks, and hills are so rare in this text. If the characters are lifted up, their tendency is to aspire to descend, as d'Arrast leaves the balcony of the *mairie* to join the *coq* below. The highest structure is the terrace of 'La Femme adultère'. It is undoubtedly significant that in Camus's six stories there is only one female principal character, and she is drawn to this elevated structure.[20] The only other character who is drawn to a height is Daru. 'L'Hôte' presents two men and two journeys. In the course of the first journey, the Arab is brought, bound, a prisoner, and deprived of his humanity—a *zèbre* (1614)—to a man he takes to be his judge. The second journey is used by Daru as an attempt to reverse the first: he takes the Arab from an enclosed to an open space, puts food into his hands and tries to restore to him a freedom of choice. In vain: the Arab's progress on the eastern

---

[19] *Speculum de l'autre femme* (Paris, 1974), 165–6.
[20] For this reason I would not interpret the fort-terrace as a miniature Tower of Babel.

road inscribes the second journey within the single itinerary beginning with Balducci and ending in the French prison. What is reversed, ironically, is Daru's position: the *cellule* in which he lived his monkish life is transformed by contact with the prisoner into his own condemned cell: as the second draft of the story explicates: 'ton école brûlera, et toi avec'.[21] So the fraternity that Daru deliberately rejected when the two men slept in the same room has come about notwithstanding in this transformation, which extends to turning Daru into a guest in the country where he was born. But if the importance of the location in this narrative (Daru's bedroom) is apparent, another site fulfils a significant function. Daru takes the Arab up to a fairly high eminence, and shows him the two paths and their possibilities. Not only does he leave the Arab at that point: he returns to the spot to view the outcome of the man's decision. We saw that the renegade referred to himself twice as 'le soleil'. Daru, strangely, appears as even more closely associated with the sun. Strangely, because on a psychological reading, on the basis of which Daru is usually interpreted as a liberal humanist, it might seem inappropriate that the point at which he feels himself to be a *seigneur*—the point at which he waxes most abundant—is in the torrid summer solstice when the uninterrupted shining of the sun has produced famine and death. While the snow lies on the ground he is impatient to see it gone, and his mind returns to the sun in two of the very rare instances, in *L'Exil et le royaume* as a whole, in which the conditional tense is employed:

Quand toute la neige serait fondue, le soleil régnerait de nouveau et brûlerait une fois de plus les champs de pierre. Pendant des jours, encore, le ciel inaltérable déverserait sa lumière sèche sur l'étendue solitaire où rien ne rappelait l'homme. (1615)
Un léger vent rôdait autour de l'école. Il chasserait peut-être les nuages et le soleil reviendrait. (1620)

It is therefore fitting that he should *tourne[r] en rond* (1621), and set out towards the east.

With respect to the senses, those doors between the self and the world without, Daru gives marked priority to vision. Twice he thinks he hears noises around the schoolhouse but does not trust his auditory faculty; he cannot interpret what the Arab was doing outside until he is able to *see* him again. Equally, Daru feels secure in

[21] *Théâtre, récits, nouvelles*, 2052.

the schoolhouse because he can see people approach (or so he thinks), can *calculate* their time of arrival. On his blackboard he inculcates knowledge (or ideology) through vision. The snow which obscures is, in his terms, a temporary aberration: the 'real' nature of the landscape is revealed when the stones re-emerge into view. By contrast, Daru cannot comprehend that which does not itself seek visibility. Twice, the narrative states that the Arab did *not* look up: Daru himself looks out of windows and into distances. He feels uneasy at night, when the Arab goes and comes; he inhabits— indeed can only live in—a desert of stones where the only soil to be found is taken by the villagers to heap on their meagre gardens, and where the only product of the earth is stone: predictably, he cannot understand the Arab's quarrel, which was over grain.

In his own rising, in his desire for the sun's reappearance and for things visible, and in the confidence and range of his language, Daru is an exception. We have seen Janine's and Yvars's reaction of aversion to the sun at its zenith. To the heat of the macumba-*case*, d'Arrast preferred 'le ciel et la nuit' (1679). The renegade associates darkness and water, for both of which he yearns: 'seule la nuit, avec ses étoiles fraîches et ses fontaines obscures, pouvait me sauver' (1588). One must beware, of course, of believing all the characters say. But neither should one construct too hasty a gender-argument on the basis of such observation of the sun, and for one specific reason: water and darkness inform two other spaces in which the self may form relations, and to which one must now turn.

So far, the self has been considered only in particular terms. Such i(n)solation may be illusive, and the metaphor of Daru spinning solitary in his firmament, a misrepresentation. On the ethical level there would be a great deal to be said in terms of the individual and society, with respect to marriage and the family, the means of production, and the functioning of ideology, and reference has been made to this possibility in connection with the 'public' interiors. In the reading adopted here, and the 'horizontal' traversing of the narrative journey, it is indeed first of all the inner/outer antithesis which comes into sight, since human relationships are set primarily in interiors and have as their lowest common denominator the factor of contiguity. Janine and Marcel's relationship thrives on, in fact depends on, proximity. Despite Jonas's brief excursion into adultery, he gravitates continually around his family. Yvars commutes between home and work and is bonded in both places; daily rites of humiliation and submission assure the renegade's fidelity and his hobbled feet guarantee his safe return or recuperation. More revelatory than this somewhat dull prospect is the way in which new human encounters are narrated: there are two principal examples in *L'Exil et le royaume*, in 'L'Hôte' and 'La Pierre qui pousse'. The former has already been discussed at sufficient length to emphasize how suggestive are the 'counter-references' to water, and how their placing in the text occurs in conjunction with the theme of encounter and the possibility of fraternity. The Arab comes to Daru in the snow-time; Daru makes tea and coffee for his guest(s), but he fails to give the Arab liquid for his journey, and he interprets as escape the man's need to go outside to pass water. It is noteworthy also that Yvars and his fellow-workers regain their lost sense of mutuality in the shower/changing room. But the story which stands most clearly 'under the sign of' water is 'La Pierre qui pousse'. The journey opens with the river-crossing and ends at Iguape set on another river by the sea, with its streaming skies, inundated houses and profusion of liquids which are applied, imbibed or exuded: mineral water, alcohol, sweat. D'Arrast, who has come to dam the river and prevent further devastation by flooding, meets the *coq* (who has survived death by drowning) in the Jardin de la Fontaine. The contrast with Daru's kingdom of stones could hardly be more marked. We have seen how, *nolens volens*, a certain fraternity/identity was established between Daru and the Arab: the *coq* verbalizes a similar process of identification when he tells d'Arrast: 'puis tu vas m'aider à tenir ma promesse, c'est comme si tu la faisais toi-même' (1672). And of course d'Arrast assumes the *coq*'s burden. Rateau, *alter ego* of Jonas, in one sense takes over the latter's function of provider, by constructing furniture appropriate to the dimensions of the flat and thereby making the interior more *vivable*. Indeed these examples of human relationships reveal an equal balance between identity and alterity. This is further imaged in a pattern common to the encounters in 'L'Hôte' and 'La Pierre qui pousse'; that of initiation/contract/repayment. Following the giving of hospitality in the form of a shared meal, the *coq* takes d'Arrast to the macumba ceremony, having engaged him to help him leave early. The *coq* goes back on the agreement to the extent of refusing to leave the dancing, but d'Arrast 'completes the work', if not exactly as the *coq* has envisaged. Daru shares his meal with the Arab and seemingly initiates him into a racial/cultural equality, in contradistinction to the man's treatment by Balducci. But Daru leaves him without comment, and the Arab fulfils the (perceived) obligation by taking the colonizers' road. Whereas Daru leads the Arab outside, d'Arrast and Rateau are invited into, or come close to, the interior space of their friends: in what the narrative relates, Rateau comes closer to Jonas in his *soupente* than does even Louise. Difference, *per se*, is not an obstacle to communication, but rather a catalyst of possibility: it is the acquaintance who tends to reduce perspectives to the identical: 'Vous peignez, continua l'autre. Moi aussi' (1644), the intimate who confronts: Rateau continually differs in his assessment from Jonas, and from the latter's disciples, beginning with his wonderment at what Jonas could possibly see in Louise. Thus the relation with the other offers both a new perspective and the concomitant possibility of redefining or reaffirming the self's own.

An obvious feature of inter-human relationships is that they are characterized primarily by speech. It was mentioned earlier that a common denominator of the downward movement of the self's journey was the interruption of communication, and the self's reduction to a thing observed. It is apt that the conclusion of the stories should foreground the question of speech or its replacement or suppression. The renegade's mouth is stopped with salt, Jonas leaves us with writing, and writing confronts Daru. But the narrative of 'La Femme adultère' ends with speech of the not-normally-loquacious Janine; Yvars, silent at work, at least *vis-à-vis* his employer, is able to tell all to his wife, and it is the taciturn brother of the *coq* who invites d'Arrast to sit with them: all three examples stress communication regained. In fact, continuing speech is brought out in two of the narratives in a curious way. While in the first part of 'La Femme adultère' it is frequently Janine's silence that the narrative communicates: 'Janine suivait sans répondre' (1567); 'Janine ne répondit rien' (1568); 'Janine ... restait sans voix' (1569), in a later section mention is made, repeatedly, of her forming speech without sound, whether that speech is addressed to Marcel: 'en elle-même, elle l'appela du nom d'amour qu'elle lui donnait autrefois ... elle l'appela de tout son cœur' (1572), or whether it is not even clear for whom it is destined: 'elle parlait, mais sa bouche n'émettait aucun son. Elle parlait, mais c'est à peine si elle s'entendait elle-même' (1572). Even though the renegade has no tongue, 'une autre langue, je ne sais pas, marche sans arrêt dans mon crâne' (1579). One is reminded of Meursault's 'en même temps et pour la première fois depuis des mois, j'ai entendu distinctement le son de ma voix. Je l'ai reconnue pour celle qui résonnait déjà depuis de longs jours à mes oreilles et j'ai compris que pendant tout ce temps j'avais parlé seul.'[22] Regarding what is articulated by the self and perceived by the other, it would seem that there is no proportional relation between volubility and significance, which in turn might suggest that, if significance is sought, it might be found on the edge between speech and silence. This of course is familiar territory for all readers of Camus, but the 'unspoken speech' seems to be saying that the voice of the self continues to seek expression, even if the self does not understand. Clearly, self-expression is not synonymous with communication, can result in solipsism. *Solidaire* or *solitaire?* From the angle adopted here one cannot claim to resolve this problem, but can only say that *if* the impulse is towards speech, then the seeming opposites presented in these stories: feigned dumbness and deprivation of the power of speech, are not so far apart.

Ethical discourse—one thinks of Kierkegaard's Agamemnon—could both explicate and be comprehended, but the doubt that reigns in this text over production and reception is part of a more general unease. Reference has already been made to the way in which the text questions whether the self can adequately be described in nominal or adjectival terms, but uncertainty informs all levels of these narratives, as a problematization of both articulation and representation. The narrative structure does not reveal 'what happened next' after the individual crises, in the sense of how the characters' perspectives and subsequent activities might have been transformed by their experiences.[23] Narrative explicitness[24] is no summary of the experience previously described; rather than providing a point of convergence, it seems to be beside the point, tangentially orientated: 'Ah, c'est de sa faute!' (1608). 'Ce n'est rien' (1654).[25] How confident, by contrast, are the workings-out of Clamence, that lover of heights: 'Ça fait tant. Vous êtes un pervers,

---

[22] *L'Etranger*, in *Théâtre, récits, nouvelles*, 1183.

[23] Although, presumably, the renegade dies.

[24] The reference here is to a truism: to what the narrative actually states, as opposed to what it does not say or could have stated differently. A term like 'explicity', were it more elegant, might serve the purpose better.

[25] Cf. p. 1575.

un satyre, un mythomane, un pédéraste, un artiste, etc.'[26] How sure he is that the interlocutor's story will be, essentially, *the same* as his own. If there is a myth-figure whose hidden presence illuminates the narrative, it is not the robust and stoical Sisyphus, but the unfortunate Icarus. Falling away from the heights of intelligibility, the characters, mute, mutilated or manically talking, exist on the edges, in the margins, in the zones of representational obscurity. Even those instruments by means of which Art and Knowledge traditionally re-present themselves, the canvas and the blackboard, are subverted: the lambent white space s(p)oiled by a word which is not even properly a word, since one word is defined by being distinguishable from another; the blackboard commandeered to question authority and the right to represent. But however profoundly it questions its own certainty, the narrative does not conclude with an unqualified negative: the blackboard still carries a message, and the canvas a representation. Even if expression has become the silent speech of an absent tongue, the narrative makes it quite clear that this is not the same thing as silence itself.

There is, however, a domain of the self's experience associated with silence or with speaking with other tongues, and it remains to ask, in conclusion, whether the text posits any relation between the self and some form of absolute. Three of the stories refer to the possibility of some form of mystical experience: 'La Femme adultère', 'Le Renégat' and 'Jonas', and here it is darkness which surrounds the narration of the experience. In each of the stories, the character is presented with something hidden: indecipherable, the 'étrange écriture dont il fallait déchiffrer le sens' (1569); invisible, the fetish-god behind the small door; incomprehensible, 'ce secret qui n'était pas seulement celui de l'art' (1652). Janine on the terrace at night and Jonas in his *soupente* are in darkness, and thereby hidden from the view of others; the same applies to the renegade when he is first taken to the house of the fetish, but when the door is opened it is light enough to see the features of the god. And here there is a significant difference between 'Le Renégat' and the two other stories, in addition to the fact that the exposure to the fetish does not take place in the renegade's own chosen location, as happens with the mystical experience of the other two characters. The difference is that the renegade sees the fetish face to face: 'sa

---

[26] *La Chute, Théâtre, récits, nouvelles*, 1543.

double tête de hache, son nez de fer tordu comme un serpent' (1586). Not only can the fetish be seen, but the description (for once) accords with the perception. This triple adequacy makes the fetish not a god, but, exactly as the renegade says, a representation of 'le principe méchant du *monde*' (1589).

The vision of Janine and Jonas is more dimly lit: by the stars and for the latter, towards the end, by a lamp. Janine responds to an 'appel muet' and no reason is given for Jonas's sudden call for a canvas. Both characters collapse. The end of the penultimate paragraph in both cases suggests the possibility of death: 'renversée sur la terre froide' (1575): 'lorsqu'il tomba, sans bruit' (1654), but the final one shows them both alive, if not well. What Jonas thought he has expressed remains ambiguous for anyone else; Janine's 'ce n'est rien' functions ambiguously in referring to the experience undergone and the impossibility of its description, as well as to nothing being the matter. What provokes the collapse? Two other instances are given in *L'Exil et le royaume*: Lassalle's little girl who falls 'comme si on l'avait fauchée' (1607) and the *coq*. But if both episodes can be read as brushes with death, there is nothing supernatural about them: the little girl had been ill the same morning and the *coq* was not built to carry that size of stone that far. Fatigue, lack of sleep and food, and the effects of cold could be responsible in the case of Janine and of Jonas. The narrative concludes with ambiguity, but again, it is a fastidious ambiguity: the fact that the narrative says nothing about mystical experience is not the same thing as there being nothing (or nothing possible) to say about it.[27]

How then does the journey end? Did the characters/does the self wait in vain? The reading proposed here is not one which permits evaluation of the characters' relative success in reaching any kingdom, and can offer no conclusion in that sense. However, 'La Femme adultère' and 'La Pierre qui pousse' are markedly similar in

---

[27] More mundanely, one might mention here that the earlier abrupt dismissal of the gender-argument (p. 199) does not mean that it could not be developed. On the contrary, and especially bearing in mind Luce Irigaray's interpretation of Plato's cave in *Speculum de l'autre femme*, one could see some of the characters' locations— notably Jonas's *soupente*, the *case* of the *coq*, and Daru's bedroom, as womb-like (tomb-like) structures. The cave of miracles in 'La Pierre qui pousse' is an interior where men on their knees, illuminated by the light of candles, chip off pieces of the ever-re-growing miracle stone. And it could be significant that the unusual references to *parler* (pp. 20–6) are made through the voices of a woman and a (symbolically) castrated male.

their conclusion, and it will be remembered that it was these two stories which represented waiting in terms of the self both waiting and being awaited. In fact all the stories can be said to show a concluding reference, in a sense, to water. This may be imaged as a negative possibility: the renegade is silenced with salt, as if the sea had run dry; Daru is left with chalk representations of rivers, while the 'terres . . . qui s'étendaient jusqu'à la mer' (1623) remained *invisibles* to him. Yvars's is a doubtful case: he sits on his terrace facing the sea, but on the other hand, if one takes his desire as reality, the sea would be eliminated: 'il aurait voulu être jeune, et que Fernande le fût encore, et ils seraient partis, de l'autre côté de la mer' (1608).

Two or three cases are rather more positive. 'Jonas' is a doubtful case for a different reason. There is little mention of water in the definitive edition. Unfortunately, as Quilliot notes: 'en l'état actuel des documents dont j'ai pu disposer . . . Jonas n'offre guère de prise à l'étude critique' (2053). However, in the *mimodrame La Vie d'artiste* one finds, *heureusement*, in the final scenario:

Les voisins entrent à ce moment et, remplissant peu à peu l'atelier, se dirigent vers le lit. Mais soudain, les projecteurs éclatent sur l'œuvre terminée, les lumières ruissellent dans un fleuve de musique. Tous, brusquement, se retournent alors vers l'œuvre et restent visiblement pétrifiés, pendant que lui, indifférent à son œuvre et à leur saisissement, pleure.   (2060)

On the terrace, Janine had been filled with 'l'eau de la nuit' (1675); back in the hotel room, 'elle pleurait, de toutes ses larmes' (1575). The resemblance to the final description of d'Arrast is striking: 'il écouta monter en lui le flot d'une joie obscure et haletante qu'il ne pouvait pas nommer . . . le bruit des eaux l'emplissait d'un bonheur tumultueux' (1685–6). The 'waters of the self' are released, whether 'really' as tears or imaged as a current: at the same time the self is 'filled' in a sense by the waters outside, again, whether 'real' or imaged. What can one say? Certainly, that these journeys end in water. But possibly also that in a rare fusion of image and 'reality', perspective and experience, the self is at one with itself and with the world.

12

The Autobiographer Astray: Leiris and *La Règle du jeu*

JOHN STURROCK

WE make free use these days of a formal opposition first thought of during the episode of modern French literary history known as the *nouveau roman*: between narration seen as 'l'écriture d'une aventure' or, by chiasmus, as 'l'aventure d'une écriture'. The distinction is seductively clear-cut and was first drawn, by the master-propagandist for the *nouveau roman*, Jean Ricardou, in order to point up the shift characteristic of that insurgent school of fiction whereby narrative was to be stripped of its mask of innocence and shown as no more than the questionable outcome of an act of narration. The adventures which we read may be made more adventurous still, if the chances, upsets and inspirations of their composition are once brought into the picture. So let those who would spin stories come clean, and show the spinning for what it is, a strenuous outlay of the imagination in which the spinner is scarcely better placed than ourselves to know what is coming, except in his or her power of veto once it has come and proved disappointing.

There was a certain cunning, however, in the efforts that the writers of the *nouveau roman* made to unseat the old and deceptive certainties of narration. What they themselves gave us were *models* of a new style of narration, exemplary fictions if anything further removed from the spontaneity of creation than the narratives whose stale devices they were set on exposing. By their own admission, novelists like Nathalie Sarraute and Alain Robbe-Grillet write slowly and with extreme fastidiousness, having to be even more patient, paradoxically, in the task of construction than traditional novelists apparently much less open than themselves to the accidents of composition. But then a greater or lesser measure of openness in this respect can only be an appearance, since the conditions of writing are the same whatever views you hold as to the proper form for fiction to take; the only difference lies in what the writer chooses to make of which accidents and that choice will be in part conditioned by the conventions he or she is following.

But the *nouveaux romanciers* had a good point to make: a false air of power and foreknowledge hangs habitually about the teller of a story; he is thereby set apart from his audience, who must wait upon his words. The story-teller is the privileged one who knows the story in advance and right to the end, for whom there can therefore be no surprises or unprescribed departures along the way, who addresses us from somewhere beyond and outside the narrative, though having condescended to return to the start so as to play the role of knowing guide. This may seem, to taste, either a false or a realistic state of affairs. Realistic inasmuch as by the time we are given to read a story, it *is* definitive and its teller to that extent entitled to possess it in its entirety; false inasmuch as in point of fact it was not always so, the story only seeming to have pre-existed its present telling, having had previously, if only the once, to be made. The democratic theorists of the *nouveau roman* wished to alert us once and for all to this grand illusion as to the independence of narrative from its maker, and to show as directly as possible, while remaining within the limits of the fictional, the true nature of an originary, first-time narration.

Why not thank them, then, for their rare conviviality in seeking to give up what looked to them an unfair and misleading advantage which they held over us, as their readers? Why continue haughtily in the pretence that the actual creation of a narrative and its eventual public re-enactment are in kind a single performance, when everyone should recognize that, on the contrary, the narrative as presented has suppressed all trace of its writing? Why not let it be seen instead that literary creation is one more process in time and a very chancey one, that a story is not something existing in advance in some Platonic repository but a sequence to be constructed *ad hoc*, and thus a compound of the fixed and the fortuitous? The fixed is the element of form, or of structure, in a literary text, whether this be preordained by a writer or not; the fortuitous is everything else, whatever comes to hand in the many moments of composition. There is merit in trying to demonstrate the fortuitousness of writing, even if no such demonstration can ever quite work. It cannot work because of the conditions of reading, which do not match those of writing. The true adventure is the writer's alone, as the philosopher-turned-writer Jacques Derrida describes it:

C'est parce qu'elle est *inaugurale*, au sens jeune de ce mot, que l'écriture est dangereuse et angoissante. Elle ne sait pas où elle va, aucune sagesse ne la garde de cette précipitation essentielle vers le sens qu'elle constitue et qui est d'abord son avenir . . . L'écriture est pour l'écrivain, même s'il n'est pas athée, mais s'il est écrivain, une navigation première et sans grâce.[1]

This is a Romantic-sounding doctrine, yet one which Derrida can defend very brilliantly by appeal to the facts of writing; I shall have cause to return to it, since nowhere is it more intelligently at work than in the writing of Michel Leiris. As readers, we are by the nature of things unable to share, except by insufficient proxy, in the adventure of this primary navigation. As readers we are relegated to a state of what Derrida calls 'sécondarité', stemming from 'ce redoublement étrange par lequel le sens constitué — écrit — se donne comme *lu*, préalablement ou simultanément, où l'autre est là qui veille et rend irréductible l'aller et retour, le travail entre l'écriture et la lecture.'[2]

Even allowing that we can never cross over, in reading, from a secondary to a primary role as navigators, it remains the case that a way of writing which seems to invite us to do so is one admirably fitted to an age such as our own, so biased against authority. The ostentatious shedding of authorial privilege which I have been adducing has its sociable aspect, whatever its tendencies in some hands to withdraw again into mystification. It is a throwback to Shandyism, that *cas-limite* in sympathetic straight dealing between author and reader so delicately practised by Laurence Sterne. Sterne it was who elevated most memorably the slightest contingencies of the authorial life into a creative principle, and who saw virtue and amusement in confessing as much to those readers who were prepared to stick by him through all the genial ramblings of his narration. His naturalism in this respect out-does anything that the far more decorous *nouveaux romanciers* proved capable of, extending beyond their carefully dramatized scenes of literary invention to the incorporation of raw data from the writer's daily life. When the narrator of *Tristram Shandy* displays vexation at the chance that has led him to throw a page of the fair copy of his manuscript into the fire, in mistake for a spoiled sheet, there is no need to suppose that this is anything other than a petty frustration that minute consummated in the fireplace of Laurence Sterne.

[1] Jacques Derrida, *L'Ecriture et la différence* (Paris, 1967), 22.
[2] Ibid.

The example is pejorative, to those who hold a higher view than this of contingency as a metaphysical force in our affairs. To anyone brought up on the philosophy of Jean-Paul Sartre, Sterne may seem a dreadful trifler. But what I am concerned with here is his philosophy of authorial nescience; that is neither trifling nor necessarily comic, as it is certainly not comic in the case of Leiris. Let Sterne's, however, be the classical statement of it:

When a man sits down to write a history,—though it be but the History of Jack Hickathrift or Tom Thumb, he knows no more than his heels what lets and confounded hindrances he is to meet with in his way,—or what a dance he may be led, by one excursion or another, before all is over. Could an historiographer drive on his history, as a muleteer drives on his mule,— straight forward— . . . he might venture to foretell you to an hour when he should get to his journey's end;—but the thing is, morally speaking, impossible: for, if he is a man of the least spirit, he will have fifty deviations from a straight line to make with this or that party as he goes along, which he can no ways avoid.[3]

From which formulation it is clear that for Sterne the demands of an ordinary sociability are what drives, indeed what should drive, the story-teller astray; to err, in the Shandyan context, is human. The story which the narrator of *Tristram Shandy* sets out to tell, and which he fails so engagingly to stick to, is his own. The book is a hopelessly botched autobiography, in which even the inaugural and suitably obstetric episode of the autobiographer's own birth proves exceptionally hard to reach. To go so consistently astray in the attempt to narrate one's own life would seem the most terrible incompetence in an author, since that is the one story before all others which he ought to have straight in his mind before starting. Indeed, his incentive to become an autobiographer in the first place derives, you might think, from knowing that there is a story there to be told, since if there were not it would be presumption or folly to see oneself as a potential autobiographer. Tristram Shandy is the funnier in his failure as an autobiographer for having undertaken what should be the most straightforward of all narrative tasks. The autobiographer's story looks to have been given, to exist already as a prescribed datum; except, as we know, that life bears sadly little resemblance to a narrative until such time as it has been written.

[3] Laurence Sterne, *The Life and Opinions of Tristram Shandy, Gentleman*, 3 vols (Oxford, 1926). i. 14.

A story like *Tristram Shandy*, however, if it be allowed to count as one, bears, we conclude, a delightful resemblance to life in its failure to observe so many of the bye-laws of fiction. As a parody of a first-person narrative it achieves a playful literalism, approximating to the life-story of an ingenious but easily distracted teller of stories. Perhaps such literalism as Sterne's is always playful, since whoever descends to it knows that he is letting literature down by presenting it as a disgracefully casual and capricious business. But it is possible to be both playfully literal and in great earnest, as Leiris is, in the four volumes of autobiography whose general title is *La Règle du jeu*. This also is a literary game or adventure founded on a notion of sociability and of willed digressiveness, though to it Leiris brought an intensity of purpose altogether foreign to the sensibility of Sterne.

In what sense, first, can a writer as seriously intentioned as Leiris be described as 'playful'; why would he take for his title a wording which suggests that what he was embarked on was a game? Because, to be brief, writing *was* a game if you compared it with living. Living Leiris had found to be difficult, and he believed that he did it shamefully badly; writing he needed as a respite from living or as a place where he could play at being himself unimpeded by the inhibitions and requirements of company. Which is nothing unusual; we are well accustomed to see the activity of writing as making up for some failure of living. But Leiris was not happy with the idea that once he stepped out of life and into literature there was no way back. 'Je me résignais mal à n'être qu'un littérateur' he wrote in a celebrated introduction to an autobiographical volume, *L'Age d'homme*, which led the way for the four subsequent volumes of *La Règle du jeu*.[4] The words were written in 1946, at a time when the urgent question facing left-wing writers and thinkers in France was that of their political commitment, but it would be wrong to give them a merely topical cast. Leiris was too lucid for his own good, too sure of his own physical cowardice to be able to take himself seriously as a man of action. Unlike Sartre, whose excitable politics he shared, he could talk himself only down, never up, and he sensed that any reconciliation which he might effect between his search for a more virile management of his daily life and the knowledge of his incapacity to satisfy it must take a literary and hence not fully serious form.

---

[4] Michel Leiris, *L'Age d'homme* (Paris, 1946), 10.

Unless, that is, he could find some way in which to make serious use of an unserious game, and persuade himself, first that the playing of it involved taking genuine risks, so that writing was something braver than a secure asylum, and second, that if he played it well it might be the very therapy he needed, might enable him to live more positively once he reverted from writing to being. It seemed to him in his younger days that there were risks which the autobiographer could expose himself to, so saving a certain kind of literature from the stigma of 'aestheticism'. The 1946 preface to *L'Age d'homme* has the ambitious title: 'De la littérature considérée comme une tauromachie' and in it Leiris, an admirer of the bull-fight for its remarkable association of aestheticism with courage, claims that it is possible for the writer as well to expose himself to danger, by the candour of his confession:

Mettre à nu certaines obsessions d'ordre sentimental ou sexuel, confesser publiquement certaines des déficiences ou des lâchetés qui lui font le plus honte, tel fut pour l'auteur le moyen — grossier sans doute, mais qu'il livre à d'autres en espérant le voir amender — d'introduire ne fût-ce que l'ombre d'une corne de taureau dans une œuvre littéraire.[5]

As time passes, and as his autobiography grows from volume to volume, this hopeful assimilation of the genuinely hazardous occupation of the matador to the entirely safe one of the writer fades right out from Leiris's view of what he is engaged on. I shall not dwell on it here, except to remark that in the volumes of *La Règle du jeu* the notion of risk survives, if only just, in his faith that the plunge into language which writing entails may be hazardous in terms of what it brings in the way of self-discovery. Of this, more presently.

The integration which Leiris proposed as his extra-literary end, between the writing of autobiography and the business of living, was by far the more realistic of these two attempts at finding serious uses for a playful endeavour. This is to treat autobiography as a version of psychotherapy, as a ladder, indeed, which could be kicked away later, were the literary cure to work, though that would be to count without the narcissism of the autobiographer, who has worked on his text not exclusively for his own immediate good but so as to attract others to it, and to him.

Surprisingly, despite the close hold that the psychoanalytic

5 Ibid. 8–9.

model has had for so many years over confessional discourse, Leir-is's remains an unusual autobiography, in both its ambitions and its form. It calls brutally into question what we would ordinarily think of as the *occasion* for autobiography. Autobiographers work gener-ally to a rule of live first, write later, so that it will be not until they have entered on the later part of their lives that they will feel quali-fied by the richness or singularity of their experience, or by the importance of their public achievement, to write an account of their lives. An autobiography crowns a life, it is not a part of it; we are asked as its readers to overlook the fact that an autobiographer may have years left to live, in which he could if he wished revise his account of his past and also extend it in the direction of this new present moment. An orthodox autobiographer, it is fair to say, is as good as dead.

It does not follow, however, that an orthodox autobiography is something less than a creative document, since the writing of it must involve multiple and prolonged sessions of recollection, and however full the documentary evidence may be from which the autobiographical text is derived, a large part of that text will belong to the inspiration of the moment of writing, not to some supposed 'pre-text' laid down in the past. The autobiographer will be more open than most writers to the creative surprises which uplift us all in the act of writing, as well as to a steady progress in the self-knowledge inseparable from any such interrogation of the events and attachments of his past life. And yet, traditionally, autobio-graphers have not drawn attention to either of these peculiar bless-ings. Leiris does the genre a high service in singling them out and demonstrating that the autobiography best worth writing is that whose actual composition is a further, possibly crucial event and attachment in the life of the writer, and whose text is not a calcu-lated index to actions that took place elsewhere, long ago and off the page, but an immediate experience in its own right. As such, it displays an openness to the contingencies of writing which mimics the openness we must all of us enjoy or endure to the contingencies of daily living.

Anyone who would write free-range autobiography such as this must break loose from that iron convention which ties autobio-graphers to chronology. The autobiographer who would do himself some good by writing autobiography can neither afford to wait until he is past the point in life where any such access to self-understanding will be useful to him, nor cling fast to chronology. To write up one's own life chronologically, as if it were someone else's, is to play safe, since chronology lays down an order for the text to follow which may be personal, inasmuch as the order is one peculiar to the writer who is recovering it, but which cannot be especially revealing, since episodes that follow one another in the anonymity of calendar-time lack the deeper closeness of those which follow one another in the private time of recollection. The contiguity of memory bears an altogether more mysterious and emotive charge than the contiguity of history. We may look on memory as spatial, and as manifesting the timeless dynamics of our selves; but the text which it supplies is discursive, and temporal. If our wish in writing autobiography is to go beyond the known facts of our lives into some cognitive adventure, then we can but prefer a text whose order is associative to one that is tamely chronological. The question the free-range autobiographer puts to himself in writing is, not 'What came next?' but 'What is coming next, now, as I write?'

We need not pretend that this break with chronology is a novelty inspired by the psychoanalytical tastes of the present age; it is a distinguishing mark of that respected branch of autobiography known as the Self-portrait, whose promise, neatly condensed by a present-day theorist, has always been: 'Je ne vous raconterai pas ce que j'ai fait, mais je vais vous dire *qui je suis*.'[6] This is a serviceable distinction, but it cannot be hard and fast, given how in autobiographical writing narrative will always intrude on self-description and self-description on narrative. No readers of autobiography, however theoretically inclined they may be, could tolerate a form of it from which narrative had been banished entirely. The story of how the text itself has come into existence may at times be gripping, but it is not enough; we ask also for dramas less literally self-regarding. Nor is there any reason to think that narrative is less sincere or spontaneous a mode of writing than description, since it too originates largely in the text, however vigorously it may seem to point away from it, towards some previous or transcendent incarnation.

Leiris's practice of self-portraiture is in one striking and profound way a departure from precedent. It takes systematically what in modern Anglo-American philosophy has come to be known as

[6] Michel Beaujour, *Miroirs d'encre* (Paris, 1980), 9.

'the linguistic turn'; it has become remarkably attentive to the medium common to recollection and to literature: to language. In the case of Leiris himself, this attentiveness is not, however, of the sceptical, deconstructive kind which either revels in or despairs over the ultimate metaphoricity of all natural language; on the contrary, Leiris's philosophy of language is of a strangely optimistic, quasi-magical kind. Language is the nearest thing he knows to a source of grace, able to deliver to those who hand themselves willingly over to it, unexpected, potentially saving truths.

He is an autobiographer seeking to find himself in life by first losing himself in language. He came originally to autobiography in his twenties as a 'poet', and as a writer deeply marked by the quite short time he had spent as a loyal Surrealist. He was full of the —for him, especially convenient—idea that deep down the political revolution and the literary one had a common purpose, and that the truly revolutionary task was to make something marvellous from the nothingness of ordinary life (what else should bourgeois auto-biography be for?):

La poésie avait remplacé pour moi le mysticisme proprement dit . . . Je ne croyais à rien — en tout cas pas en Dieu, ni en une autre vie – mais je par-lais volontiers d'Absolu, d'Eternel, et je pensais que par l'usage lyrique des mots l'homme a le pouvoir de tout transmuer. J'accordais une importance prépondérante à *l'imaginaire*, substitut du réel et du monde qu'il nous est loisible de créer. Le poète m'apparaissait comme un prédestiné, une manière de demiurge à qui il incombait d'effectuer cette vaste opération de transmutation mentale d'un univers, vrai dans la seule mesure où l'on veut bien lui attribuer cette vérité. Je croyais qu'au moyen des mots il est poss-ible de détecter les idées et que l'on peut ainsi, de choc verbal inattendu en choc verbal inattendu, cerner l'absolu de proche en proche et finalement, à force de déclencher dans tous les sens des idées neuves, le posséder.[7]

This commentary, without need for irony, marks a certain distance between the author and the credulity of his youth. By the time he wrote it Leiris had outgrown once and for all his belief in the trans-cendency of Poetry. Whatever revelations were to come from the shock conjunctions of words, they would not put him in possession of the Absolute; they could do nothing so cosmic or so final. But they could put him more fully in possession of himself. His ambitions had in the meantime become more reasonable, they had

---

[7] Leiris, op. cit. 216–17.

not changed direction; the writer's encounter with words continued to promise him the revelation of previously unknown, beneficent truths, and this promise remains as a motif in his writing as well as a fortifying rationale for it over the many years in which the sequence of *La Règle du jeu* was being written.

Revelation is a good for Leiris because he allows it a power to redeem, or to bring a new, hitherto hidden coherence to a subject-matter—himself—that must otherwise have remained without rhyme or reason. Prose leaves the world as it depressingly is; poetry raises it up. And if here by 'the world' we mean the brute data of the autobiographer's life, then Poetry alone can make something of them. As an autobiographer Leiris will pursue a method that courts revelation. All autobiography inescapably makes sense of a life, but usually by picking out from the past those high moments that endow it with a significant relief in public terms. Leiris goes instead to the low moments, the anti-autobiographical moments, since if it proves possible to raise these to the level of Poetry, then salvation really is at hand. To locate the marvellous in the everyday: the Surrealist dream, and Leiris's compulsion. But since there is no knowing where the marvellous may turn out to have been hiding, he needs in writing to go wherever the everyday may carry him, to be driven literally out of his way. Revelation is dramatic, provided that his readers can be assured of its genuineness and immediacy; and it is also a recurring inspiration for the writer, who must cultivate a certain automatism of his pen.

Derrida has taught us to see wisdom in such a recognition, that a writer has no authority over the language in which he writes. It is wise, and it seems also modest, to give up at least some of the authority of authorship voluntarily. But in Leiris there remains an element of conscious duplicity, of 'qui perd gagne'. In the second of the four volumes of *La Règle du jeu, Fourbis*, he associates the power of revelation with his distaste for everything that is showy or brilliant. True brilliance may not be manifested straight off, but made to appear suddenly from behind some unpromising exterior, when its effect will be very much greater. Leiris, recalling at this point the glamour of the jockeys who were among his earliest heroes in life, imagines the deferred triumph of the runner that, as racing commentators like to say, 'comes from nowhere':

Excitante sera toujours la minute où débouche victorieusement le coureur qui, jusque-là, semblait avoir un retard trop grand pour jamais parvenir à le rattraper. Un tel instant saisit parce qu'il est révélation: le traînard qui n'avait l'air de rien prend le meilleur sur tous les autres, le dieu caché apparait dans le rayonnement de sa force, moment comparable à celui où l'on met bas les masques, où l'imposteur sort confondu et où la face du monde semble soudain changée, une seule chose s'étant avérée contraire à ce qu'on avait cru.[8]

In the theatrical terms which Leiris himself so often favours, given his unsleeping awareness that as a writer he is also necessarily a performer, one could call a dramatic disclosure of this kind a moment of anagnorisis, marking a passage from a state of ignorance into one of knowledge, and inviting us in the light of this new knowledge to reinterpret what has gone before. This is to 'read' a race in terms of its result. We would not normally read autobiography with the same expectancy, when there is no possible denouement to look forward to. But even without the prospect of that ultimate resolution, we can still appreciate Leiris as the supreme *traînard* of autobiography, a writer who will make a virtue of dawdling, knowing that in the end we will love him all the better for his still unredeemed mediocrity.

It seems to be the case that originally he believed that his life itself might constitute for him, as its biographer, a sudden revelation; that it might take form in writing as a single and invulnerable whole, exempted from the fearful erosiveness of time. Life might become Poetry, that is. But unfortunately he could pursue this fantasmal Poetry only in a prose that must forever deny him satisfaction: 'Attendre d'une méthode discursive, prosaïque, l'impression de présence absolue et de saisie totale que seule peut donner la poésie, dans son surgissement apparemment sans racines, c'est— bien sûr—espérer l'impossible . . . '.[9] 'Présence absolue' and 'saisie totale' are concepts hard if not impossible to recognize, except as tokens of the presumptuousness of Leiris's youthful literary credo. Transcendental objectives of this high order imply that Poetry and prose are no longer continuous with one another but are rooted in incompatible experiences of the world, the one magical, the other rational.

What Leiris so remarkably asked for then from autobiography

---

[8] Leiris, *Fourbis* (Paris, 1955), 98.
[9] Leiris, *Fibrilles* (Paris, 1967), 223.

he at no time received; in that sense, the hundreds of pages of *La Règle du jeu* are the protracted record of a failure. Far from making compensation to him for the perceived failure of his life outside literature (a failure misleadingly harped on within the text, as if its author had achieved much less publicly than we know that he did), they compound it. The Great Revelation is forever withheld. But such is Leiris's tenacity and will to understand that each realization of failure is recuperated as a textual motif, reinforcing his pessimistic view of himself and at the same time ensuring that the writing will go on. The revelation that something cannot be achieved counts among his useful discoveries about himself, while his changing perspective on what it is that he is doing is evidence that the lucidity he has been seeking from the outset is slowly widening its scope. There is an ambiguity, therefore, about the many disclaimers to which Leiris treats himself, at those times when his enterprise seems to him to be foundering:

En commençant ce livre, je marchais à tâtons vers une découverte, puis a grandi peu à peu, avec mon besoin croissant de réunir des éléments susceptibles d'entrer en liaison, l'idée que je faisais un *livre* . . . A mon exaltation de défricheur s'est substituée par degrés l'excitation maniaque de celui qui, au hasard des brocantes, voit s'augmenter son stock de meubles. A mesure que le livre, page après page, s'alourdissait . . . l'élan initial se perdait; il n'est bientôt plus resté des *bifurs* que le nom . . . et pas grand'chose n'a surgi de la 'mise en présence' . . . Nulle flambée poétique ne monte, je perds de vue mon but ultime qu'étouffe la foison de détails plutôt qu'elle ne concourt à y mener, et je m'engonce, à chaque pas, davantage dans mon lugubre petit traintrain de collectionneur.[10]

It is a mistake, no doubt, in quoting at length like this from Leiris, to economize by means of vicarious dots on the full imbroglio of his subordinate clauses, when the length and ramification of his sentences have themselves a lot to tell about his failure to strike Poetry from the chance conjunctions of his prose. The volumes of *La Règle du jeu* give the impression of an unnerving plenty, of a 'Baroque profusion' in Leiris's own rueful description of it. But this profusion is not to be mistaken for the fluency of the writer who is never at a loss as to how to go on, it is an effect of a deliberately digressive way of writing in which every *écart* is treasurable for what it may contribute. It might seem that a writer like Leiris, although reliant

[10] Leiris, *Biffures* (Paris, 1948), 264.

in part on an extensive collection of pre-textual *fiches*, would necessarily work fast, it being his wish that his own inventions should come as a surprise to him; for freedom in verbal invention surely goes with speed in its pursuit. Yet each of the volumes of his autobiographical tetralogy took him seven or eight years to finish. Such a time-scale is destructive of the naïve idea that a book—any book—can be the product of a unitary act of composition; it brings into view the discontinuities of writing as well, in the case of an autobiographer, as the writer's awareness that, between writing one page and the next, the world has moved on, he has moved on, the text has moved on, and that all of these movements will condition what he now finds himself adding to what he has earlier written. There are sad admissions here and there from Leiris that he no longer knows for sure what he *has* written, because his text has extended well beyond his power to recall it in any detail.

Time passes, even for autobiographers, and may in the speed of its passage easily falsify a text like Leiris's that is searching for an absolute authenticity. In *Fibrilles* he reflects, for example, on a decision he has taken to move his autobiographical *fiches* and working notebooks into the country, at a moment when he thought that they, like himself, might be at risk in Paris from the attentions of colonialist *plastiqueurs*. But by the time this decision finds its place in his text, giving rise as it inescapably does to further reflections on one of the great cruxes of his writing, to wit, how to reconcile his revolutionary political ideas with his timidly bourgeois mode of life, he has reversed it, has decided that the danger is past and that the archive may safely be carried back to Paris. The time-lag between the decision to evacuate it, and the writing-up of that decision, means that he has been acting (writing, that is) 'en mauvaise foi'. Hence the admission which, by its extreme scrupulousness, raises the autobiographer on to a level of playing straight with his readers that few of us ask for in autobiography. In terms of the ethics of the genre, as observed by Leiris, we have another instance here of *qui perd gagne*, of the defaulter coming doubly good in the end, thanks to this autobiographer's mania for owning up.

Such culpable discrepancies as this, between an event and its textualization, merely magnify the discrepancy in time which is inherent in the act of writing itself. This time-lag we usually disregard, for all its obvious and denaturing effects on mental process. We can none of us write as fast as we think, with the result that if, as Leiris is, we are trying to transcribe with some if not total immediacy the present flow of our thought, we can never in truth catch up with it. To invite the pen to wander, *à la* Leiris, is not the same thing as to invite the mind to wander, since the pen has more work to do than the mind and by the time it has done its work of transcription, the writer knows that he has fallen behind himself, so to speak. Or alternatively, if this last phrase obscures his sense of his own duplicity, he knows that his 'self' is only ever behind him, never entirely with him. A coincidence between thought and its transcription is, Leiris recognizes, an 'impossibilité radicale'—unless we hold the sensible view that thought *is* its transcription, and only that, on the grounds that we cannot gain access to anything beyond transcription—but so far as he is concerned it is an impossibility without practical consequences, even if the knowledge of it pains him.

Leiris's Grand Design was undone not by any inadequacy on his part but by the temporalization constitutive of the medium in which he meant to realize it: language. Undone, or rather turned into a grand design of another kind, immanent where the other was transcendental, sociable where that was autistic. *La Règle du jeu* begins with the recollection of a vital discovery, made early in childhood, about the nature of language. The discovery serves as a *rite de passage* for Leiris, the ethnographer of self, first into life in society and then, years later, into the life of the text. It is that language cannot, by definition, be private; it belongs not to an individual but to a community, it is not purely expressive but also indicative. The child Leiris passed from using faulty forms of words, peculiar to himself, to using right forms, common to his fellows, so setting the stage for the vast communicative endeavour of his autobiography. The solidarity with others which Leiris has always felt himself to lack in everyday life, or on which he has been unable to act to his own satisfaction, is a quality intrinsic to language, so that as an autobiographer, however self-obsessed, he is assured of being no longer alone.

In the end, the prolongation of his text, through so many years and many hundreds of written pages, marks his dependency on it, once its elaboration had become an end in itself rather than the key to successful living. We read it as an astonishing exercise in the rationalization of a life, written by someone who first set out with much irrational baggage that had to be jettisoned along the way. The conclusions that he comes to about himself, in the course of this constantly renewed adventure, are not comfortable ones, but then he began writing in the conviction that the honourable thing was to show himself up, not show himself vainly off. Comfortable or not, much is made clear to him as he writes. There is no one saving truth to be revealed about his nature, but many smaller, local truths, so that even the proliferation of the text, which he claims to deplore and which is the proof of its inconclusiveness, can itself emerge as a large step forward in self-understanding:

C'est, en fin de compte, à cause d'une lenteur telle que ma pensée me semblait s'émietter au lieu de se fortifier, que l'idée du temps m'a occupé jusqu'à l'obsession, tandis que s'affermissait ma folle exigence à l'égard de l'écriture, sommée de le mettre en échec. Je sais fort bien, au demeurant, qu'un certain goût du baroque m'incite à accumuler (comme si elles participaient directement de ma recherche) les fioritures et les digressions au lieu de marcher droit au but, manière de faire qui contrarie mon désir d'aboutir rapidement. Mais je sais tout aussi bien que je ne pourrais y renoncer sans m'écarter de mon propos, puisque ce goût représente (que je le veuille ou non) l'une de mes tendances en matière d'esthétique et que ma quête d'une vérité trop sensible pour ne pas être inextricablement mêlée à la beauté doit passer par ce qui, dans la vie, m'émeut et me séduit et par ce que, sur le plan littéraire, une attirance invincible me conduit à introduire dans le jeu.[11]

Of all the tensions to be felt in reading the wilfully vagrant prose of *La Règle du jeu*, that between completion and incompletion is the strongest; what is archetypal about this extraordinary series of volumes is their author's initial setting of a 'poetic' objective for writing which writing can never attain to, and the consequent realization that he has in sober fact opened up for himself a delectable, boundless space in which publicly to disport himself without any need ever to reach the conclusion that would bring his mind back to the hated fact of his mortality. Seldom in literature are we able to share so directly in the equivocal pleasures of going nowhere.

[11] Leiris, *Fibrilles* (Paris, 1967), 230–1.

List of Contributors

MALCOLM BOWIE is Professor of French at Queen Mary College, University of London

GEORGE CRAIG is Reader in French at the University of Sussex.

PETER FRANCE is Professor of French at the University of Edinburgh.

S. BEYNON JOHN was until his retirement Reader in French at the University of Sussex.

ROSEMARIE JONES is Lecturer in French at the University of Sussex.

GABRIEL JOSIPOVICI is Professor of English at the University of Sussex.

ROGER LITTLE is Professor of French at Trinity College, Dublin.

MARGARET MCGOWAN is Professor of French at the University of Sussex.

JEAN MESNARD is Professor of French at the Sorbonne.

BRIAN NICHOLAS is Lecturer in French at the University of Sussex.

JOHN STURROCK is Assistant Editor of the *Times Literary Supplement*.

ANTHONY THORLBY is Honorary Professor of Comparative Literature at the University of Sussex.

Index